Praise for *Subjectified*

"Authentic and moving. Challenging and uplifting. This book couldn't be more relevant to the battleground that is women's bodies."

Victoria Bateman, University of Cambridge, author of
Naked Feminism: Breaking the Cult of Female Modesty

"Weiss is one of the best sex writers out there. Her voice is one that lifts and carries you. This book has the power to change the way we think of ourselves as women, as people – to know our power and agency when we so often have been left wanting."

Gigi Engle, psychosexual therapist and author of *All the F*cking Mistakes: A Guide to Sex, Love, and Life*

"*Subjectified* is a highly original, irreverent, and refreshing perspective on what it means to be a woman. I hugely enjoyed Suzannah Weiss's debunking of the sacred cows of female sexuality (I use that term deliberately – you'll see why). I guarantee you'll never look at 'the divine feminine' the same way again."

Cindy Gallop, founder and CEO of MakeLoveNotPorn

"This is the inclusive feminist manifesto of destigmatization and personal power we need today. Weiss asserts a unified imagined future of possibility that can speak to anyone who has grown up in the last several decades. An important voice in the modern fight for liberation and human thriving."
Kiran Gandhi, musician, activist, and free-bleeding runner at the 2015 London Marathon

"*Subjectified* is a book that will make you think long and hard about sex and the way we talk about it. Weiss shows how a simple sentence flip or reframe can dramatically change the way we think about ourselves and our partners, as well as what it means to be sexually free. Readers stand to become informed and empowered 'subjects' of desire."
Justin J. Lehmiller, host of the 'Sex and Psychology Podcast' and author of *Tell Me What You Want: The Science of Sexual Desire and How it Can Help You Improve Your Sex Life*

"Taking us on a journey of sexual liberation, *Subjectified* is a deep dive into what it means to be objectified and how we can talk, think, and action our way into becoming the subject of our own lives."
Erika Lust, indie erotic filmmaker and author of *Good Porn: A Woman's Guide*

"Weiss perfectly breaks down the dehumanizing split between subject and object, detailing the myriad ways in which the enforced position of 'object' is profoundly destructive for women. Her deep dive into the consequences of this process is both illuminating and liberating."
Nina Menkes, director of *Brainwashed: Sex-Camera-Power*

"*Subjectified* will make you think – about the words we use to describe women, sex, and men. More than that, it will inspire readers to consider their role in the world and how they want to create their own sexual narrative and life journey. Using cultural critique, linguistic analysis, surprising facts from science, and her own journey as both a woman and a sex writer, Suzannah Weiss invites readers into her world so that they can choose if they want to change their own. I plan to recommend this book to students and clients for years to come. I am certain that all will have 'Aha!' moments and be inspired to make changes to the way they approach the world of sex."

Laurie Mintz, University of Florida, author of *Becoming Cliterate: Why Orgasm Equality Matters – and How to Get it*

"*Subjectified* is a deeply heartfelt, thought provoking, and gripping account of Suzannah Weiss's personal journey toward empowerment in a world that still frequently treats women as objects. It is a gift to any woman who wants to get in touch with her own true north and make choices that honor her body, mind, and feelings, across each and every part of her life."

Tiffany Pham, founder of Mogul and author of *You Are a Mogul: How to Do the Impossible, Do It Yourself, and Do It Now*

"Suzannah Weiss rediscovers sex-positivity as she returns our agency, worth, and subjectivity to ourselves, our own voice and vision, our 'I.' This radical script-flipping of women's selfhood sees Suzannah dancing with language and gifting us the wonderful, powerful identity 'subject of desire.'"

Carol Queen, staff sexologist at Good Vibes and author of *Exhibitionism for the Shy: Show Off, Dress Up and Talk Hot!*

"What Suzannah Weiss has achieved in *Subjectified* is remarkable. In a marketplace packed with 'pop feminism' books she has written something fresh, absorbing, and important. This is persuasive, groundbreaking material."
Emma Rees, University of Chester, author of *The Vagina: A Literary and Cultural History*

"*Subjectified* is a super thoughtful, heartfelt, generous story that dives into many important and interesting topics – such as menstrual blood, dick pics, the politics of pubes, sex work as play, behind the nipples, easy money, sex and divinity, body sizes, and more – all in one nicely written book. Suzannah Weiss asks, and answers, many questions about our bodies and ourselves, which many women ponder – if they dare."
Annie Sprinkle, sexecologist and author of *Assuming the Ecosexual Position: The Earth as Lover*

"*Subjectified* is delightfully nerdy, zeroing in on the details of how language informs our feelings and framings. The way Suzannah Weiss weaves personal and societal together is absolutely stunning. Thanks to her for sharing this with me, and the world."
Jessica Stoya, porn icon and sex columnist

"*Subjectified* takes you on a journey that's equal parts playful, poetic, profound, silly, sexy, and full of titillating twists and turns. Weiss is a trailblazer, expanding minds and pushing boundaries with a refreshingly approachable warmth and tenderness."
Maitland Ward, actress and model

Subjectified

Subjectified
Becoming a Sexual Subject

SUZANNAH WEISS

polity

First published in 2024 by Polity Press

Polity Press
65 Bridge Street
Cambridge CB2 1UR, UK

Polity Press
111 River Street
Hoboken, NJ 07030, USA

ISBN-13: 978-1-5095-6018-9
ISBN-13: 978-1-5095-6019-6(pb)

A catalogue record for this book is available from the British Library.

Library of Congress Control Number: 2023939814

Typeset in 11 on 14pt Warnock Pro
by Fakenham Prepress Solutions, Fakenham, Norfolk NR21 8NL
Printed and bound in Great Britain by TJ Books Ltd, Padstow, Cornwall

For further information on Polity, visit our website:
politybooks.com

Contents

To everyone who has ever been treated like they were there to be used, rather than simply to be.

Preface

Subject verb object.

This is the basic structure of a sentence. This is the basic structure of the world. Boy meets girl. So the story goes. Man sees woman. He pursues her. He woos her. He proposes to her. He marries her. "You may now kiss the bride." Husband kisses wife. She is kissed. She is taken. She is claimed. By him.

Male subject, female object. Subject verb object. Man verb woman. He verb her. In these sentences, a man acts on a woman. A woman gets acted on. If she's a subject, she is in the passive voice. And the other pronoun is still "he."

> Objectification (n): the action of degrading someone to the status of a mere object.[1]

This term is often invoked in a visual sense: Women are mere things to look at. But objectification happens with many verbs: "use," "take," and even more neutral words like "ask" and "admire." If women are always the objects and never the subjects, any action can objectify with repetition.

Instead of objectifying women, how can we *subjectify* them? How can we make women the subjects of more sentences and actions? How can we put "she" before more verbs? How can we create a world where she sees, she pursues, she acts, she knows, she desires, she loves?

I see the irony in these questions. When I ask "how can we subjectify women?," women are the objects of the verb "subjectify." When I talk about "making women the subjects," women are the objects of "make." Even the title of this book, *Subjectified*, is in the passive voice. But I embrace this paradox. It leaves room for each woman to exist in any spot in a sentence she likes. Being an object once in a while doesn't mean you cannot be a subject. A subject is not confined to one position. She cannot even fit onto a page. She dances between sentence fragments, hops from clause to clause, and somehow gets home in time to write a whole new story. To live a whole new dream.

I am taking about women because women have been denied the subject role for so long. But subjectification is for anyone who uses the pronouns I/my/mine. It is for all who seek to be the authors of their lives and the starters of their sentences. Accordingly, each chapter begins with the pronoun "I" and then a verb, inviting readers to imagine how they can be subjects of each action.

I am writing for those who use gender-neutral pronouns like "they," who get omitted from every kind of clause. (I personally use "she" as well as "they.") I am writing for those whose partners' pronouns are the same as theirs and those with more than one partner, with love stories full of plural pronouns. Subjectification is for all bodies and all varieties of relationships. It's for people like me, who say exactly where they want to eat, when they want to talk, and how they like to be touched. And it's for people like me, who have fun putting on flowy dresses and cooking sweet recipes to surprise someone they love.

This is a book about the grammar of everyday living. The ability to stand on any side of a verb we like, then jump back and forth over it, switching or sharing sides with others. And how we can revise the sentences that shape our lives so that every type of person has the chance to do, to be. This is a book about the female I and our female eyes, and how to position yourself at "I" level. How to speak in the first person, to say "I" and mean it, when you've been confined to "you" and "she" and "them."

And this is a book about me and my career as a sex writer. I draw upon this work to show how I came to understand subjects and objects, how I've played with the grammar of my actions. I've been immersed in this field for nine years and have formed many opinions, which still shift as I grow. So, consider this your invitation to accompany me to clothing-optional beaches, pleasure workshops, and other assignments as I discover what it means to be a subject. It won't all be so serious. I am not writing to persuade or debate or convict or accuse. I'm an artist, not a lawyer. My goal is not to argue but to share my thoughts so you can apply them as you wish, even if that means doing the opposite.

I am not trying to tear down the movements I critique but to expand them. You can think of this book as a "yes, and," not a "no, but." Most people I describe here are doing good things. *And* we can do even better. Nor am I posing as an authority on scholars' philosophies or histories. When I draw upon thinkers' ideas, I'm taking poetic liberty to expound what they mean to me, how they've shaped my life, and how they might impact yours. I am writing to dance with language, in all its contradictions and its silliness.

Perhaps, as you whirl and twirl with the words on the pages, you'll find inspiration for how to subjectify yourself. Or, you may become more enamored with the thought of being an object. Don't be alarmed if it's both. The body loves to rebel against whatever role it's placed in. The body doesn't like boxes. Tell it that it's one thing, and it'll take extra care to become the opposite.

Is it trying to have it both ways? Yes, but that's what it means to be human. To be everything and its opposite all at once. All at twice.

But let's start this story from a time when I didn't know that. From a time when I wondered if an object was all I could be.

If that's where you are now, then maybe, you can follow my footsteps and walk this path out of objecthood.

Or, even better, forge your own.

Chapter 1

I Walk: My Path Out of Objecthood

I remember just what it was like to be a child. Every sight I saw, down to each yellow forsythia outside my bedroom window, had its own spot on my retina. My face in the mirror was just one of these sights. And when I saw it, I saw inside it: the light, the laughter. All people begin life as subjects; a child's eyes are globes. On each little sphere is a map of that person's growing world. But during adolescence, my eyes started to shrink. I realized the Earth was not inside them. No, I was just a coordinate inside others' globes.

This awareness began with little comments: an older man telling me I looked "developed"; another warning my parents to "watch out" for me. Boys in class describing efforts to peer down girls' shirts. One murmuring about my "nice ass." By age thirteen, it was as if my eyes had floated outside my head, always on the watch. I stood with my shoulders hunched, trying to protect the beginnings of breasts that I could sense were there for show. I'd stare in the mirror, crossing my arms over my chest, trying to squish it in and make it disappear. I could not love my body because it felt dangerous to live there.

I wished I didn't have to live the life of a person with breasts, which may seem odd, since we so often learn that breasts are attractive and women should be just that. But that's precisely why I felt this way. In the back of my mind, I knew that life with breasts would be different from life without them. That I would face sexual advances, wanted or not. That people would perceive me as motherly, hormonal, and everything else they project onto women. After all, I'd seen breasts depicted in only two ways: as objects of men's sexual appetite and children's literal appetite. I was never taught they could be body parts you bare on a beach without sexual connotations. Or that you can cover and keep to yourself – and either way, they're not asking for attention. Or that a partner can notice and like without a hint of aggression or entitlement. Or touch for your pleasure, checking in with you every step of the way. All I knew about having a "woman's body" was that people would want to use it and possibly abuse it.

Since I couldn't determine what my body signified for myself, others defined it for me. My dad scrutinized my eating habits, warning me that as I got older, maintaining my figure might not be so easy anymore. I remember eating my favorite dessert, Oreos with peanut butter, when he told me that once gymnastics season was over, I'd have to cut back. So that was another thing a "woman's body" made me: an object of men's opinions. I grew aware that I was no longer just me. I was "you." I was "her." Even to myself.

It turned out my eyes did not hold the world. Some powerful, collective eye held me. This eye seized me and sized me up: Look at that body. This eye, this I, this mysterious masculine voice told me what I – what she – was and wasn't. If this was what being a woman meant, I wanted out. I wanted to fight for the world I saw, for the self I was.

Recovering the "Me" I'd Always Been

My thirteen-year-old self didn't know about rape culture or objectification. All I knew was that I didn't want an objectifiable body. I'd go to great lengths not to have one. And I did. I limited my intake of carbs, fats, and food altogether – until I didn't have to squish my breasts inward or wear tight bras to erase the woman-ness lumped onto me. At last, my form was slight enough to slip into the peripheral vision of this eye staring at me. With less meat on my bones, I could finally stop feeling like a meal. I'd found an (albeit unhealthy) way to subjectify myself, to retain my identity as "I." Not "she," not "you" or "that" or "those," but the "me" I'd always been.

By age fifteen, my efforts had paid off. While most of my peers were gaining weight due to puberty, I'd quickly lost 20 pounds and hadn't gotten my period in a year. Thus began two long years in and out of therapists' offices. One of them spoke to me about intuitive eating and heeding my internal signals. I hadn't known my body had a voice. It had been spoken of, but nobody had asked it what it had to say. Yet as I paid attention, I learned that my stomach had its own sensibilities, my hands their own creativity.

I spent that summer taking writing courses in New York City, and as I learned to tune in to my physical needs, I listened to my everyday instincts. I wandered through the buffet at the Metropolitan Museum of Art cafe, putting salads, grains, and fruits on my plate as if I were splashing colors on a canvas. I wrote poems that flooded my ears from up above the skyscrapers. I strolled the streets of Greenwich Village with no destination, my feet deciding for me which alleyway to go down, which shop to pop into. I met up with a friend to get my nails done and knew which peachy pink I wanted right away. I was beginning to experience myself as the subject of verbs like "sense" and "feel" and "like." I sensed what I sensed, felt what I felt, liked what I liked for no reason. It was subjective. No one else could tell me what my body was craving. No eye could size me up and say what size I should be. Like a seed sprouting a tree, a subject knows which direction to grow in.

Yet I couldn't stop monitoring my body as it grew, trying to make sure it stayed small enough to remain unnoticed. When my period and shape returned, I remembered I was defined as "feminine." Defined by whom, what subject, I can't say. But I could tell I was the object. I sensed that people associated curves with sexiness, passivity, and other "womanly" traits. And I did not want to take all these characteristics on. I at least wanted a choice. I sensed that people were looking at me, and as I struggled to connect to my body's own voice, others continued speaking about it, about me, for me. Telling me to make sure not to gain *too* much weight, not to eat at night, not to eat too many carbs – but also not too few, lest I fail to boast a big enough butt and boobs. For two more years, I fell in and out of disordered eating habits. These were my only safety mechanisms at a time when no one could even explain why I felt unsafe. Nobody around me had the language.

Body for Sale

At last, my parents sent me to live at an eating disorder treatment center the summer between high school and college. There, I ate supervised meals and attended therapy sessions. During one appointment, my therapist had me draw myself and label each part with the connotations it carried. Over my breasts, I wrote, "FOR SALE." I didn't label anything between my legs. When my therapist asked which body part was scariest, all I could do was point there.

The words she then told me are ones I've spent my career passing on: "You don't have to do anything with it. You don't have to have sex with anyone. You don't have to have kids. You don't have to do anything." With these sentences, I became the subject of "do" and "have." My body could do and have, not just have things done to it, not just be had. I realized then that my eating disorder was fueled by the perception that my body existed for other people. I *did* want to do those things with it. I just wanted to be the one to do them – and the one they were done for. I wanted to be "she" and "you" *and* "me." I yearned to grow, to thrive, to expand, to rejoice in my physical vessel. I simply hadn't found a way to do so that felt safe.

I'm unsure where I learned that my body wasn't my own, but there were plenty of opportunities: the scantily clad women in men's (and even women's) magazines; the models presented as rewards for buying products on TV; the predatory male behavior in movies and music, which always seemed to blame women's irresistible figures. "Look at those gazongas!" a devil on a frat boy's shoulder in *Animal House* exclaims as he contemplates whether to sexually assault a thirteen-year-old girl. The angel on his other shoulder wins and he resists, as if not raping is so difficult, it's angelic. "She takes her vitamins," a high school boy in *American Pie* comments while spying with a group of peers on a girl undressing. "I like 'em round and big … just can't help myself, I'm actin' like an animal," rapper Sir Mix-a-Lot broadcasts in "Baby Got Back."

It was clear to me that the woman my society wanted me to be was curvaceous, vapid, and submissive – yet the more I fit that description, the more I'd be viewed as an object for men's pleasure. And the less safe I would be. I'd heard that the pressure for women to be sexy contributed to eating disorders, but I saw another force at work: fear of being sexy. It seemed that my value lay in my sex appeal, but that if I had sex appeal, I was vulnerable to degradation. Being sexually desirable felt obligatory but dangerous. The same internalized male gaze that made me think I wasn't beautiful made me fear my beauty. By attaining a body that felt less objectifiable, I'd been trying to protect my freedom.

I didn't have real-life experience to counter these frightening depictions of sexuality. All I knew about sex, besides the basic anatomy taught in sex ed, came from gossip about school "sluts" who pleasured guys to gain approval. Sex seemed like a favor women did for men. Women's whole existence seemed like a favor for men.

The Girl Jumped Over the Verb

But one night, the week after I got out of eating disorder treatment, those assumptions were shattered. I had my first-ever hookup on a beach during a family vacation, and it consisted entirely of me receiving pleasure. I snuck back to the beach house and tucked myself under the covers with a beam on my face. Sexuality was so different from what I'd been taught it would be. My body was so different from what I'd been taught it would be. The "womanly curves" that were supposedly there to be soaked in by male eyes had instead soaked in wonderful sensations. Sex, I realized, could be for me. My body could be for me.

My high school peers' gossip had led me to believe that, if I engaged in hookups, I'd be giving something away. But I hadn't given anything. I had only gained. And I had not just gained physical gratification. I'd gained permission to be sexual, not just sexy. I'd gained freedom. My eyes returned from that place in outer space where they'd sat sizing me up and reassumed their spots below my forehead. They began to fill again with my own dreams and fantasies. I took an interest in those around me, no longer so scared of them taking an interest in me.

As I began college that fall, I took part in a few hookups but would stop after the other person pleased me, knowing that anything more would stem from a sense of obligation. I had to derive pleasure from my body before anyone else could. I had to know someone saw me as a subject before I'd be their object. I began to understand that female bodies were not passive or powerless, nor were men made to be violent or threatening. There were other ways of thinking about our bodies. There were other ways of thinking about ourselves.

Over the course of this awakening, my eating disorder recovery got easier. It was as if some invisible cord connecting my stomach and brain also passed through my genitals, and once that opening cleared, everything else could flow. Spells are cast with words, and the words I used to think of myself transformed. I was no longer just the object of verbs like "see" or "want" or "pursue." I saw. I wanted. I pursued. With a skip in my step, I jumped from the right side of each verb to the left, to the beginning of each sentence, starting over. Rewriting myself. Rewiring myself.

I began to make new meanings of my body, part by part. My vagina was no longer a place to let men in or keep them out. It was a source of sensation I could act on. My breasts didn't have to be objects of partners' or children's appetites; they could provide me with pleasure – or not. I could decide if, when, and how others touched them. My disordered thoughts fell away as I inhabited a place deeper inside myself. Instead of being hyper-aware of being observed, I felt. Others could look at me, and I knew they would. But I was still in there, still living, existing, looking back.

My recovery had forced me to develop a mature female body, the kind of body typically objectified. Yet by exploring pleasure on my own terms, I saw that this same body could produce sensations for me and me only. Though I'd learned that men were predators and women were prey, I could find people who defied that framework. I could be one of those people. By changing how I spoke to myself, I forged a path out of objecthood. I still struggle with self-consciousness, as women probably will until society itself changes. But that first semester of college sparked a fascination with how sexuality can both damage and heal women, how it can both enforce patriarchy and liberate us from it.

"No Such Thing as a Woman"

To understand the transformation I'd experienced, I studied feminist theory. Two quotes by psychoanalyst Jacques Lacan stuck with me: "Woman does not exist"[1] and "there is no such thing as a woman."[2] He stated that "there is no woman who is not excluded by the nature of things, which is the nature of words."[3] While the meaning of these quotes is complex and debated, what I took from them is this: A culture that objectifies women has no concept of a female subject. We've defined "woman" in the negative: as someone lacking what men have. Men can be "emasculated"; they can lose their masculinity. But there's no "efemination" because femininity is already defined as something lost, a state of lack, an absence of maleness.

Since it's how we learn what it means to be male or female, sex is the first way we learn to associate women with lack. From childhood, girls are taught that they have a vagina but not that they have a vulva or clitoris. Our genitals are depicted as an empty hole, a negative penis. A few years later, when we're taught how sex works, we hear that we get penetrated. We're literally the objects of the sentence: "Man penetrates woman." This is how we learn to relate to the world: to take it in rather than move into it. A similar sentence, "man looks at woman," governs how we're portrayed in the media, teaching us to direct our gaze toward ourselves rather than all that's around us.

Whether or not a woman has a body that society deems desirable, she likely knows what it's like to be an object – if not of desire, then perhaps of scorn or stereotyping. And objecti-fication is faced not just by women, but by all disadvantaged groups. LGBTQ+ people, people of color, those with disabil-ities, and more are objectified in their own ways, whether they are objects of pity, fear, or mockery. They – or I'll say we, as

I belong to other objectified groups – are judged, monitored, spoken for, and placed in the passive voice in a million other ways. Yet we fight for our right to be subjects.

To the Unheard Teen in All of Us, Who Always Was a Subject

It's all too common for people to seek subjectivity through destructive methods like disordered eating. But once I learned there were joyful, healthy ways to become a subject – ways full of blossoming and growth rather than self-denial and erasure – I made it my career to explore them.

I became a sex and relationship writer in 2015, when feminist blogs, books, and celebrities had begun spreading sex positivity. The #FreeTheNipple movement and SlutWalks were advocating for women's right to wear as little as they pleased without judgment or victim-blaming. Sex educators were evangelizing vibrators as tools for independence. Celebrities were promoting vaginal adornments and spa treatments to help women feel good about their genitals. Affirmative consent advocates were spreading the word that a woman's partner must hear "yes" to know she consented. Body-positive Instagrams and fashion campaigns were teaching us that every woman is beautiful. They still are.

As a journalist, I've explored these movements firsthand. I've sought subjectivity at singles' and couples' retreats, sex parties, and masturbation circles. I've reviewed dozens of sex toys, from smart vibrators to crystal dildos, that promise to literally put women's pleasure in their hands. I've modeled for figure-drawing classes and traveled to clothing-optional resorts to gain comfort with my naked body. I've thrown myself into the study of sacred sexuality and orgasmic meditation to experience "feminine" forms of pleasure. I've interviewed everyone from feminist pornographers to dominatrixes to discover how they've cultivated authentic female perspectives in a culture built around male ones. I have also trained and worked as a sexologist, sex educator, sex and love coach, sexual assault counselor, and birth doula, sharing the knowledge I've gained while learning from real people's experiences.

All the while, my inner thirteen-year-old tagged along, seeking the same thing she sought in front of her childhood bedroom's white wicker mirror: to be something other than an object. To be a subject. Toward that end, many of these adventures fell short. Feminism and sex-positivity aim to help women embrace their sexuality. But at times, I've seen such movements cater to men's sexuality instead. Too many women's empowerment advocates still teach women to flaunt their bodies but not to enjoy them. Too many are teaching women to love their looks but not their inner beauty. Teaching them they can say "yes" or "no" to others but not asking them what they want. Telling them not to give themselves away for free without questioning whether they should have a price tag.

The thirteen-year-old in me deserved better than this cheapened version of empowerment. She deserved to find enjoyment in her own gaze, not just to be the object of a man's. She deserved to feel confident for reasons independent of her looks, not to be reassured she was sexy. She deserved to be looked in the eye no matter what she was wearing, not to be told how arousing her naked body was. She deserved to be celebrated not just for her "femininity," but for all the precious qualities that made her a well-rounded person.

The problem is, many efforts toward women's liberation encourage us to be sexual without distinguishing between sexual objects and sexual subjects. By focusing on women's right to be looked at, feel wanted, and otherwise have things done to them, the recent explosion of movements bringing feminism into the bedroom does not always afford us subjectivity. Sometimes, it objectifies us.

There's a saying attributed to French writer Anne Louise Germaine de Staël: "The desire of the man is for the woman, but the desire of the woman is for the desire of the man."[4] But it only seems that way because male desire is the only desire we talk about. A sexual subject has desires of her own. She is the subject of the sentence: "I desire." In a world where we get to be subjects, we're at the beginning of many new sentences: "Woman envelops man." Or "woman touches woman." Or "woman loves non-binary person." We get to ask ourselves: What would our sentences say if we were the subjects?

We've been doing things to women for long enough. It's time for women to do. It's time to take women out of the passive voice. It's time to subjectify women, as I call it: to create space for women to see themselves as desirous, desiring beings. Not just desirable beings. Subjectification leaves room for women who are horny on days when they look like crap, women who look without being seen, women who would rather forget about their looks than love them, and women who would rather propose their own ideas than consent to someone else's. Being a subject means having an inner world that can dream, perceive, and have objects of its own. It doesn't mean you can't be an object of anyone's desire. You can still be looked at, desired, and penetrated. But you can also look, engulf, and do everything else that makes you the subject of the verb. You can be more than the negative space men fill.

This shift must take place in the bedroom as much as anywhere else. Sex, after all, is where the status quo is rooted. The view of women's bodies as passive receptacles has led to a cultural neglect for women's needs.

But despite the expectations we internalize, women continue to desire more than being desired, to conjure up their own plans rather than just cater to others', and to take joy in what they see, hear, and feel, not just what they look like, sound like, and feel like.

The thirteen-year-old girl who felt that desire within her and used every means available to protect it, but just didn't have the right tools, lives in each of us.

This book is for her.

Chapter 2

I Feel: My Body's Size Doesn't Matter Because I Have a Big Heart

One day in eating disorder treatment, the art therapist had us draw life-size contours of our bodies as we saw them, then lie on the paper so she could trace us. This way, we could compare the two drawings and become aware of our warped self-images. I paused before beginning my artwork. I was scared I wouldn't discover I was smaller than I thought, as the art therapist expected. More than that, I feared the finished product would disappoint me no matter what size it was. I did not want to size up my figure. I knew my body hatred wasn't about my body itself. Nor would loving my body come from reassessing how it appeared. I had a hunch that would come from somewhere deeper.

I nevertheless cooperated with the activity, then stood up and looked down in dissatisfaction at my own traced shape. It was thinner than I'd guessed but still did not look thin enough. As long as I was focused on the physical form, it never would. Then, I spotted a container of red spray paint on the table to my right, and an idea struck me. I grabbed the bottle and covered the whole drawing with a giant heart. Its pointed bottom surrounded my legs and feet. The circular sides at the top ensconced my head and shoulders.

I filled it in until my shape was barely visible beneath the ruby mist.

"My body's size doesn't matter because I have a big heart," I explained as the art therapist walked over to look. She scowled with disapproval and took me outside. "It seems like you're engaged in self-defacement," she said. "You need to make peace with your body." My eyes welled up. She didn't understand. Foregrounding my heart *was* my way of making peace with my body. But I understood why she didn't understand. I wasn't being body positive, by many definitions.

The Right to Be Sexy

It was 2008, and plus-size models were appearing on catwalks. Phrases like "real women have curves" and "embrace your curves" were thrown around in women's periodicals. Each magazine had its own way of telling us to appreciate our bodies by seeing ourselves through men's eyes.

Glamour conducted a survey for "bikini season" on "what men think about women's bodies," with a breakdown of how many men prefer butts vs. boobs, to prove that "while you're busy wanting a 'perfect' body, guys are busy admiring the one you've got."[1] *Redbook* shared a collection of quotes from men praising female bodies, including "all boobs are great" and "your butt is the best."[2] *Cosmo* created a "feel great naked" guide assuring readers that "seeing yourself in your mind's eye as a super-sexy star, and envisioning yourself at the center of everyone's fantasy will trick you into acting sexier."[3]

The way to love my body, it seemed, was to look in the mirror and find myself sexy. But how could I see myself as sexy when I hadn't yet learned how to be *sexual*? How could I embrace being looked at when I hadn't even learned how to look – to really see through my own eyes and feel with my own heart? Declarations like "every woman's beautiful," "all boobs are great," and "your butt is the best" did little to mitigate the discomfort I felt around being seen. Nor did such words help me care less about beauty in the first place. Instead of helping me see myself as more than an object, these statements taught me I'd be objectified no matter my size – probably more so if I were more ample.

I confided in another patient at the eating disorder facility about my fear of being an object. "I'm scared that if I look too much like a woman, men will want to take advantage of me."

"It's true," she said. "Men are horny bastards."

"But why?"

"Because women's bodies are beautiful. If you look at people naked, men don't look very good. But women's bodies are pretty, and that attracts men's attention."

Her take confirmed my worst fears. Men were predators. I was prey. And I couldn't even help it because my body was irresistible by virtue of being female. My physical characteristics, which I had no control over – except the control I gained through weight loss – were the reason that men were horny bastards. Man hunts woman: It was a sentence supposedly scrawled into my DNA. I remembered what my therapist told me. I didn't have to accept men's advances. I could say "no" to sex. "No" to impregnation. "No" to motherhood.

But where was the joy in "no" when I had nothing to say "yes" to? Where was the fun in constantly getting hunted down? Did my ability to run from my hunters really make it better? Where was the power in being reassured that I looked appetizing? Did God or whoever created us hate women so much that we were designed to live under the threat of violence? There had to be more to being a woman than that.

Questions like these spiraled through my mind during my two months at the treatment center. But, motivated by the desire to go to college, I cooperated for the most part. I ate what they asked me to. I gained weight. The fullness in my stomach spawned feelings of self-loathing, but I learned to sit with those emotions. I was discharged that August and went back home healthier. But even after that healing experience on the beach during my vacation, there remained a discomfort I couldn't shake. An unwillingness to fully inhabit my body, listen to my hunger, or grow to my full size. Friends tried to reassure me that "men like women with meat on their bones" and "guys want something to grab on to." Men were the subjects of "want," "like," and "grab." The consumers of the meat. And I, delectable. It made everything worse.

My goal had never been to make men happy. My goal was to find happiness myself. If I recovered from my eating disorder to look pleasing to men, was that really recovery at all?

Don't Worry, You Get to Be Objectified, Too

In college that fall, I picked up a book in the library: *Look at My Ugly Face: Myths and Musings on Beauty* by feminist scholar Sara Halprin. This book relates a Chinese folktale about a woman named Sun Pu-erh who goes on a quest to achieve enlightenment. A man warns her: "You will be the target of men who desire your beauty. They will rape and molest you." So, she scars her face before she sets out on her journey. "The ugliness she achieved" was "her way of finding freedom," Halprin wrote.[4]

I saw myself in Sun Pu-erh and other women I'd read about, escaping objectification by making themselves less conventionally attractive. Carol Emery Normandi wrote of her binge eating disorder in *Over It: A Teen's Guide to Getting Beyond Obsessions with Food and Weight*: "I felt safer because I didn't have to deal with men saying, 'Nice tits,' or 'Check out her healthy chest,' or grabbing my butt and breasts. It dawned on me that maybe having some weight on me protected me in a way I didn't otherwise know how to."[5] In these stories, women gained a sense of empowerment through invisibility.

They gained control over how they were seen – or not seen. Deflecting attention from their looks liberated them, even when that liberation came with harm.

The version of empowerment pushed in magazines and online was very different from Sun Pu-erh's. It was all about women's ability to be the objects of "see." Dove, perhaps the first brand behind popular body-positive advertising, unleashed its Campaign for Real Beauty in 2004 with a website reading: "Real beauty comes in many shapes, sizes, and ages."[6] One of its first ads featured women who weren't professional models posing in underwear. But the ad was nevertheless promoting beauty ideals: It was for a cellulite reduction cream aimed at "firming the thighs." And the models were thin, just not super thin. The message was still to aspire toward conventional attractiveness; it was just sneakier: Love the skin you're in ... but firm it up.

Almost a decade later, in 2013, Dove created an ad that reminded me of my drawing exercise in eating disorder treatment. In a YouTube video titled "You're More Beautiful Than You Think," an artist drew women's portraits, based first on their own self-descriptions then on how others described them. The women realized they were more attractive to others than they thought – "more attractive" seemingly meaning skinnier, whiter, and younger-looking. One woman is described as "thin" with a "nice thin chin." Another observes that she looks "fatter" in the drawing guided by her own self-image. In one cut, a Black man characterizes a white woman: "She had blue eyes, very nice blue eyes."[7]

The video's goal was to let women know they were pretty – by a Western, ageist, fat-phobic standard – rather than question whether they should work toward prettiness at all. In fact, it stressed the importance of feeling attractive. "I should be more grateful of my natural beauty. It impacts the choices in friends that we make, the jobs we apply for, how we treat our children," one woman said. "It couldn't be more critical to your happiness." She presumably meant that your feelings about your looks, not your looks themselves, are paramount. Yet there's a fine line between the two, especially when the focus is on drawings of your face. Especially when the message is tied to a brand promising to enhance your appearance.

Dove made headlines again two years later with a video where women had to walk through one of two doors: one reading "beautiful" or one reading "average."[8] They were shown debating whether they were beautiful or average – one exclaimed "oh my gosh" when another confessed she chose "average" – and at the end, large text read "choose beautiful." This ad made me wonder if all women really had to label themselves beautiful, or simply to free themselves from the expectation to be. Maybe some women who chose "average" considered themselves conventionally average-looking and were at peace with that. Maybe the issue was not some women deeming their looks average, but Dove implying that women had to have above-average looks – then categorizing and dividing them based on their looks.

All around me, I saw women invited through the beautiful door. A 2015 Lane Bryant ad featured plus-size models in sexy underwear purring words like "hot," "beautiful," and "honey, have you seen all this?"[9] That same year, women's publications circulated a photography series showing women of varying body types naked in piles of flowers. The photographer was recreating an *American Beauty* scene – where a forty-two-year-old man lusts after a high school girl – for "women who are hungry to see themselves represented in a beautiful way."[10] Beauty pageants cropped up around the world for plus-size women to compete in lingerie and evening gown contests.[11] Music also embraced body positivity: In 2014's "All About That Bass," Meghan Trainor imparted the advice not to "worry about your size" because "boys like a little more booty to hold at night." It felt like a step forward to encourage women to accept their size, yet a step backward to tell them not to diet so they could be more grabbable, the objects of "hold."

The range of women celebrated for their bodies was also expanding, with trans women like Laverne Cox and Caitlyn Jenner appearing on magazine covers as commentators remarked on how lovely and womanly they looked.[12] As trans activist Carter Brown has said, there's a difference between visibility and representation, and the sentiment of "oh wow, she's a beauty, she looks 'real'" doesn't constitute representation.[13] A singular focus on beauty constitutes objectification. And objectification is not the antidote to any woman's self-esteem struggles.

Women Don't Exist to Produce Erections

There's nothing wrong with plus-size women or trans women participating in photoshoots, pageants, or whatever helps them shine. It's OK for artists to sing about looks. Looks are a part of us, even if just one part. And I can't blame advertisements for focusing on how to improve your outer shell. That's the point of fashion and beauty products. Models, like people of every profession, should come in all shapes and sizes. It sets a good example to show a variety of people feeling good about themselves.

Yet I had a sense there was something more to confidence than seeing my figure as alluring. As I began writing about body image, I investigated various movements to figure out what that something could be. I spoke with the late fat-positive activist Cat Pausé, who considered fat positivity a more radical alternative to body positivity. Body positivity didn't always include fat people, she told me, because it capitalized on women's role as objects. "Women don't exist to produce erections," she declared.

Since fatness had not been absorbed into pop culture's depictions of beauty the way curviness had, fat positivity focused on celebrating those who weren't deemed objectifiable. Fat-positive Instagram accounts advocated for women's ability to live and thrive outside the male gaze, with quotes like "I see you taking up more space for yourself … the world is truly a magical place with you in it"[14] and "Why should I have to alter the natural state of my body to be seen as socially acceptable?"[15] The focus was less on women's right to be sexy than their right to exist – as everything they are. This is a helpful lens for people of all sizes who want to be subjects of a sentence – "she takes up space" – rather than mere objects: "she is seen."

Leah Vernon, a plus-size hijab model who identifies as a fat, Black Muslim, told me that fat positivity is for those who pioneered body positivity but are now excluded from it. "The body-positive space has been white-washed and is now fatphobic," she explained. "Which is interesting because the body-positive space was created by Black women, queer women, fat women, and dark-skinned women." For them, declaring fatness worthy of celebration is a way of defying objectification-based norms.

From Being Seen to Just Being

I learned about another movement, body neutrality, from a 2015 article by feminist writer Melissa Fabello. Fabello wrote that body neutrality aims "for the acceptance of our bodies as-are, for the understanding that we are already enough, [and] for the freedom to go about our days without a strong focus (positive or negative) on our physical shells – either as a step toward body positivity or as a goal in and of itself."[16] Body neutrality is more about taking the focus off your appearance than loving it.

I later took a course with body neutrality coach Summer Innanen, where she explained that self-love is not about "liking how you look" or "lusting after yourself." You can embrace your body without being the object of "like" or "lust." In an interview with me, Innanen elaborated on this point with an analogy:

> You may not be a very good parallel parker, but you don't let that really damage how you feel about yourself as a whole. Our perception of our appearance is going to change on a daily basis, and so if we are hinging the way we value ourselves on that, then it creates this rollercoaster. The goal is really to look at what love is. It's really about the actions that we take. It's about respecting yourself, it's about having compassion for yourself, it's about being kind to yourself – and we can do those things without liking the way we look.

The term "body neutrality" was popularized by body image coach Anne Poirier. "Body-positive social media figures continue to highlight, focus on, and share pictures and videos of their bodies," Poirier told me. "It is their bodies that are speaking the loudest, not their words or thoughts." Through body neutrality, however, "people are able to shift their attention away from how the body looks to what the body does." In other words, we can celebrate our bodies for their ability to move, provide sensory experiences, and bring us joy. "Think about your body as being the vehicle you get to experience life in, rather than an object to be viewed," Poirier advises.

Body neutrality is a subjectifying movement: We are not just the objects of "see" but the subjects of "do." I would also add "feeling" and just "being" to the list of verbs to value. We do not always need to be doing something, nor are those who can do more superior. We do not have to look good *or* do a lot. It really is enough just to be.

Out of the Looking Glass

Right before the pandemic, I moved into an apartment full of mirrors, and quarantine gave me lots of time to look in them. My bathroom had mirrors on every wall, so I could see my face from different angles. I'd reflect on my reflections. I'd stare at myself and fall down rabbit holes of appearance-related worries. A women's coach had me do "mirror work." I was to stare into the glass and praise what I saw: "I am beautiful, I am a goddess, I am physically blessed." This didn't alleviate my insecurities. I fell deeper down a tunnel of outward fixation.

And as I strove to see myself as attractive, both subject and object of "see," I realized I was posing the wrong question. "Am I beautiful?" didn't yield productive answers. That inquiry treated beauty as something to observe from the outside, not to cultivate inside. "Do I love myself?" was not too helpful either. That made me the object of "love," always striving to be lovable. To gain approval, albeit my own. It kept me in the role of the observer.

Then, a friend gave me advice so clichéd I'm almost reluctant to share it, but it's what finally got through to me: "Focus on *acting* beautiful, and you'll feel better about yourself inside and out." In that sentence, I'd catapulted into the active voice. Beauty was not just something I could be seen for; it was something I could act on. Something I could bring into the world. My goal was no longer to detect my luminosity; it was to shine it. The question was no longer "how can I find myself lovable?" but "how can I show love?" It was through loving acts – for others and myself – that my confidence would rise.

The insight I'd had in art therapy twelve years prior came back to me: "My body's size doesn't matter because I have a big heart." I knew this to be true because I saw the beauty in me when I behaved in beautiful ways. When I reached out to friends, volunteered to help others, or said kind words, I could feel the light inside me radiate outward, color my face, and, more importantly, color my surroundings. It was as if the lost Alice in Wonderland within me had climbed up the rabbit hole and out of the looking glass.

I went from asking myself "am I beautiful?" to asking how I could share my beauty with the world. And the answer was in my seventeen-year-old self's wisdom: to focus on my heart. When I expand and share my heart, it feels as if its warm glowing red really is spray-painted all over and around my body. Physical characteristics like my shape and size matter less. What shows is that luminous color, a hue detected by the spirit, not the eyes. And I can see this beauty, not when I look in the mirror, but when my gaze is focused on others.

Trying to see myself as thin or pretty reinforced the objectification that made me think I wasn't thin or pretty enough. Aspiring toward skin-deep beauty kept me outside myself, fixated on pleasing others' eyes – or, just as detrimentally, my own. As long as I was looking at myself, there would always be some flaw to find. It was not my evaluation of my looks that had to change, but my habit of evaluating them.

And so, I discovered a new antidote to my body image woes. It was not to put on lingerie or skin cream or to tell myself my curves were sexy. It was simpler: to get out of the looking glass and into the world. To reach out and connect. To pay someone a compliment, call a family member, pet an animal, or create art that shares who I am. And then I can feel the beauty that was in there all along, waiting to be expressed, coming out.

When your heart expands beyond the parts of you that can be transferred onto a piece of paper, when you color outside the lines of your outline, you begin to see your real size.

You begin to want to be big.

Big enough to hold the whole world in your heart. Your open, ever-growing heart.

Chapter 3

I Reveal: Freeing the Person Behind the Nipple

I strove to stay tuned in to my heart. But the rest of the world's attention seemed to linger just outside it – on my nipples.

Like body positivity, the #FreeTheNipple movement defended women's right to be seen, with the display of breasts in particular presented as a liberating act. "Nipples are beautiful things, don't hide them," model Cara Delevingne told *Elle* in 2014.[1] "When did the women's [*sic*] body start being something to hide?" actress and singer Willow Smith echoed in a 2015 tweet using the #FreeTheNipple hashtag.[2] A woman's body was not something to hide, according to these celebrities and their feminism. It was something to proudly reveal.

I did my best to embrace this idea, but the truth was, it frightened me, as I wanted to hide. Between *Girls Gone Wild* ads featuring drunk college women flashing cameras, *The Man Show* segments devoted to ladies on trampolines with their clothes falling off, and warnings about dressing modestly so I would not get assaulted or distract male classmates, I'd gotten the impression that an army of men was constantly encroaching upon my breasts, poised to seize control of them the moment I looked away. A male friend once told me that a woman in a low-cut shirt was like an opened bag of potato chips: Men would see what was hanging out there and instinctually go after it, whatever their morals told them.

I had no way to define my chest except in terms of how men experienced it. The question of what I could gain from it was never posed. There was no space for such considerations when I was so busy protecting myself. Facts I did not learn: that nipple stimulation activates the same brain region as clitoral stimulation.[3] That nipples possess sexual sensitivity for many people of different genders. That some can even orgasm through breast play. That breastfeeding is not just good for a child but improves a mother's health.[4] What I did learn: that men's deepest, wildest dream was to see and touch a pair of boobs, and they'd go to great lengths to realize that aspiration. Simply possessing this body part felt dangerous. During my earliest hookups, I preferred to keep my shirt or bra on. I was afraid my partners would become out-of-control animals if they saw what lay underneath. Removing my top felt like the ultimate concession, surrendering to being under siege.

Looking Through the Male Gaze

Some of my early experiences cemented this terror and dread. When I was nineteen, someone I'd just started dating tried to reach under my shirt while we were making out. I said I wasn't comfortable with that, but nevertheless, he managed to unbutton my dress without me knowing. I only realized he'd done so when I saw a rabid stare in his eyes, then looked down to notice my bra exposed. I could not let my guard down for a second.

The haunting ogle I saw on his face felt like the same look I had felt on me my whole life. My sophomore year of college, I learned a word for this large, masculine eye that seemed to follow me: the male gaze. Film theorist Laura Mulvey coined this term to mean exactly that: an imagined gaze that peers at women from a stereotypically male perspective.[5] The male gaze is not the same as an individual man's gaze, which can be loving or gentle. But its omnipresence in the media can affect how men see women in real life. And how women see themselves.

The male gaze functions through *Playboy* centerfolds that show off naked ladies alongside their weight and measurements, through camera lenses in sex scenes that zoom in on women's breasts, through art gallery walls filled exclusively with nude female paintings, and through song lyrics that wax poetic about women's curves. Along with the male gaze, there is a white gaze, a heterosexual gaze, and all sorts of gazes that assert themselves over less valued perspectives. Usually, they function together: The male gaze is a stereotypically white, heterosexual man's gaze.

Because women can be objects of the gaze and still be subjects, the male gaze can be showcased within art, film, and literature without oppression taking place. The problem is when the male gaze is *the* one and only gaze. When this typified male perspective has a monopoly on media, it appears objective. Why aren't there many sex scenes where someone sensually undresses a male lover? Why is male nudity more often used for humor? Why does heterosexual sex dominate porn and other media? Why do woman-on-woman sex scenes seem more catered to men than women? And why do we rarely wonder why?

That is the male gaze at work: The man's role is as the looker, not the looked-at. The subject of the gaze, not the object. The perceiver of women, not the perceived. The beholder of beauty, not someone contained within the eye of the beholder. When the male gaze becomes universal, the female body becomes a symbol of "to-be-looked-at-ness," as Mulvey called it. Even women peer through their own eyes with this gaze. We become our own observers, experiencing our bodies from the outside, noticing every line, every crevice, every asset, every flaw. Without the instruction or examples necessary to focus on how we feel inside, we view our bodies as objects.

There's a term for this, too: objectified body consciousness. Psychologists define this as "the tendency to view oneself as an object to be looked at and evaluated by others."[6] The authors of one study on objectified body consciousness wrote: "Repeated objectification experiences might lead to females' self-objectification and facilitate such individuals to assume and internalize an outside observer's gaze."[7]

The Split Self

My own objectified body consciousness created a divide between my eyes and the rest of my body. My eyes looked at me. My eyes didn't feel like mine. They didn't feel like mine because they were the eyes of a subject, and I was an object. My eyes had internalized the male gaze. Peering at the glass, they possessed a piercing look detached from the eyes in the reflection. Eyes covered in makeup, made up to dazzle, to be seen, yet not to see. I split into two parts: the part of me evaluating my body, and the part being evaluated. I fell out of touch with my sensations, seeing my face as a mask, my body as a thing, rather than feeling what it was like to be in it.

Not all women look upon themselves with the same gaze. Some of us look at ourselves in scorn, deeming ourselves not beautiful enough. Some of us survey our bodies with a predatory gaze, frighteningly aware of our "tits and ass." Some enjoy this gaze, aroused by another's imagined arousal. Many, including me, find it's a combination of all three. I somehow simultaneously felt that I never looked good enough, that men would not be able to resist me, and that I *wanted* to be irresistible.

How can we feel all these ways at once? Because the male gaze is the subject of varied verbs: Criticize. Lust after. Admire. Loathe. Attack. Adore. The aggressive, attacking male gaze made me uncomfortable with anyone seeing or touching my chest. The scrutinizing gaze made me wonder if my breasts were too big or small or droopy or lopsided. The admiring, ravishing gaze caused me to fantasize about being desired. I felt all those gazes on me, even if no one in the room possessed any of them. Even if no one else was in the room. Though not all these gazes were unpleasant, what was unpleasant was always being gazed upon. Even when I was alone, this sense of being watched clouded what I saw and felt. It was as if my five senses were inverted, directed at me rather than the world around me. I'd walk down the street, not taking in the sights, but wondering how other passersby perceived my face and body.

Especially my breasts. I'd heard so much about men looking at breasts, yet so little about what how women could enjoy them. Or what was underneath them. I longed for that heart I had spray-painted in art therapy to be seen, not hidden behind this ... rack. These knockers. These jugs. Or whatever word people wanted to use that I didn't invent or consent to. All I wanted was to get this imaginary male eye off my chest. To simply exist without any eyes stuck to me. To be witnessed without being surveilled. And so, when women began fighting for the right to appear topless, I had trouble relating.

All Eyes on the Nipple

The #FreeTheNipple movement began in 2012, when filmmaker Lina Esco was creating a movie about double standards in shirtlessness. Not only was she pursued by New York City cops while filming – despite toplessness being legal there[8] – but she was also censored by Facebook and Instagram while promoting the film.[9] The movie pointed out that men were allowed to go nearly anywhere without shirts, while women were socially – and in some US states, legally – required to cover up.[10]

Two years later, actress Scout Willis's Instagram page was deleted after she posted a photo of a sweatshirt with two topless women in the design. To protest this penalty, she walked shirtless around New York City and tweeted a photo from her stroll with the hashtag #FreeTheNipple.[11] Other celebrities like Rihanna and Miley Cyrus expressed support for the movement on social media.[12] Meanwhile, in-person events were affirming women's right to be shirtless, including an annual Go Topless Parade in New York and a book club where members read topless in Central Park to "make reading sexy."[13] #FreeTheNipple spread around the world, with Icelandic women adopting the hashtag for their shirtless photo-sharing.[14] It was also folded into body-positive advertising: An Adidas sports bra ad featured a collage of bare breasts with the text: "We believe women's breasts in all shapes and sizes deserve support and comfort."[15] Some praised the brand for breaking stigma and showcasing diversity. Others pointed out that Adidas was doing something that had been done many times over: They'd used pictures of boobs to sell stuff.

Efforts like these, despite their positive intentions, did not feel liberating to me in their impact. I'd grown up with images of breasts all around me, and now there were even more. Mostly of young, white, thin, cisgender women, underscoring the male gaze's ever-presence. It seemed that any female celebrity who posed topless for a sexy magazine shoot was now lauded as "freeing the nipple." #FreeTheNipple itself sold shirts with pictures of full, perky, Caucasian breasts.[16] The fight against breast cancer was even sexualized: I saw bracelets sold in shops to raise money for cancer research with the words "I <3 boobies" engraved on them. My culture's obsession with breasts, these mythical symbols of sex appeal that I somehow carried below my shoulders, only seemed to have grown.

Not all these phenomena were direct consequences of #FreeTheNipple, whose goal I understood to be the opposite. It was trying to desexualize breasts by making toplessness normal. The aim was to treat female shirtlessness just like male shirtlessness: as no big deal. I could get on board with that mission: Women shouldn't have to wear anything to be safe or to be deemed respectable. I shared this vision, but I could not feel liberated by it because I didn't see it manifesting in reality. What I did see was that even the fight against sexualization was sexualized. When *Vice ID* covered the Icelandic #FreeTheNipple campaign, 72 percent of the article's views came from men, even though the publication's readers were mostly female.[17] Nor were men's magazines like *Playboy* and *Esquire* shy about using the phrase "free the nipple" to tease and share sexy photos of women.[18] I could not throw myself behind the fight to be seen – one that often recreated the ways women were already seen constantly – when I still felt deprived of the option *not* to be seen.

Where did this movement leave women who felt empowered by having attention off their bodies? Did being empowered mean being looked at? This was how it seemed when Kim Kardashian explained her choice to post a nude selfie to Instagram with: "I am empowered by my body."[19] And when the 2018 *Sports Illustrated* swimsuit edition – where models posed nude with words describing themselves written on their skin – claimed to be giving women "control" and showcasing their "strength."[20] A *Vanity Fair* article presented the spread as an act of solidarity with #MeToo, as it made the models "as much participants as objects." *Sports Illustrated*'s swimsuit editor observes in the piece: "At the end of the day, we're always going to be sexy, no matter what is happening."[21] Even, apparently, if what is happening is that women can't be "participants" without being "objects."

Concealing as Revealing

Where was the movement for women's right not to be sexy? Where was the movement that accepted awkward under-boob sweat and nipple hair just as much as pert, pink nipples? Where was the movement for women's right to be seen for the heart underneath? Or to see, in the active voice? To emerge from behind their nipples, to shine beyond the confines of their skin? Where was the "free the person" movement?

It's not that this kind of feminist movement doesn't exist. It just hasn't been the white, mainstream feminism dominating North America or Western Europe. Some Muslim feminists, for instance, defend their choice to cover up as liberating, as a statement that they don't owe anyone visual pleasure. The pressure they receive to display themselves instead shows how deeply objectification is woven into Western ideals of female freedom. In 2021, a New Jersey teacher allegedly pulled a hijab off a seven-year-old girl, declaring: "Your hair is beautiful."[22]

Anti-hijab sentiments are "rooted in Islamophobia as well as the objectification of women," says Leah Vernon, the hijab model I interviewed. A woman hiding her body is supposedly disavowing her beauty, failing to celebrate herself. But what if this choice is instead a declaration that her body is hers and no one else's to look at? What if celebrating ourselves does not require celebrating our looks? Philosopher Frantz Fanon wrote of Westerners' hijab aversion:

> Unveiling this woman is revealing her beauty; it is baring her secret, breaking her resistance, making her available for adventure. ... There is in it the will to bring this woman within his reach, to make her a possible object of possession. This woman who sees without being seen frustrates the colonizer. There is no reciprocity. She does not yield herself, does not give herself, does not offer herself.[23]

More simply, Muslim American researcher Dalia Mogahed asked Trevor Noah on *The Daily Show*: "What are we saying when we say that by taking away or privatizing a woman's sexuality, we're oppressing her? What does that mean? What does that say about the source of a woman's power?"[24] It says that Westerners define women's power by their accessibility to others' eyes. By their right to be the objects of "look at." I did not want my power defined that way. But, as a white woman in the US, other options were not presented to me. So, I searched for novel ways to free my body from the male gaze, to resuscitate my floundering subjectivity.

My Body as Art

When I was eighteen, a good friend suggested I model for a figure drawing class to improve my body image. She told me that modeling for this class had helped her to look at her shape and size non-judgmentally, the way someone might look at a vase or a tree they were drawing. I cringed when she told me that most of the students were male and most models were female, but she said she'd never felt sexualized there. I trusted her, so I took a leap of faith and went.

As I posed in a dim wooden basement with Iron & Wine humming from an old-fashioned record player, I felt the students' eyes on me – indeed, all older men – but to my surprise, I did not feel the male gaze on me. There I was, naked in a room full of men, all staring at me. And none reacted in a sexual way. The artists spoke to me during breaks just like I was one of them, even if I didn't bother to put my clothes back on. This was when I realized that the male gaze is different from an individual man's gaze. Men can look at you with all kinds of gazes. These men looked at me with an artist's gaze.

The male gaze breaks women into parts: breasts, butts, vulvas. The artist's gaze sees shapes and lines, shadows and lights. The male gaze wants to do things to a woman. It views her body as a conquest. The artist's gaze isn't interested in that. It simply wants to observe. The male gaze sees women as the only viable objects and views male objects as unnatural or perverse. The artist's gaze does not uphold this duality or these judgments. One man in the class told me he preferred drawing men because he found the lines more intricate.

So, perhaps I was not designed to arouse uncontrollable lust after all. Perhaps being an object of someone's gaze did not always mean being objectified. I saw that my unclothed skin did not have to be arousing. It did not have to signify sex appeal. It could signify art. And if my nudity could signify at least one thing other than sex, then maybe, it could signify whatever I wanted it to. My naked body could signify pleasure. It could signify wildness, freedom. It could signify privacy, sacredness. Its significance could change at my whim, for my purposes. And men could celebrate that significance with me, with their gracious eyes and conversation, without imposing any perspective on me. I modeled for several classes over a semester, then did not return. I'd accomplished my mission of looking at myself without the male gaze coloring my vision.

Stripping Under the Sun

Once I'd conquered my fear of falling into an abyss of male pupils, I felt no need to revisit public nudity – until, eight years later, an invitation graced my email inbox. This email presented another opportunity to explore how to be the object of "see" without forfeiting my subjectivity. It came from a PR rep for a clothing-optional resort in Jamaica called Hedonism II, offering me a trip so I could write about my time there. "Hedo," as they called it, was full of swingers and other sexual adventurers and home to sex shows, erotic theme parties, and a "playroom" where X-rated activities took place. The representative dubbed Hedo a "judgment-free haven perfect for sex-positive millennial women" to "take charge of their sex life" and "empower themselves sexually, but more importantly, personally."

Sexual and personal empowerment were just what I was seeking. I'd been writing about women's bodies for two years, on a quest to figure out what it meant to be sexually liberated. I'd become more, though not completely, comfortable with my body by that time. I'd been in a relationship for a year with a man who honored my boundaries and never pushed me. He liked and frequently complimented my looks but never peered at me with those devouring eyes that guy in college possessed. I was seeing how I could be an object of desire and still a subject.

And yet a worry lingered that if I were too sexual, too free, I'd lose my subjectivity. The thought of being naked among strangers gave me pause. I feared objectification was something I could not escape in such a setting. That was why I had to go: to see if I could prove my fears wrong. Since I was in a monogamous relationship, I went strictly as a journalist. The PR rep assured me there was no pressure to do anything at Hedo. From dancing to swimming, there was plenty of non-sexual fun to be had. Perhaps this would be an opportunity to be naked and not be sexualized. To have my boobs hanging out without people looking below my eyes. To make my body signify whatever I wanted, as I'd begun to dream of in that art class. That was, to me, what it meant to free not just the nipple but the entire person.

I flew to Jamaica on a sunny afternoon, and a staff member escorted me around the resort grounds. "Women have all the power here," he declared. In the span of ten minutes, I saw a painting of the Mona Lisa with a breast hanging out on the lobby wall, statues of female busts flanking the salad bar, a photo of a skinny yet busty nude woman behind my bed, and a TV screen in front of it where two women were giving a guy a blowjob. I lay on my mattress and peered up at the ceiling, which supported a giant mirror. As I saw myself reflected back in it, I couldn't shake the feeling that I was another decoration adorning the room. Another object to be admired. Was this what it meant for women to have power?

Our Eyes Are up Here

The following week confirmed my suspicion that the power to be looked at was not real power. My relationship status didn't serve as a boundary circumscribing a container for freedom, as I'd hoped. Instead, it was a challenge for the men there. When I resisted their advances, they pushed back and explained that my "boyfriend wasn't there." In the hot tub, several men swam up to me and touched my breasts and thighs without asking. Another woman in the jacuzzi reminded the man across from us, "My eyes are up here," as he ogled her. He replied, "You have eyes?"

She had eyes, and so did I, but it didn't seem to matter. When I sat on a cushion in the playroom and watched two couples have sex on adjacent mattresses, I got kicked out for not "participating." Women at Hedo were there to be objects of "look," not subjects. We were not the ones with eyes. We were not the ones with "I"s beginning sentences like "I explore" or "I connect" or "I pursue." We were the "you"s. Our nipples were free, but were we?

Hedonism's Instagram displays no shortage of skin freed from clothes. Pictures captured from the vantage point of someone staring down a woman's bikini top and checking out her thong from behind. Scrolling through it, I sensed that I was looking through the lens of a horny man's eye. It was vaguely the same eye that had been darting around, trying to spot me in the sand, locate me on my balcony. It followed me as I dashed through the waves, splashing water on my skin, covering myself with foam, longing to be exposed and hidden at the same time. Exposed for what I was, and hidden for what I wasn't. For what I was made out to be: an object.

On that beach, in that hotel room, in that ocean, I'd been part of so many sexual sentences. So many that still began with "he": "He notices her." "He invites her to the playroom." "He asks her to have a threesome with him and his wife." "He tells her she has nice breasts." "He knocks on her door at 1 a.m. to see if she's awake." "He describes her pubic hair as a 'lobster trap.'" I was told this was empowerment. Sexual empowerment. Personal empowerment. I was included in sexual and personal activities, after all. Yet I was rarely the subject of these activities. To many, that concept did not exist. Empowerment was simply inclusion, even if I was included as an object. But sexual empowerment requires more than placing women in sexual sentences. It means women get to choose where in the sentence they sit. Or stand or run or walk or lie down, clothed or unclothed.

The same goes for trans and non-binary people, who I did not see at Hedo, with its heavy marketing to heterosexual cisgender men and couples. What sentences would they fit into in a world of male subjects and female objects? Men, as well, should be able to occupy any position in a sentence. Yet at Hedonism, men were strictly subjects, reluctant to assume the feminized object role. I saw men attend dinners in simple shirts and slacks, hand in hand with women in lingerie. I witnessed threesomes involving two women, but guy-on-guy action happened "behind closed doors," one guest told me.

Women are "just pretty creatures," she said of this dynamic; this was just the way it was. Many things appear to be "just the way they are" when one perspective is treated as universal. The stereotypical heterosexual white man finds female bodies most attractive, so they just are. He finds thin, curvy, white, able-bodied, cis women the prettiest, so they just are. The male gaze considered me someone who was born to be objectified, so I just was.

On my flight back, the man next to me on the plane struck up a conversation with me. I instinctively avoided eye contact, accustomed to being visually broken into pieces from the past week. I did not want to acknowledge his gaze. When I finally did, I realized he was looking at my face. He was only talking to me to be friendly, person to person. How odd, I thought, that this was the one time I'd felt empowered or comfortable in my body all week.

Our "I"s Are in Here

I was invited to more clothing-optional resorts over the following years as I built up my reputation as a sex writer. And again, I saw female sexual liberation equated with female sexual display. At the top-optional Temptation in Cancun, Mexico, the management had renovated the facility to appeal to women, which meant putting a picture of a nude woman's body on the bottom of the pool and spray-painting female silhouettes on the bedroom walls. The word "topless" appeared throughout the resort's website, and among its main attractions was the "boobs cruise," where bikini tops came off in the ocean. My breasts were not just there to be looked at; they were there to sell hotel rooms. So, it wasn't surprising when other guests' eyes – and sometimes hands – found their way below my neck.

Another Mexico resort, the couples-only Desire, offered to host my boyfriend along with me. Under the Riviera Maya sun, between champagne glasses and chocolate-covered strawberries, I enjoyed non-sexualized nude moments like I did in that figure-drawing class. A staff member complimented my shoulder tattoo, unphased by the rest of my bare skin. Other couples met us in the pool and asked about our relationship and jobs, as they would if we were clothed. The fact that I was with a man probably helped. I was seen as taken. And since we were together, I was treated the same way he was. I got to see what liberation through nudity looked like for a man, and it had little to do with being declared "sexy" and aggressively pursued.

Desire was not making any special effort, like Hedo or Temptation, to appeal to women. It was, strangely, some places' focus on women that always seemed to become a focus on women's to-be-looked-at-ness. It was as if the world did not have the language to consider women's sexuality from a female perspective. It was as if there were no female perspective. Jacques Lacan's words echoed through my mind: "Woman does not exist."[25] Sexual freedom as seen through women's eyes did not exist. A woman's desire, supposedly, is for a man's desire.[26] And so affirmations of female desire just end up affirming male desire.

There's little precedent for anything else. The most prominent efforts to allegedly showcase women's desire have centered men's desire from the get-go. When Hugh Hefner founded *Playboy* in the 1950s, he saw himself as liberating women sexually. "*Playboy*, very clearly, from the outset, has fought against the historical repression of women," he once said.[27] But the accounts of his bunnies themselves, rife with stories of sexual abuse, hardly paint a picture of female freedom. Even Marilyn Monroe's famous centerfold was published without her consent.[28] She wasn't the only one: *Playboy* published at least nine minors' nudes, with the *Playboy*-owned publication *Sugar and Spice* showcasing a naked ten-year-old Brooke Shields.[29]

Upon Hefner's death, *Refinery29* wrote that *Playboy* gave women a space to "put [their] sexuality on display," wondering out loud if these women were "simply expressing their sexuality and using its power in their own favor."[30] Yet whose sexuality is really displayed or expressed in homogeneous photos of naked women and girls, some of whom did not consent? Who really holds power when these women are selected, styled, and photographed to appeal to male consumers? Calling *Playboy* an expression of women's sexuality is like calling a McDonald's commercial an expression of a cow's appetite. If an image's goal is to arouse men, it depicts men's sexuality, or at least someone's idea of it. Not women's. A woman performing sexiness is not the same as a woman expressing her sexuality. A woman's sexuality lies within her, not within images of her.

There's a difference between being sexy and being sexual: being sexy means provoking someone else's desire; being sexual means having your own. This should be obvious, but it isn't in a culture where women's sexuality is conflated with their sexualization. Women's ability to be sexual has been confused with their ability to be sex objects. And so, many attempts to appeal to the female gaze recreate the male gaze. Arousing images of women stand in for women's own arousal. Attempts to instill confidence in women devolve into declarations that women are beautiful – and initiatives to enhance and exhibit that beauty.

Behind the Breasts

The way to free the whole person – not just the nipple – isn't to admire women's bodies. It's to look into their eyes and let them look back. It was not in sexualized settings but through reverent connections that I shut that watchful eye that was always scanning the room for men staring down my shirt. It was through partners who expressed an affinity for my appearance while seeing everything else I was. Who looked at me, perhaps with desire, but with more: with curiosity, affection, or warmth. Who acknowledged my breasts and the heart behind them.

And it was through experiences I savored on my own, with no one else's gaze on me. A year after visiting Desire and Temptation, I discovered an app full of sex meditations, including one on breast massage and pleasure. It prompted me to tune in to my nipples, ribcage, and heart. To caress and breathe into these spaces, allowing the air to flow. To put the disjointed pieces of my body back together. It grew easier to gain pleasure with someone else once I could feel it by myself, while performing for no one. Once I felt safe taking my shirt off in front of a partner – as the object of "look" and "touch" but the subject of "look back" and "feel" – I could explore how I myself might enjoy being seen and touched. Nerve endings that were previously numb woke up. I came to love having breasts for reasons unrelated to how anyone perceived them. They went from decorative ornaments to bundles of sensation. Newfound rapture emerged as my awareness shifted from outer appearance to inner feeling.

As I journeyed from fragmentation to wholeness, every part of my chest began to feel like part of me. The thought of others' eyes there didn't feel so threatening. I grew excited about being noticed, about the possibilities that brought. I could be sexy because I knew I could be sexual at the same time. And those were two of many things I could be. It was as if, not just my breasts, but my heart was freed from the protective wall I'd placed around my chest. When someone grazed their hands over my nipples, I could feel them touch a piece of me. My skin, my soul touched back. There was no longer a split between my body and my subjectivity, between the part of me being touched and the part touching the other person's hands.

Breasts as Gazelles, Deer, and Lightsabers

In mid 2020, as I was coming to these realizations, I noticed a cartoon on Instagram featuring a large pair of breasts with the caption "sexy" and a small pair with the caption "also sexy." "Comment ' ♥ ' if you agree that all boobies are pretty," the post read, prompting comments like, "HELL YEAH I LOVE ALL THE TITS."[31] I tweeted a screenshot of the cartoon with the text: "Instead of telling women their breasts are sexy no matter their size, how about we stop sexualizing breasts?"

My phone flooded with responses, including an email from a doctor and sex therapist. "I was always taught that the primary reason nature bothered to keep women's breasts rounded even when they're not pregnant or lactating is to serve as an erotic cue," he wrote. "So, according to that assumption, it would have been nature that sexualized women's breasts, not people." He pointed out that in most mammals, breasts only grow during pregnancy and lactation – yet in humans, they enlarge during puberty and stay that way. Some googling convinced me this could be the case: breasts may serve as markers of fertility and sexual maturity.[32]

Maybe desexualizing breasts was beside the point. A body part can be sexy and still be honored as part of a subject. No body part, in fact, should need to be desexualized to be honored. Still, I wondered how this erotic cue, this maturity, might be seen as sexual, not just sexy. If not filtered through the male gaze, breast development might be something for a woman herself to celebrate: a sign of her growing capacity for pleasure and desire.

Another reply to my tweet argued that the sexualization of breasts was natural based on a very different source. It cited the Biblical book the Song of Solomon as proof that this phenomenon was as old as time. Yet when I read the Song of Solomon, I found descriptions of a woman's body that were altogether different from modern-day sexualization. In fact, these descriptions showed how breasts could be eroticized without being objectified. Two lovers call out to each other in a poetic duet, speaking sensual lines such as "your breasts are like two fawns, twins of a gazelle" or, in a different translation, "your breasts are perfect; they are twin deer feeding among lilies." Another Bible passage in the book of Proverbs speaks of husbands' regard for their wives: "Let her breasts fill you at all times with delight; be intoxicated always in her love."[33] This portrayal of breasts was not about the surface but the passion and sacredness underneath. The eyes witnessing these "fawns" and "twins" were tender ones, admiring the bosom as an expression of the heart.

"Bosom" is a word with multiple meanings: "a woman's chest," "loving care and protection," "the chest as the seat of emotions."[34] The bosom is a living, feeling entity that receives as much as it gives. In the Bible, the breasts are the bosom. They are the subjects of the verbs "be" and "fill," creatures with their own will. They spill their light and feeling out into the world. They "feed," even though some may feed from them; they hunger and fulfill themselves. They are almost animate, like "fawns" exploring their terrain. In neotantric philosophy, the breasts are the seats of love, and just as a penis penetrates a vagina, a female heart penetrates her lover's heart.[35] She feels love, shows love, goes after what she loves. Her breasts represent this affection she exudes; they are not separate from it. They are the part of her that points outward and moves in toward others.

This is what it means to be a subject: to have a body that feels, senses, and radiates. Once I came to understand myself as possessing both a physical and spiritual bosom, I saw that I could be an object of the gaze with a physical form *and* a subject expressing myself through this form. The form and the feeling were inseparable. When someone touched my physical frame, they touched a part of me. Through my chest, they touched my heart and opened it. When I undressed with a partner, I stopped imagining their view. Instead, I felt myself fall into their hands, extending myself further so that more of me could be reached. Spilling myself out from the inside, from the inside out. And having a woman's body, that thing I had been fearing, took on a whole new heavenly meaning.

Open Chest, Open Heart

If all we're taught growing up is to show off our bodies or guard them against incoming advances, we won't get the chance to enjoy them as the living, breathing entities they are. Amid all the messages about how much men love boobs, we don't learn to see our breasts as participants in pleasure, play, and love. When we learn that our bodies are objects for others to see or hold, we detach from them as if they are not ours. We divide our outer shells from the self that sees and feels, which deprives every part of us of feeling.

It was as if I'd built an invisible barbed-wire fence around my ribcage, so nobody could truly see or touch me. I did not feel safe inside my own chest, so the sensation there shut down until I could reimagine it as mine. This happens not just for breasts but for vaginas and other body parts that we learn exist for male pleasure or for our offspring. If all we hear about our nudity is that others are aching to witness it, we can't inhabit our vessels enough to enjoy being naked, physically or emotionally. The irony is that when we can't enjoy our sensuality, others can't either. Neither we nor our partners can step into the feedback loop of reciprocal honoring where each person, embodied and free, soaks in the other's pleasure and offers their own.

When someone else gains enjoyment from our bodies, we will feel used unless we gain from that interaction too. To foster mutual pleasure rather than exploitation, we must beat objectification to the punch. We must teach everyone from a young age how their bodies can serve them. Only then can they free their nipples – if and how they choose – with an understanding of what they themselves can reap from that. Each person can create their own definition of "freeing," whether that means baring or covering. Which one they choose is not important. When you're hyper-aware of being looked at, neither revealing nor hiding is liberating. But if you are living inside your own skin, you can feel free in any state of dress or undress.

Once you so are immersed in the tingle of the air – or your shirt – gently grazing your skin that you're not watching yourself through anyone else's eyes, that is when you can truly be free.

Once you learn how to derive pleasure from your own body, that's when you'll feel at ease with others enjoying it, too.

Being looked at stops being so scary when you are given the space to look back.

Chapter 4

I Look: Reclaiming the Dick Pic

Every woman is beautiful.
Every woman deserves to be seen.

From body-positive billboards to boob-themed bracelets and cruises, the message was loud and clear.

All breasts, all butts, all hips, all thighs are worthy of attention.
All stomachs are sensuous, whether they are round or flat.
All vulvas are delicate roses, designed to be admired.

All penises are …

Wait. Why doesn't that seem to fit? The notion might sound humorous to some. While supporting movements that prompted people to look at women, many feminists have maligned a phenomenon that involves looking at men. Yes, I'm talking about the dick pic. No image knows the internet's wrath quite like a photographed penis.

Unsightly or Unwanted?

"Your dick is ugly. No one wants to see your dick in any context," comedian Samantha Bee said in a public service announcement to men on her talk show. "Even the straightest, horniest woman who loves you the most is hoping you can get it inside her without her having to look at it ... Your dick is objectively the worst thing about you."[1] Online publications were quick to join the war on dick pics: "The woman on the receiving end usually ends up losing her lunch," *Bustle* declared.[2] "The assumption that a penis photo is sexy reflects men's total misunderstanding of women's turn-ons," *Mic* concluded.[3] While any part of a woman was sexy no matter its shape or proportions, this did not appear to be the case for men. Dicks – especially those deemed abnormal in size or appearance – were ugly, the consensus seemed to say.

"Your dick looks like I wouldn't even feel it if it was inside of me. ... Look! You grew a pube! Oh wait, that's just your dick,"[4] one woman wrote in a text reply to a dick pic, dubbed the "perfect response" by *Buzzfeed*.[5] In a 2015 YouTube video called "Women React to Dick Pics,"[6] which was shared by popular publications like *The Huffington Post* and *Bustle*,[7] women respond to penis photos – all presented to them with their consent – with laughter and disgust. "Ew, that's not circumcised," one woman says. One penis is deemed a "huge monstrous elephant dick," while another is a "sad little one" that's "more balls than dick."

The positive responses this video garnered from progressive sites speaks to women's frustration with non-consensual dick pics. Over half of US millennial women have received dick pics, and while 69 percent of them asked for one at some point, 78 percent had received uninvited penis photos.[8] One study in the UK even found that three quarters of adolescent girls had received unsolicited dick pics.[9] Such photos are, of course, a violation. But they're a violation because they're unwanted. Not because they're dick pics. Not because the penises in them may be big or small or uncircumcised. Rather than starting a conversation about navigating consent in the digital age, these photos started a conversation about how gross male genitalia supposedly are, especially when they do not fit societal ideals.

This pattern of criticizing men's looks carried over into the #MeToo movement, when the media focused on shaming sexual predators' bodies, rather than their choices. Tabloids covering Harvey Weinstein's trials described his "odd" and "deformed genitalia" as photos of his penis appeared in court to corroborate victims' accounts.[10] *The Mirror* and *The Sun* reported that he'd earned the nickname "the pig" in France due to his size and tendency to sweat.[11] Howard Stern called him "this big fat guy ... there is no girl on the planet that wants to see Harvey Weinstein naked and is going to get aroused."[12] Age-related stigma came into play too, with talk show host Seth Meyers saying of TV personality Charlie Rose, who was accused of flashing several women: "Usually, when someone that old is walking around naked, a couple of male nurses lead him right back to his room."[13]

OK, so it is kind of funny. It's hard to sympathize with these men or care when they're insulted. After all, they imposed their bodies on others; why should we honor their boundaries? But disparaging their looks – or the appearances of people who send unwanted dick pics – detracts from the real issue, which is the ugliness of their actions. It thwarts discussions of ethics and respect in favor of superficial judgments. It shames not just sexual predators who happen to be "fat," "old," or "undesirable," but anyone who shares those traits, regardless of their character. And when the shaming is directed toward penises in general, that includes everyone with one.

All Breasts Are Sexy and Penises Pretty

Not only are penis owners made to feel bad about their bodies, but anyone attracted to them is made to feel perverse for wanting to see and touch something so "ugly" and "disgusting." Especially if that person is a man who is choosing other men over women's supposedly superior beauty. But not everyone with a penis identifies as a man – and the conflation of penises with masculinity is part of the problem.[14] The idea that "male bodies" (and therefore penises) are there to *do* – while "female bodies" (and therefore vulvas) are there to *be seen* – colors views of genitals themselves.

You can see this binary at work in how we talk about small breasts vs. penises. "All boobies are pretty," as that Instagram post declared, is the dominant body-positive message that flat-chested women hear. Though penises, like breasts, could be considered erotic visual cues, we don't typically hear that all penises are pretty no matter their size. Those insecure about penis size are instead advised: "What matters is how you use it." No one tells them the gorgeous curve of their glans is just as luscious despite its modest size. No one reminds them that their genitals are flowers, each unique yet lovely in its own way. These ideas sound comical in a world where beauty is almost synonymous with femininity. Where penises are called "equipment." Where male bodies are there to get shit done and female bodies are there to get shit done to them.

Beauty (n):
1. A combination of qualities, such as shape, color, or form, that pleases the aesthetic senses, especially the sight. "I was struck by her beauty."
2. A beautiful woman. "She was considered a great beauty in her youth."[15]

With femininity baked into our very definition of beauty, it may be hard to imagine someone other than a woman as a visual object. Body-positive advocates reinforce this when they say that all women – but not all people – are beautiful. Many seem to agree that women, by definition, are the attractive ones. "Women look like beautiful, soft, gorgeous angels when they're naked. We look like hairy ogres or little scrawny trolls," singer Jason Mraz told *Cosmo* in 2009.[16] Or, as the character Elaine observed in a 1997 *Seinfeld* episode: "The female body is a work of art. The male body is utilitarian. It's for gettin' around. It's like a jeep."[17]

All ~~Women~~ People Are Beautiful

Such views are often expressed in an attempt to boost women's self-esteem. Women shouldn't feel self-conscious in front of men, the thinking goes, since they're far more attractive. Yet such words validate women's ability to be desired at the expense of their ability to desire. It's as if female bodies were made to be objectified, the objects of "see," while male bodies were made to be subjectified, the subjects of "function" and "get around." And, of course, to enjoy female bodies.

With men there to enjoy and women there to be enjoyed, this is not just heteronormative but totally imbalanced. And this imbalance is so normalized, we rarely question it. "Women don't love the penis. If they love the man, they'll tolerate the penis. The best your penis can ever hope for is, 'well, all right,'" continued Seth Meyers' diatribe against sexual predators. As if, once again, the real issue with these criminals is that they have penises. This expectation that men just love women's bodies while women "tolerate" men's sets us up for inequality within heterosexual sex. If a man's eyes are feasting on a woman's body and loving every second of it, while the woman is merely putting up with her partner's body, how can they enjoy themselves equally?

If women learn this dynamic is normal, they'll never expect equality in the bedroom. They'll come to accept partners they feel "well, all right" about instead of seeking partners they're turned on by and excited to be with. They'll come to accept sex that their partners relish but that they merely put up with, rather than seek out sex that they themselves can't get enough of. And the adjacent stereotypes of women as "less visual" and "less sexual" encourage women of all sexual orientations to settle for sex they're lukewarm about.

Return of the Peacocks

I've heard people say this is nature. That men care more about physical pleasure, while women enjoy the sentimental dimensions of sex. That men look for visual cues like large breasts and butts to assess whether a woman is fit to bear a child, while women care about how emotionally available a man is and what's in his bank account. One woman in the "Women React to Dick Pics" video complains: "Please stop sending me pictures of your dick. I wish you would instead send me records of how much money you make." Anthropologist Helen Fisher echoed to *The New York Observer* in an interview about sexting: "A man wants to see a woman's body, and a woman may want to see a man in the picture with … a Rolex watch or a business suit or a pair of cool jeans."[18]

People often bolster such statements by evoking our hunter-gatherer instincts, claiming that males want to spread their seed to the most fertile females, while females want males who can provide sustenance and shelter. But if one wants to draw upon evolutionary psychology, the opposite argument could be made. In most animal species, it is males who have eye-catching features. Male birds are more colorful than females.[19] Male lions boast fluffy manes, demonstrating their ability to withstand the heat.[20] Male peacocks have bright, five-foot-long tails that they fan out to put on a show for females, whose tails only span a few inches.[21] Contrary to the view of male bodies as utilitarian while female bodies are works of art, à la *Seinfeld*, the male peacock's tail actually compromises its ability to move. Yet this feature has survived in the species because it serves as a visual cue.[22] And lest I leave penises out of the equation, male chimpanzees and bonobos display their genitals as part of a mating ritual to get females' attention.[23]

Like animals, human males possess visible features that provide cues of reproductive fitness. Male humans have beards, which appear to serve no function except as ornaments, signaling sexual maturity.[24] Scientists have also speculated that human penises are larger than is functionally necessary because they serve as visual signals of fertility, similar to female busts.[25] Nor is vision a smaller part of women's arousal than men's. Women's bodies respond just as much to erotic images as men's do.[26] And the idea that women's focus is on men's finances and careers may be more cultural than biological. In prehistoric communities, everyone hunted and gathered.[27] It was not until agriculture became pervasive that roles were divided along gender lines and men's money and property mattered.[28] Queer and non-monogamous people's existence should be enough to question whether we're wired for relationships consisting of masculine-feminine dyads, where one person supplies sex while the other offers financial support.

Why is it, then, that it seems like straight men care more about women's appearances than vice versa? "We've been training men to be sexually visual since the time they were born," Tulane University sociologist Lisa Wade told me in an interview. "In a society constantly bombarding one type of person with visual stimuli, I wouldn't be surprised if they became more visual."

Uncovering Adonis

The "just so" nature of the male gaze leads to many justifications of women's objectification. Another is that the human eye is wired to find women more pleasant to look at. As my fellow guest at Hedo explained the uneven gender dynamics there: "Women are just pretty creatures." Or, to quote a more influential figure, Hugh Hefner defended *Playboy* in a 2010 interview by claiming that "the beauty of women, and the fact that they are the focus, that they are sex objects in a positive sense, is the reason we have civilization."[29] Such reasoning explains away the tendency for media to assume a straight male viewer and ignore everyone else: Women's bodies are just *that* aesthetically pleasing.

But if one wants to appeal to aesthetics, the opposite argument could be made as well. In the 1980s, 85 percent of nudes in New York City's Metropolitan Museum of Art were female, according to research by the feminist art group Guerrilla Girls.[30] But male nude statues filled ancient Greece and Rome – the origins of Western "civilization," to use Hefner's term – where men were subject to elaborate beauty ideals. A beautiful man possessed "a gleaming chest, bright skin, broad shoulders, tiny tongue, strong buttocks, and a little prick," wrote the ancient Greek playwright Aristophanes in the play *The Clouds*. Penises were prized for being graceful and elegant, not huge and dominating.[31]

While today you hear male singers wax poetic about women's beauty – à la John Mayer's "Your Body Is a Wonderland," James Blunt's "You're Beautiful," and Ed Sheeran's "Shape of You" – ancient Greek poets described male bodies with flowery language. "He shone among the other pentathletes as the bright moon in the middle of the month outshines the stars; in this way he showed his wondrous body to the great ring of watching Greeks," one male poet, Bacchylides, wrote of a male athlete. The ancient Greek male athlete's body was "a spectacle, a body performed, observed, admired, and desired," writes Ruth Allen, curator of Greek and Roman art at Emory University's Michael C. Carlos Museum.[32] It was the object of many verbs and gazes. And how could we forget Adonis, the Greek god of beauty, whom Aphrodite hid from the other goddesses in a chest due to his stunning appearance?[33] I think it's about time he came back out.

I'm not suggesting we reverse the male gaze and objectify men. I am suggesting that gendered beauty ideals are culturally relative – and that women are not "just more beautiful," at least not to everyone's eye. The notion that people only want to look at women is "not true in the West; it's not true anywhere," Thomas Laqueur, Professor of History Emeritus at the University of California, Berkeley, and author of *Making Sex*, told me in an interview. Female figures began dominating nude paintings during the Renaissance because such paintings were created for male patrons, according to Laqueur.

Fast forward several centuries to 2012, when a viral image circulating through social media contrasted photos of petite models and actresses like Keira Knightly and Nicole Richie with older stars like Marilyn Monroe and Bettie Page. "When did this become hotter than this?" the accompanying text reads.[34] Yet both referents of "this" are basically the same. The celebrities of earlier generations are – like their modern counterparts – thin and white with rare, idealized proportions. And they're all women. I sometimes wonder when *all* those women became hotter than the male athletes of ancient Greece.

The idea that men can be objects of the gaze is not reserved for ancient times, though. Donatello's David sculpture from the 1400s is full of erotic cues, with a wing on the giant Goliath's helmet inching up King David's leg.[35] "When the city of Florence wanted to have a great statue by the great sculptor of the day, they didn't have a female," says Laqueur. "They put up a male. They told Donatello, 'Do the spectacular naked David.'"

And, of course, you can find examples of male bodies visually appreciated today. *Magic Mike*, a movie whose main draw was footage of Channing Tatum and other male actors stripping, raked in $170 million worldwide.[36] Women's second-most-viewed category on Pornhub is gay male porn – a genre watched by 21 percent of straight men as well.[37] This should not seem strange. What seems stranger is expecting women to want penises inside them, yet also be repulsed by them. What seems stranger is expecting straight women to willingly have sex while despising their partners' bodies.

Which brings us back to the dick pic.

The I of the Beholder

From the time I was a teenager, I was aware that while men looked at images of women in magazines like *Maxim* and *Hustler* geared toward pleasing their own eyes, the magazines I read also featured sexy photos of women on the covers. They instructed us on pleasing men's gazes, with advice on fashion, diet, and looking good naked. Their makeup application tips taught us how to look at our eyes, not through them. I saw art on walls of restaurants and museums showcasing elegant female bodies, while portraits of men portrayed their status, accomplishments, character, and stories. I saw music videos like Robin Thicke's "Blurred Lines," where nude women dance alongside clothed, libidinous men directing them to "shake your rump" and "do it like it hurt."

The message I received from this disparity was that what I looked like was important, but what I looked at was not. My ability to pose and seduce and enchant was important, but my perspective was not. And this disparity between men's and women's ability to look was a disparity between our enjoyment. Men got a show, while women got to be the show. And those outside this binary got nothing.

Even efforts to appeal to the "female gaze," from art exhibits to feminist porn, still made women the show. The New York City Museum of Sex's 2017 "female gaze" exhibit, which included work from twenty-eight female artists, consisted mainly of female bodies.[38] Mainstream porn sites' "female-friendly" videos often portray a softer version of male-centered porn, featuring male actors' hands – and/or the camera itself – gliding over women's breasts and butts. The feminist porn site Bellesa hosts thirty-two pages of videos classified as "lesbian" and thirty-five pages of "girl on girl" porn, compared to five videos total under "guy on guy" and no similar classification.[39] Articles on women's sexuality feature sexy photos of women, rather than images of what women themselves may want to look at. Like clothing-optional resorts' attempts to empower women sexually, "female gaze" initiatives end up making women objects of the gaze.

This convention comes out even in media that's not visual. When I was hired to write audio erotica scripts geared toward women, including one featuring a man getting aroused as he draws a female friend, the site instructed me to include details about the female protagonist's appearance. They wanted the women listening to put themselves in that woman's shoes and feel desired. So much effort goes into helping women feel desired. So little goes into helping women feel desire – or allowing men to feel desired. We've defined beauty as something men witness, rather than something they possess.

The Fear of Female Subjects and Male Objects

Maybe that's why dick pics are really so hated across the board. They pose a conundrum to the patriarchal gaze. Nude photos of men flip the script that says men should look and women should be looked at. They challenge the assumption that the only legitimate taste is heterosexual men's. When women request such images, they are female subjects with male objects. "We have this idea of women interested in sex as being scary, voracious, hungry in a way that's dangerous," sociologist Lisa Wade told me. "To actively seek out dick pics is to be an agent of one's own sexuality, and I think being the active member of a sexual pair, as opposed to the passive member, is something women are taught to not do. So, it is to break out of a gender box for women to actively seek and request sexual images."

It bucks gender norms not just for women to be desirous, but also for men to be desired. Being an object of the gaze is seen as a feminine, debased role, since it's been associated with male predation for so long. On her blog *Sociological Images*, Wade theorizes that homophobia is rampant in part because the thought of being desired by another man causes men to "feel what it's like to be prey."[40] It's not that gay men are out there preying on straight men, but since we don't always imagine women possessing a lustful gaze, it's sometimes when the gaze comes from a man – even if imagined – that it hits men: They, too, can be objects. "It's like they've been treated like a human being their whole life and then, POW, they're a piece of ass and nothing more," Wade writes.

But gazing doesn't have to be predatory. We can gaze in a way that honors someone when we acknowledge that they're in there, gazing back. For someone to be a subject, they *must* be able to gaze back. And that's why we have to acknowledge a variety of people as potential visual objects. Male-on-male activity happening "behind closed doors" in settings like Hedo goes hand in hand with men looking at women's breasts instead of their eyes. As long as it's taboo for men to be desired, it'll be taboo for anyone attracted to men to be sexual subjects. And the reason why is simple: Part of being a subject is having an object. "I see" and "I desire" are incomplete sentences. Those verbs take direct objects.

We can't end the objectification of women unless we challenge the constant subjectification of men, their confinement to the role of viewer – not just because many women are attracted to men (98.6 percent in the US, according to a government survey),[41] but because the "male subject, female object" construction leaves out many sexualities. Granting all people subjectivity requires validating images outside women performing for the male gaze as objects of visual pleasure. These non-standard images cover a vast spectrum. They include images geared toward queer women, where women are objects of desire without exuding passivity and patriarchal beauty norms. They include genderqueer people. All these representations are scarce, and no matter our sexual orientation, women can sense when our subjectivity is denied.

You Show Me Yours

Despite feeling this denial myself, I always knew my sexuality lived within the two globes of my eyes, not the mirror that I battled each morning. I knew that what I saw mattered more than how I was seen. I knew my pleasure mattered more than my ability to please. And so, in my first sexual relationships, I made sure I got to soak in sights, not just provide them. That included sexting. And yeah, sometimes, dick pics. Requesting photos felt like a feminist rebellion. I'd been taught my own body was a work of art to enjoy, yet here I was, enjoying others' artwork.

When I began writing about sex, I received my first unwanted dick pics – and my visual and emotional experience was completely different. Even though I was a subject of the gaze, I felt like an object, a receptacle for strangers' exhibitionist fantasies. That was when I understood that the hatred of dick pics was a hatred of boundary violations. The issue was not with the shape, size, or appearance of anyone's dick, but with the sense of entitlement conveyed by these photos' random appearances in women's DMs. Men who send unsolicited dick pics have been found to hold exceptionally sexist attitudes.[42] Their intent to degrade emanates through the photos they send. That's what makes them unsightly.

Instead of condemning acts or bodies, we should condemn entitlement, abuse, and intimidation. Otherwise, people will feel ashamed over consensual acts or for simply having the bodies they have. Sexual violence involving acts and bodies deemed desirable, such as that perpetrated by women, will appear less severe. And survivors will receive less compassion: How could a woman assault a man? Not only are men horny bastards, the thinking goes, but the female body is beautiful. Maybe not when it is tied to ugly actions.

Changing the World, One Dick at a Time

The truth is, bodies are shapeshifters. They take on beauty or ugliness depending on what they do – and what we associate with them. When we see female bodies dressed in bikinis and skirts, posing seductively on screens, they come to signify prettiness. When we see vulvas depicted with floral imagery, they represent softness and delicacy. When we hear about male bodies as vehicles for war and crime, they signify violence. When we think of penises as responsible for assault, they signify aggression and disgust. Especially for those of us who have been violated ourselves.

But we can create new associations through new interactions. Interactions where women ask to see exactly what they want and receive only that. Where we undress partners at our pace and touch them exactly where we like, waiting for our own hands to guide us. Things look and feel different when we are in control. Then, maybe men's bodies won't signify aggression, disgust, or violence. Maybe one day, they will signify the warmth men have shown us. The times they used their power to amplify our voices. The times they looked, not just at us, but into us. The times they helped us discover how much we could feel. The times their vulnerability cracked our hearts open. The experiences they facilitated where we witnessed how passion and gentleness could coexist. Where we could step out of our comfort zones and be held. Where we felt safe.

It's up to men to lay the framework for these new associations. Women can't suddenly view penises more positively if their experiences with them have been negative. But men can pave the way for love and trust where there was previously fear and pain. Having a penis is an immense responsibility. It's a gift. One you can use to make a partner feel their absolute best or their worst. One you can use to make the *world* better or worse. And that starts with believing in the loveliness you already possess, dick and all.

That's why I'm really writing this chapter: so men know they were not made to add ugliness or darkness to the world. In fact, they have a precious, cherished role in adding beauty. They are so much more than what's in the tabloids and talk shows. Their manhood is medicine, not poison. Their dicks can be lightsabers, life savers: healing, uplifting. And when they own and recognize that light, their actions have so much power. Even small actions – like telling a woman "forget about me for now; tell me what you want" or "I won't proceed unless you're a full 'yes'" – have the power to heal our collective trauma.

I am not particularly invested in a world where women's phones are blowing up with dick pics they've requested.[43] I'm invested in a world where women's partners, whatever their gender or genitals, are giving as much consideration to delighting them as they are to their own delight.

Where each woman's, each person's, partner contemplates: What can I do to make her light up when she sees me walk through the door this evening?

What can I do to put a smile on her face when she opens her eyes in the morning?

Her gaze matters. Her perspective matters. She is the beholder whose eyes hold beauty.

Chapter 5

I Ask: From Consent to Desire

Things look and feel different when we are in control. This doesn't just apply to sexting. Any act can take on a beautiful new life when we're in charge of whether and how it happens. On the flip side, sex itself can become aversive when we're constantly fending it off rather than seeking it out. When we're receiving others' desires without the chance to tune in to our own. When the only power we're granted is the power to consent or say "no."

Consent (n): voluntary agreement to or acquiescence in what another proposes or desires; compliance, concurrence, permission.[1]

Some synonyms for consent, according to our friend Google: agreement, assent, concurrence, accord, authorization, sanction, clearance, acquiescence, acceptance, approval. Almost all these words refer to someone else's ideas. If you're the subject of "consent," it's because you are the object of "ask." You are agreeing or concurring with what someone else suggests. You are authorizing or sanctioning them to do what they want, giving their desire clearance, acquiescing to it, accepting it, approving it.

Where is the desire of the person consenting? Often, it is hovering on the periphery of the conversation, not quite making it into questions like "can I ... ?" or "is it OK ... ?"

The Keepers of Consent

I'm grateful that the question that launched my first sexual experience began with "do you want me to," not "can I." That it concerned what I wanted, not just what my partner wanted. That it was a question at all. I'd soon learn that hookups were often attempted based more on assumptions than questions. The assumption that, if I went to someone's room, I was open to sexual activity. The assumption that, if someone pleased me, I owed them pleasure in return. The assumption that intimacy followed a script, escalating from one act to another. My desire was nowhere in those assumptions.

My role, it seemed, was more often to veto or allow men's desires. Advances were coming at me, and it was my job to filter them. To filter out the ones I didn't like by stopping them. To filter in the ones I liked just by letting them continue. Even in that inaugural experience that helped me see myself as a subject, my partner was the one asking the question. My second sexual experience was not as affirming. My partner used phrases that were not questions but directives, like "let's go" and "come on." I couldn't quite pinpoint why I left with an icky feeling, not the sense of nourishment that characterized my first hookup. I'd consented, after all. I'd agreed. I'd acquiesced.

Then, in college, I went to a talk called "Doing What You Desire, Not What You're Just OK With." It was about making sure you enjoy your sexual encounters, rather than just tolerate them. The speaker emphasized that people of all genders can be victims and perpetrators of sexual violence, and everyone's consent mattered equally. It was the first time an expert had spoken to me about sex without depicting it as some military operation, where a man tried to seize control of a woman's body. It was revelatory to hear someone acknowledge that women had desires, let alone that they should follow them and nothing less.

Up to that point, the discussions of consent I'd been privy to centered on ensuring a woman was not protesting. The silence around our wants and needs made "doing what you desire" seem like an impossible standard for women. It implied that women didn't desire much. That notion didn't match my experience, but it matched the little sex ed I'd received. My high school's instruction on consent was limited to one harrowing talk, where a rape survivor shared her story and explained why men must honor that "no means no." The focus was narrowly on male–female dynamics, and stereotypical ones. Women were afforded the right to say "no" – to lack desire, not to express it. Women were the objects of "assault," "exploit," and "use," not the subjects of "want," "request," and "enjoy." The focus was on our trauma rather than our desire and pleasure – neglecting that sex devoid of desire and pleasure can itself be traumatic. Instead of feeling empowered, I felt unsafe and scared to be female.

The Consent Double Standard

Today, there's an alternative to "no means no," dubbed affirmative consent: "yes means yes." Instead of assuming consent in the absence of a "no," affirmative consent makes the standard a clear, verbal "yes." Affirmative consent is encoded in law in several US states and Spain.[2] Some educators and activists also use the term "enthusiastic consent," meaning that everyone involved in a given sexual activity should actively be into it.

What even affirmative and enthusiastic consent leave out is an examination of who is saying "yes" or "no" and who is posing the question. If we're taught that it's men's role to initiate sex and women's role to consent, we're still living in a sexually unequal society – unequal for those whose encounters don't involve one woman and one man, and for women who would like to be initiators instead of mere responders. PSAs on college campuses, a setting where many of us first learn about consent in depth, often reflect this "man asks, woman answers" dynamic. A poster distributed at Coastal Carolina University in 2008 reads:

> Jake was drunk. Josie was drunk. Jake and Josie hooked up. Josie could not consent. The next day Jake was charged with rape. A woman who is intoxicated cannot give her legal consent for sex, so proceeding under these circumstances is a crime.[3]

The message is phrased as if the man were responsible for the encounter, even though they were both drunk. Jake was the subject of "rape," and Josie was the object. Consent campaigns now make an effort to be gender-neutral, yet even in 2021, a study of 194 American and Canadian consent posters found that "women are rarely positioned as the initiator and thus have an implied responsibility to say yes or no; that is, monitor the gate," the authors wrote. "When an emphasis is on women's strength and decision-making, there may be more than a hint of the returning of the old-fashioned idea of a gatekeeper, one that permeated sex education texts and advice columns from a century ago, which presented the idea that boys' lust was girls' job to manage."[4] It's almost as if the woman is even less than the gatekeeper: She's the gate, opening and closing to let others in or keep them out.

The assumption of a male perpetrator and female victim is baked into the US government's definition of rape: "the penetration, no matter how slight, of the vagina or anus with any body part or object, or oral penetration by a sex organ of another person, without the consent of the victim."[5] This definition, from 2012, is an improvement on the previous one – "the carnal knowledge of a female, forcibly and against her will" – yet a clear descendent of it. The narrow definition of rape as penetration reveals a cultural view of insertion (as a penis does) as active and possibly violent, while engulfing or enveloping (as a vagina does) is considered passive and powerless. Rape, supposedly, can happen to a vagina, mouth, or anus, yet the formidable penis is immune.

"Pockets of Vulnerability"

The depiction of women as vulnerable and rape-able makes rape seem like a natural occurrence that happens because of how our bodies are formed. This view comes out even in feminist thinking. In her 1990 book *The Beauty Myth*, feminist author Naomi Wolf characterizes vaginas as "'pockets of vulnerability' subjected to assault."[6] Perhaps she was describing a cultural vulnerability, but in the classic 1975 book about rape culture, *Against Our Will*, Susan Brownmiller posits a biological vulnerability, stating that "man's structural capacity to rape and woman's corresponding structural vulnerability are as basic to the physiology of both our sexes as the primal act of sex itself."[7] But women don't get raped because we have vaginas. We are not designed to be violated. We get raped because of the very belief that makes vaginas appear as "pockets of vulnerability": that we are passive objects.

Any unwanted sexual contact counts as sexual assault, and what makes it devastating is the violation of boundaries – not the specifics of what happens to what body part. The focus on rape as penetration trivializes assaults that don't line up with the typical gendered narrative. The only way a man can be raped, under the legal definition, is if he's in the feminized position of being penetrated. Yet according to the Centers for Disease Control and Prevention (CDC), one in fourteen men in the US has been "made to penetrate someone."[8] The CDC defines "made to penetrate" as "a form of sexual violence that some in the practice field consider similar to rape." Yet somehow not rape. When a man is the subject of "penetrate," it is difficult to imagine him as the object of "rape." His genitals are seen as instruments of violence, not pockets of vulnerability. And so he is clumsily both the object of "made to" and the subject of "penetrate," as if he is an active participant in his own violation.

Rape is not described this way for women. We do not hear "he made her have sex with him" or "he made her put her vagina around his penis." This language would border on victim-blaming. If we thought of women as subjects, we might consider women capable of assault, which they unfortunately are: 83.6 percent of male survivors of sexual coercion and 53.1 percent of male survivors of unwanted sexual contact report only female perpetrators.[9] And sadly, it's more common than many realize for women to assault other women.[10] When men are seen as the sole subjects of "assault," women become the sole objects of "ask." And consent education stops at teaching men to ask women's permission – if even that.

From Gatekeepers to Move-Makers

Objectification also affects how we talk about consensual sex. Women miss out on the chance to pursue what they want, and people are left in the dark if their encounters don't always involve one cis man and one cis woman. I talked to several LGBTQ+ people about this, including Kate, forty-one, who is non-binary and queer.

"As a kid, the idea that I had agency to say 'no' was vaguely there," Kate said. "But the idea that I could initiate wasn't clear until I was in my first queer sex situation in college. I had no idea how to make a move. I had no words for what I needed to do. I didn't see someone who wasn't a man asking someone out in the media. I didn't see it modeled at home." Rachel, twenty-six, who identifies as lesbian, echoed: "It's hard for me to say what I want or don't want before it happens, and sometimes even until one or two days later. I guess it stems from society and my family telling me that as a woman, I can't want sex, and therefore, it's hard for me to even access any feelings connected to it."

When we're preoccupied with when to open or close our legs for others, we become desensitized to the desires between them. Or, we are hesitant to act on them. A survey by Kinsey Institute fellow Justin Lehmiller found that 22 percent of straight American women in relationships rarely or never initiate sex, compared to 13 percent of men.[11] But 28 percent of women said they'd like to initiate sex more, and they might be happier with their sex lives if they did. Despite clichés about women needing to be swept off their feet and carried to bed, women who initiate sex report higher satisfaction and less regret.[12] It makes sense: When we make the first move, the choice is born from desire, not a weak idea of consent that means being OK with it.

"Many women do seem to feel as though something is holding them back, but many men seem to feel pressure to be the initiators," Lehmiller told me. "I suspect adherence to traditional gender roles of women as 'gatekeepers' and men as 'initiators' has something to do with this." There's nothing wrong with a woman's partner initiating sex, but when you haven't had many chances in life to dive into your desires, it's empowering to ask for what you want, not just consent to what someone else wants. It means that the desire came organically from you.

I, Too

The same gender roles that dissuade women from initiating sex deem it natural for men to not just desire sex but push for it. In a 2016 survey, a quarter of Australians ages twelve to twenty said it was normal for men to pressure women into sex.[13] "Baby It's Cold Outside," in which a man convinces a woman to stay with him after she repeatedly tries to leave and calls him "very pushy," is celebrated as a cute holiday song. And when a woman under the pseudonym Grace recounted actor Aziz Ansari pressuring her into sexual activity, pundits called it mere "bad sex,"[14] while Ansari's defenders rallied around the hashtag #AzizDidNothingWrong.

Debates about "grey" cases of sexual misconduct often center the question of whether the accused committed assault and should be punished. This question matters in courts of law, but when it dominates media conversations, the focus on what these men deserve detracts from the question of how women – or anyone – should feel during sex. And this question is bigger than whether someone feels she's been raped. We rarely ask: Does she feel honored? Does she feel physically and emotionally nourished? Have her desires been heard? Is she leaving with a smile on her face? These standards might sound unrealistic, which is why we should ask these questions: to create new standards – for everyone including ourselves. We can ask ourselves these questions to see if a sexual relationship is working for us. We can turn down future encounters with people who leave us less than beaming. And we can make a point to leave our own partners feeling amazing, not just OK. We can ask "do you want to?," not just "can I?"

There is power in women supporting one another by saying "me, too" – as in, "someone violated me, too." But how can we go beyond sharing our past and create a new future for ourselves? What would an "I, too" movement look like, where we get to be subjects? What would conversations about consent look like if we centered women's desire? Grace may have acquiesced to Ansari's requests. But when she describes getting up and moving away, it's hard to imagine she was dying to be close to him. When she describes moving her hand from his crotch, it's clear she wasn't aching to get her hands on it.[15] To suggest a woman could have such feelings bucks standards of femininity. They make her sound "unladylike." Uncharacteristically lascivious. Masculine. And maybe that's why it can look like no big deal when a woman has a sexual experience devoid of those drives.

On Putting Out, Getting It in, and Asking for It

It's hard to view strong desire as womanly when we speak of sex the way we do. Straight men casually refer to sex as "scoring" or "getting it in," as if the woman is the opponent, trying to block him out of her vagina. The woman's role, in turn, if the man "gets lucky," is to "put out" – defined by Google as "agree to have sex with someone."[16] A definition eerily similar to the definition of consent.

You can hear these tropes at work in the arguments of incels – those who complain about being "involuntarily celibate." Not all but most of these people are men who believe women owe them sex as a natural right. And while you can find them on Reddit, they're not just an obscure online community. In 2018, four years after incel Elliot Rodger shot and killed six people, George Mason University professor Robin Hanson wrote of Rodger in a blog post: "One might plausibly argue that those with much less access to sex suffer to a similar degree as those with low income, and might similarly hope to gain from organizing around this identity, to lobby for redistribution along this axis and to at least implicitly threaten violence."[17] *The New York Times* gave a voice to this cause, with opinion writer Ross Douthat describing Hanson as "brilliant" and suggesting that we leverage "sex workers and sex robots" to meet the demands of the sexually underserved.[18]

The fact that many people are deprived of human touch, sometimes because of factors like race, size, and disability, is worth discussing. But when we talk about "access" to sex as if it's a right, it is almost always women who are the objects of the verb "access." When we put women in the same category as sex robots, we normalize a view of sex as something with only one enthusiastic participant – a man. Why not examine whether sex might be "unevenly distributed" due to the limited options that feel safe, respectful, and pleasurable for women? Or how to give women "access" to sex with people who treasure and uplift them? Imagine how many willing partners straight men could have if they learned from a young age how to empower and please women. Then, women – sex workers included – might have more space to ask for the sex they want, not just reject or submit to others' asks.

Instead of acknowledging women's capacity to ask for sex – and creating a world where they have sex worth asking for – people often tell women what they're "asking for" based on what they're wearing. It's almost as if some cannot conceive of a woman literally requesting sex. In a 2021 study, nearly 7 percent of women and 15 percent of men agreed with the statement: "When girls go to parties wearing slutty clothes, they are asking for trouble."[19] This idea even comes up in court. In Florida in 1989, a man was acquitted of rape after a juror declared that the accuser "asked for it" based on her clothes.[20] More recently, in Ireland in 2018, a lawyer displayed a seventeen-year-old girl's thong as evidence that she was "open to meeting someone and being with someone." Despite there being no signs of desire, the gate was supposedly open.

The twenty-seven-year-old man she accused of rape was also acquitted.[21]

Of course, such women are not asking for it, and those who use this phrase know that. When someone says "she asked for it" based on a woman's style of dress – or the fact that she was out at night or drinking – they don't mean she was really requesting sex. They mean that a man desired her, and she supposedly made herself available. It's because women are presumed to have little aim or will themselves that their clothes, instead of their words or actions, are treated as markers of consent. Or, signs of capitulation such as not saying "no" are treated the same way. Preventing such treatment is an uphill battle when our standard for sex – consent – is literally defined as acquiescence. Movies and TV are full of acquiescence substituting for desire. From *Gone With the Wind* to *Moonstruck* to *Fifty Shades of Grey*, men carry women off as they resist, as if this is romantic. The proxy for the woman's desire is her concession as she goes limp in a man's arms. Women, supposedly, give consent by wearing thongs, by ceasing to resist ... by doing anything but expressing interest.

Synonyms for "desire": wish for, long for, want, yearn for, crave, set one's heart on, hanker after, pine for, thirst for, itch for, be desperate for, be bent on.[22] How often do we see women on screen who are yearning for sex, desperate for sex, or hell-bent on having sex? Nowadays, we sometimes do. Yet we still live in the shadow of sitcoms where women complain they "have a headache" or only "offer" sex when their husbands offer them something in return, as if sex must be bartered for attention or love. These plotlines don't acknowledge that the sex itself can be what women gain in "return" for having it. Or that "giving" attention and love are also rewards in of themselves. Some profess that women use sex to get love while men use love to get sex. But what if we sought out love for love's sake and sex for sex's sake, free from deception or ulterior motives?

Letting the Body Speak

With men assigned the role of desirer and women assigned the
role of desired, many women end up having sex based more
on partners' wishes than their own. That's why twenty-seven-
year-old Maya, another woman I interviewed, said her first
sexual experience wasn't wanted, but she didn't say "no" either.
All she sought, all she was taught to seek, was to be an object
of desire. "I think media had taught me that the more you do
with boys or men, the cooler and more desired you are, and I
just wanted to be desired – whether or not *I* truly desired what
was happening in the moment," she said. "I felt like I always
had to put on a show and didn't know how to articulate what
I wanted ... because the show was for him! I wanted him to
think I was sexy."

How can a woman know what she wants in a world full of
adages like "the desire of the woman is for the desire of the
man"?[23] How can she be a subject of desire when the pressure
to be sexy overrides her ability to be sexual? How can men
know what they want either when they're "supposed" to want
anything and everything sexual? How can LGBTQ+ people
know what they want when the only culturally sanctioned
desires are between straight, cis people? How do you tease
apart what you desire from what you're OK with, or what you
feel obliged to desire? People of all genders and sexual orientations are flooded with messages about what they "should"
want from the day they're born.

Doing what you desire starts with the skill I learned in
eating disorder treatment: allowing your body to speak. Our
minds internalize social prescriptions for what we should
and shouldn't want. Our sensations and the emotions they
point toward tell a different story. Our feelings are subjective;
they make us subjects. When we tune in to what our bodies
want, this is called embodied consent. Practicing embodied

consent means checking in to see how you feel about a situation, act, or partner. This offers a way to understand what you desire, beyond the desire to be desired. Someone's genuine desire, in the embodied consent framework, can be felt physically. You may feel heat in your chest, relaxation in your face, or tingling in your pelvis when you want something. Conversely, when you're uncomfortable with a sexual possibility, you may feel clenching in your throat or knots in your stomach.

This sensation of "yes" or "no" may not even be a sexual feeling. Asexual people, for instance, may not feel sexual attraction, but they may feel a different kind of "yes." They may have a desire for emotional intimacy, sensual connection, or pleasure, which may or may not correspond to genital arousal, asexual sex educator Aubri Lancaster told me. Even if someone is not asexual, their decision to have sex may stem from a non-sexual desire. A couple that's been together for years may lack strong sexual passion but still crave the intimacy of sex. Either way, Lancaster says, "we need to have ways that we can check in intrinsically with our own feelings about something without having to gauge that against another person."

Body awareness is the key to this self-knowledge. "If we only try to communicate from our brain without noticing how our bodies are feeling, we can't be in consent with ourselves," Carey French, a sex educator who teaches embodied consent, told me. "We have to be in consent with ourselves first – and able to attune to ourselves – before we can navigate consent with a partner." By visualizing different scenarios and identifying the sensations and emotions they bring up, you can begin to decipher what your body's "yes" and "no" feel like. French, who learned about embodied consent from *The Survivor's Guide to Sex* by Staci Haines, suggests starting with non-sexual situations: Figure out what a "yes" to your morning coffee feels like, or a "no" to getting on a long line. Then, when you're presented with a sexual opportunity, you can ask yourself whether the

sensations arising in your body feel more like a "no" or a "yes."
French explains:

> For me, that looks like taking a full breath and closing my eyes,
> focusing internally while I consider a decision, and noticing.
> Do I feel openness across my chest, my head tilting back,
> a smile lifting my lips? For me, that means "yes." Do I feel
> energy moving down my body, my feet rooted to the floor, my
> head tilting down, my belly tight? For me, I know that means
> "no." Everyone's sensations will be different. It just takes a
> willingness to build a relationship of attunement to your body,
> and a willingness to feel.

As you practice this, you get in touch with what you want
to ask for. You also learn to respond with greater confidence
when someone else presents an opportunity. You won't always
be the one to ask. But you can still apply the standard of desire
when you're the one being asked. One litmus test is whether
you *would* have asked, had the other person not. Another is
whether you feel like you *should* say yes. If so, it may be helpful
to tune in to your body and see if you feel a true, desire-
based yes.

Hearing Your "Hell Yes"

An even simpler question to ask yourself: Is it a "hell yes"? If
not, it's a "no." I first learned this at age twenty-five at a cuddle
party in New York City. That's what it sounds like: a party
strictly for cuddling. There, the hosts told us to say "no" to
any cuddles we were less than excited about. Even if we were a
"maybe," they advised, it was better to say "no" and revisit the
possibility later.

Over the course of the event, several people asked me to
cuddle. Before the talk we'd just received, I would've told them

"yes," and it would've been fine. But fine was no longer good enough. When I thought about that guideline – if it's not a "hell yes," it's a "no" – I realized, one by one, that I didn't want to cuddle with any of them. So, I turned them down. I spent the afternoon sprawled out on the carpet, speaking to fellow guests about travel and music festivals, but not touching anyone. It was a novel experience: No one had asked me if I wanted to cuddle before. Previously, if someone wanted to cuddle with me, they'd just start cuddling with me. Then, I'd decide if I wanted it to end. Not if I wanted it to begin. Never again was I going to merely tolerate physical contact.

When women tolerate intimacy for a partner's sake, they can feel like objects. But when we give ourselves the chance to feel what we're a "hell yes" to, we get to discover who we are as subjects. "Learning that consent meant I could initiate, be rejected, and have a different place in the interaction as a whole was liberating and also terrifying," said Kate. "It also helped me realize how often I actually wanted sex versus how often I wanted romance or other things." This kind of self-discovery requires more than "yes" or "no" questions. Sometimes, sex educators use the phrase "negotiating consent" to describe pre-sex conversations where each person shares their vision for the encounter. But to me, "negotiating" sounds too much like bargaining or persuasion. The goal is not to get as much as you can from someone, but to understand their wants and needs. Boundaries are not up for negotiation. So, instead of negotiating consent, how about we discuss desires – before, during, and after our encounters?

"There's a lot of times when women and people walk away from sexual situations with a level of discomfort, maybe sometimes with a level of regret, maybe that it didn't go the way you wanted," sex therapist Marissa Nelson explained to me. "We want to move from that to having pleasurable embodied experiences, and that starts with a conversation. You can have a conversation even before sex starts – like,

'hey, this is how I like to receive pleasure. This is what matters
to me." Someone can also have a dialogue with themselves
before talking to a partner, Nelson adds, asking themselves
(and I paraphrase her): "How do I like to be kissed?" "Do I
like my partner to look into my eyes?" "Do I prefer to be more
dominant or more submissive?" "If I prefer to be submissive,
what does that look like?" (You *can* be submissive and be a
subject – more on that later.)

The Asker's Advantage

I started having these conversations with myself when I
graduated from cuddle parties to sex parties at age twenty-
eight. Once again, those are what they sound like: parties
where sexual activity takes place. I would decide before each
event what I was looking for and what did not interest me. I'd
make peace with the possibility of nothing sexual happening.
Most often, I didn't feel a strong pull toward anyone, so I
embraced evenings spent people-watching and chatting with
other guests. When someone did catch my eye, initiating
connections was nerve-wracking. But when I mustered up
the courage to walk up to someone, start a conversation, and
ask "can I kiss you?," I felt the empowerment that comes from
being the subject of "ask." From executing your own ideas and
seeing your machinations materialize.

I grew more emboldened to be the pursuer in my dating
life as well. Popular dating advice tells women to wait to be
pursued. Yet it's simple statistics that those who pursue end
up with more desired prospects, since their pool of possibilities is hand selected. Women who send the first message
on the dating site OKCupid, for instance, end up in conversations with more highly rated users than those who wait to be
approached.[24] This statistical phenomenon is not specific to
dating. In multiple areas, from hiring to school admissions,

the initiator ends up with a better outcome, simply because the prospects they reach out to are more attractive to them than those who reach out to them.[25]

This means that when women are the askers, not just the asked, they up-level their reality. When we are the creators – inviting others into our worlds, not just stepping into theirs – our whole lives shift. We learn to do what we desire, not what we're just OK with, in all realms. Embracing my own inner huntress emboldened me to advocate for my health, pursue work that intrigued me but had never fallen into my lap, and go after people I felt drawn to romantically, professionally, and platonically. It wasn't that I was suddenly in charge of everything in my relationships. But the leadership was shared. Voicing my preferences invited others to do the same. Letting people know I desired them made them comfortable expressing desire for me. Contrary to the "man pursues, woman gets pursued" paradigm, I discovered how two people can pursue each other. How they can both stand in their power – not over each other, but with each other.

Desire Cannot Be Rationalized

I thought I'd mastered it. I spent years enjoying sexual encounters that I was a "hell yes" to – or that the other person was, because I posed the question. I initiated a three-year relationship by visiting someone I'd met on vacation in another country ... then just not leaving. After that relationship, I began dating multiple people, hand-selected from message threads I started and a Tinder bio reading: "Looking for someone to make me cum really hard then lie next to me and talk about cognitive science." I asked three different attendees at a polyamory meetup for goodnight kisses, then had my Lyft driver circle back to get one of their numbers. I chased someone down over snail mail when my texts and calls weren't going through. I built a sex life and love life that matched my desires, not just my consent. One based on what I wanted, not just who wanted me. One based on what I asked for – verbally asked for – not just allowed.

Then, when I was twenty-nine, I met a man who taught me how to meditate. He worked at a spiritual shop near my apartment and made it clear he was attracted to me. I made it clear I didn't feel the same way. He said that was all right, so we meditated together occasionally on the beach, as friends. He taught me about various spiritual beliefs, and that November, he started offering to come over and give me a "healing" massage. (Note: Some may find the following story upsetting; feel free to skip to "Where Do Your Hands Feel Led?")

I said "no" the first few times. I didn't know him well enough to feel comfortable having him in my home. I wanted to avoid him trying to take it further. Then, one December evening, he asked again, and in a vulnerable moment, I texted, "all right, come. Just don't hit on me, OK?" Looking back, I wasn't a "hell yes," but I was recently heartbroken and lonely, and I thought a free massage might boost my spirits. He agreed not to hit on me and came over. But quickly, things started happening that were not part of a normal massage. He reached under my dress.

"Why are you touching my boob?"

"It's not a boob; it's holy food. I have to bless it."

More and more odd things started happening, and each time I objected, he gave me another explanation shrouded in spirituality: that touching my genitals would "heal my sacral chakra," that he had to massage me everywhere to "get all the oils in," that I seemed intent on "playing by the rules" and he needed to "open me up." He made me feel like I was wounded and in need of fixing, so I let it go on – until he got on top of me and said he had to "finish." At that point, I panicked, pushed him off, and told him to leave, even as he warned me I was "rejecting the healing."

I went to bed telling myself that this was just a very strange massage. That it was a cultural misunderstanding, as this man was from another country. That I was lucky it didn't escalate. How could I, after all, have been taken advantage of? I was in control of my body. Yet my heart pounded as I lay in bed and his voice reverberated through my ears, claiming my resistance was a symptom of a "suspicion toward men" he had to cure. Telling me I was "caught in my ego" and had to "let our souls merge." Complaining that by standing up for myself, I'd "drained his energy." I called a friend the next day, telling him the weirdest thing had happened.

"That sounds traumatizing," he said. "How do you feel?"

"To be honest," I said, "I do feel kind of traumatized. But I don't feel like I have the right to be. I said 'yes' to the massage. I let it go on for as long as it did."

"Suzannah," he said, "I'm just going to say it. This man molested you. And now you're doing the typical victim-blaming thing and thinking it was your fault."

I swallowed those words like a brick in my throat. He'd molested me. And suddenly, I felt all the feelings I'd pushed down: the shock when he announced he was going to perform a sacred ritual then humped me, the rage when he pulled my underwear to the side and asked why I didn't shave, the trepidation when I realized how easily he could overpower me. How had I not felt those feelings then? Where had I been?

The following week, I spoke to a mentor, Faye Hermine, a somatic sex educator who helps people heal trauma. "I still feel confused about what that was," I said. "I felt so torn at the time. I really did want to be healed. And his arguments were so convincing."

"Consent is about feeling a 'yes' or 'no' in your body," Faye reminded me. "Right now, you're trying to figure it out with your mind. It sounds like your body wasn't comfortable, but you didn't trust those feelings and were told they were wrong, so you're trying to rationalize it."

I realized I'd been so disconnected from my feelings, I'd let someone's skilled wordsmithery override them. I'd let him convince me that my subjective emotions, my very subjectivity, didn't matter. That what mattered was his supposedly objective view of the situation. And by proclaiming his status as an objective observer, by asserting his interpretation of events over mine, he'd made me the object of his theories. Faye explained that shutting down and making excuses were normal responses to trauma – and to being socialized female – but we could strengthen my ability to recognize when a boundary had been crossed and speak up. So, we practiced how to feel a "yes" and "no" in my body. And as we did that, it sunk in that I never had to justify a "no."

My perpetrator had formulated the most convincing arguments for why my "no" was wrong. Yet nobody could argue with my body's inner truth. My consent could not be intellectualized. My desire was not up for debate. My "yes" and "no" lived in my heart and stomach and voice. I didn't need to back them up with evidence. They were true just because they were felt. In that moment, I understood what being a subject means: that you have that inner compass pointing you one way or another, your own question, your own answer that nobody can challenge because it's yours. Subjectivity is subjective. A subject feels things they don't need to explain, don't need anyone to agree with. A subject can say "no" even when all outward circumstances point toward "yes" – or say "yes" when outward appearances point toward "no" – simply because their sacred, sovereign bodies tell them so.

Another mentor of mine pointed out that this man, who liked to bargain with customers at his shop, seemed to have been "haggling" with me. I'd said "no" to dating him and sleeping with him, so he'd tested me to see what he *could* get. This is what happens when we take the view of consent as negotiable to the extreme. We think in terms of giving and taking, as if bodies were goods to exchange. We think in terms of calculations and gains, as if one person's goal is to win while the other loses.

That was the most harrowing thing about this incident. As bizarre as it looked on the surface, so many ways people think of "normal" sexual encounters were at play: The role of a man as a hunter and persuader. The confusion of consent with acquiescence. But nothing about this was normal. Nothing about interactions where one person is a subject and the other is an object is normal. That idea is just as twisted as the events of that December night.

Where Do Your Hands Feel Led?

A year after this happened, I began reentering sex clubs, and during one New Years sex party in Manhattan, I got into a conversation with another guest. "What do you like to do at these events?" he asked, and once again, I was invited to step into the subject role, to state what I desired. The question was not what I was willing to do, not what I'd be up for, but what I liked. It was a difficult question. It was a question that had taken me time to learn to answer again. It's hard to like or want anything when intimacy itself feels dangerous. It's hard to hear the voice of a body you've detached from. But after that incident the prior year, where I felt numb, I was learning to feel again.

"I like to talk to interesting people," I said – then hesitated before adding with a playful laugh, with the boldness that was slowly coming back to me, "and sometimes I like them to play with my boobs."

"Oh yeah?" he laughed. "That sounds fun."

"It's a low-pressure activity for me," I explained.

"Well, let me know if you'd ever like me to do that for you."

"Is now a good time? I've got nothing else to do." Yup, the boldness was coming back. And this would be done for me, not to me.

A moment later, we were lying on a bed in the back of the club, and I was taking off my lacy black bra and giving instructions: "No pinching or squeezing, just gentle touches, please." It was a stark contrast from that previous experience and other experiences I'd had, where I needed to guard my chest from men's hands, too fearful to feel sensation there. I lay there, let out an exhale, and felt his touch light up my skin. I'd missed this feeling: losing track of space and time as my body melted into a puddle of receptors.

A few minutes in, he told me, "If you'd like, you're welcome to touch me between my legs."

"Let me consider that," I chuckled. "It's a kind offer." I was serious. It was. It was kind of him to be vulnerable enough to state his desires, to give me a no-pressure invitation, and to share the gift that was his body. I asked myself how the prospect felt to me. It didn't seem aversive. He was clothed; I'd merely be grazing his pants. He wasn't bad-looking. And he was being nice. I felt a little bad lying there, enjoying his touch, and not touching him back.

Yet even though he'd asked the question, I flipped it in my head and asked myself: Would I want this if he hadn't asked? No, that idea would not have occurred to me. I did not light up at the thought of it. I'd be just as happy without it. I didn't desire it. My hand wasn't feeling drawn between his legs. And, thankfully, I finally understood that my hand's inclinations mattered just as much as his penis's. It wasn't a "hell yes," so it was a "no."

"You know what, for whatever reason, I'm just not 100 percent to that," I told him.

I told him I wasn't 100 percent to make up for the times I'd been 90 percent and ignored the other 10. I told him I wasn't a "hell yes" to make up for the times nobody had even asked me. Then I asked my own question: "How about I run my hands through your hair?" Because that was something coming from me, something my hands wanted to do.

Starting Sentences with "I"

In a world where women are subjectified, where everyone is subjectified, teaching consent means teaching people how to feel where their hands want to go. What their bodies want to do. How their limbs have their own voice, their cells their own consciousness.

It doesn't just mean teaching men to respect when women don't want sex. It means teaching all people that everyone has their own wise inner guidance system, one that leads them toward certain things and away from others, sometimes for reasons we don't understand, and we must all revere the incomprehensibility and uniqueness of that. It means people asking their partners what they want and what they like, not what they'll accept. It means acknowledging that women *can* want and like, not just accept. It means building lives we want and like, not just accept. It means we can say not just "me, too" but "I, too."

I, too, feel desire. I, too, want to feel good. I, too, have fantasies, likes, and dislikes. And I, too, honor others' likes and dislikes.

Once we're allowed to open our mouths and state our wants and wishes in sentences starting with "I," we may discover an endless pool of desires in there. Desires that hadn't been heard because we were too busy fielding others' advances. Or because there was nobody to listen.

To communicate our consent to others, we first must listen to ourselves.

To that fluttering in our hearts that accompanies a much-anticipated kiss. To that panicked skittering that says, sometimes for no clear reason, "get out." To that lost piece of us that knows exactly what we want and what we don't.

It is there, and it is begging to be heard, by ourselves and others alike.

And that starts with asking ourselves, our partners, and everyone: What do you desire?

Chapter 6

I Create: My Body, My Voice

I t's not just sex where women learn to settle for what they acquiesce to. It's in every area concerning our bodies that our desire is silenced.

The verb "acquiesce," in fact, describes a trying year of my life. Not a year of sexual mistreatment but a year spent in and out of seventeen doctors' offices, hoping for them to diagnose me, treat me, and make me the object of all these actions they were trained to perform. I first came to them in late 2017 complaining of bladder pain and frequent urination. Each had their own theory and plan. They would put me on this medication. Give me this procedure. Try this other thing if that didn't work. Call it anxiety or stress if nothing showed up on a test. I was along for the ride. None of these protocols were pleasurable. Some were painful: Invasive tests. Medications with side effects. Hours in waiting rooms followed by cold and rushed appointments. I was drained and knew no better, so I acquiesced.

Yes Means Yes in the Doctor's Office, Too

I caught my first glimpse of something different when I visited a pelvic floor physical therapist. She didn't operate like most healthcare providers. Rather than tell me what was wrong with me, she had me lie on a table, massaged the muscles around my bladder, then asked, "What do you think your bladder's saying?" Could my bladder speak? Did it have a voice? Could it be "I," not just "it"? I remembered back in high school, when I'd learned that my stomach had its own taste. Maybe every part of my body had a perspective, a subjectivity. I wasn't sure quite how to listen to my bladder, so I said the first words that popped into my head: "I need a break."

"Yes," she echoed. "I need a break." It was the first treatment plan that came from my mouth. I pondered over the next few days: What kind of break did I need? Almost on a whim, on a rough night, when I couldn't take any more medication merry-go-rounds, I booked a flight from New York to Los Angeles for the following week. I didn't know what was out there for me. Just that the one time I'd gone there before, I'd felt more relaxed than I'd been in years as I strolled down Venice Beach. During the ensuing two-week vacation, I walked down that same beach every evening. I got massages, cooked nutritious food I enjoyed, and visited healers I liked working with. I developed a wellness regime based on desire, not concessions or capitulations. As I grew stronger in my sense of what I desired for my health, it no longer felt right to be a mere object of "diagnose" and "treat."

The urologist I was seeing at the time had diagnosed me with interstitial cystitis, a chronic, incurable bladder pain condition. The more research I did, though, the more I realized how often this label was placed on cases of bladder pain like mine, with no known cause, mostly in women. I started to question this diagnosis and prognosis. How could I be sure my condition had no cure when nobody could tell me where it came from?

As additional symptoms appeared, I gathered the strength to take charge of my healing. I texted and emailed everyone I knew who might have information that could help me. Through a work connection, I found a holistic doctor, who diagnosed me with chronic Lyme disease. I sensed my road to healing would be long and winding, so I adjusted my mindset to frame the process as a spiritual journey, not just a series of medical treatments. I found ways to embrace it. On the sleepless nights when the symptoms felt unbearable, I told myself, *you get to go deep to heal this. You get to take your self-love to a new level. This is not an impediment but an awakening. It is not a deterioration but a blossoming.*

I searched for solutions I could feel a "yes" to in my body. I paused, breathed, and noticed what sensations came up when I considered an intervention. The path I ventured down was unconventional, involving sensual yoga, cacao ceremonies, breathwork, Himalayan salt rooms, and many hours on the beach, along with acupuncture and modern Western remedies. Not all these activities directly addressed my physical symptoms, but they were part of a greater task: learning to hear and heal my body on all levels. Finding my desire and pleasure in a situation that was undesired and painful. Some treatments were grueling, but remembering I chose them made all the difference. I viewed myself as the curator of my therapies, my own primary care provider, enlisting professionals to guide me toward my vision of health rather than being an object of their orders.

This had not been my norm. This had not been *the* norm. In the medical clinic as well as the bedroom, women are often objects of providers' plans. It's an ongoing fight for women to be participants in their healing. Without the chance to be co-subjects of "diagnose," they end up objects of "misdiagnose." Endometriosis, a condition that causes debilitating period pain and painful sex, takes ten years on average to identify.[1] Often, the misdiagnoses are mental health conditions like depression and anxiety.[2] Interstitial cystitis is on a long list of "female" diagnoses – fibromyalgia, vulvodynia – that have no agreed-upon cause or cure. Chronic Lyme, which might be behind some of these conditions, is not recognized by many mainstream doctors, perhaps in part because it's more common among women.[3]

Women have historically been excluded from medical research, and doctors aren't always abreast of new break-throughs that may help them.[4] They do the best they can, but women's input on their own bodies would frequently be useful. Too many women are told "this is just how it is." "You simply have to live with it." "Take this pill to lessen the symptoms." The doctor assesses and prescribes. The woman gets treated. Not always well. Our consent is sought, but our desire is rarely considered. I understand why. Desire is a strange concept to apply to the treatment of illnesses. In this context, desire does not always look like excitement. It can look like relief. It can look like certainty that you're choosing the best option. For me, it looked like trust – in my providers, myself, and my resilience.

"I Had Been Like a Machine"

Three years after the height of my own health journey, I became a birth doula, someone who provides emotional support and education throughout pregnancy and childbirth. In this work, I have witnessed doctors and nurses inadvertently undermine women's role as subjects of "birth" by making them objects of "push." Pushing medications on them. Literally telling them to push or refrain rather than working with the wisdom of their instincts.[5] It's not unheard of for medical professionals to make parents objects of "consent," using phrasing like "did you consent her?" to describe the distribution of consent forms.[6]

When someone has a baby, they are a subject, and that cannot be taken away. In English, someone "gives birth," the subject of "give." In Spanish, to give birth is "dar a luz," to bring to light. The French term is "donner naissance," to bear children. The Arabic word is "wulid" – "mother," "father," or "beget." In Hindi, they say "janm dena," or "procreate."[7] Each verb makes the parent the subject. Yet the system in which this process takes place finds ways to make pregnant and birthing people objects.[8] As we decide whether to become parents, we get parented by politicians. We feed our children, yet we are fed myths and directives. We conceive our children, yet we are conceived of as passive-voice patients.

This was not always the case. Home births assisted by midwives, friends, and family used to constitute the norm in the US and still do in some cultures. Parents were in their own space, and others were present to support them, not to be in charge.[9] In the early 1900s, childbirth moved to hospitals, utilizing techniques like C-sections that minimize parents' roles and maximize doctors' roles.[10] Today, 71 percent of US births involve epidurals, which restrict parents' motion, since they're hooked up to a catheter and numb in the lower body.[11] Those giving birth are typically asked to lie on their backs, even though more active positions can facilitate birth through the help of gravity.[12] Interventions such as episiotomies (cutting underneath the vagina) and even C-sections have been employed without parents' consent.[13]

Alicia, a forty-five-year-old writer in Portland, Oregon, was pressured into an induction and a C-section the first time she gave birth. Though it was unclear when her due date was, as she didn't remember the date of her last period, the hospital deemed her overdue and told her they legally had to induce her. After 27 hours without food, she still had not gone into labor. A new obstetrician came on shift and stormed in angrily, asking, "Why is she still here?" This doctor said Alicia had no choice but to get a C-section.

"I personally feel that I was forced, though of course, I signed the papers," she told me. She consented in the weak sense of the term. She gave in to that which she did not desire. "I had been like a machine – opened up by someone who was looking at numbers and liabilities, but not at me," she remembers. "I struggled with postpartum depression for the next year and a half, which I think had a lot to do with the way I felt about the birth – as if I could not make decisions for myself and my daughter. As if I were in some sort of system where the doctors had all the power and I was helpless."

For her second birth, Alicia had another C-section. But this time, she chose it because her son's heart rate was low. "I fully consented to this C-section and feel 100 percent different about it," she said. Such interventions can be helpful and even life-saving. The issue is when parents' desires – or lack thereof – are not considered. When they are either denied choices or given choices geared toward avoiding problems, not creating desired experiences.

Most expectant parents I speak with don't know about positive elements they can incorporate into childbirth, such as breathwork, massage, and aromatherapy. Almost none know about the ecstatic and orgasmic birth movements, which help people find pleasure in birth. This may sound like an oxymoron, but one survey by midwife Ina May Gaskin found that one fifth of 151 mothers she knew – most of whom gave birth at a midwife center – had experienced orgasmic births.[14] Considering parents' desires, not just their fears, opens up a world of life-affirming experiences.

Deprived of Delivering

I trained to be a doula at age thirty-one. Part of my motivation was to help people exercise all the autonomy they had within the medical system I'd struggled to navigate. But I also did it for myself. I knew that if I didn't educate myself before having children, I would be deprived of options too. A few months later, I found myself painting a portrait of my ideal birth to someone I was newly dating. "I'd like to be in a pool of hot water outside, with my partner's arms around me," I said. "I'd like to sway to music to move the baby down, with a midwife and a doula to support me. And if I need pain relief, I'd prefer laughing gas to take the edge off difficult contractions but stay present."

"I've never heard someone talk about childbirth so positively – or think about it so far in advance," my partner responded in a flabbergasted tone.

Now I was the flabbergasted one. How could someone go into such a monumental moment without thinking about how to craft the best experience they can? But it's understandable that many do, because we've neglected women's desire in favor of their consent. The same way mainstream doctors didn't think to offer me treatments that might feel good to me, doctors don't typically focus on how to make pregnancy or childbirth positive experiences. They more often contemplate how to make them less bad. How to help the mother get through the birth, not be present for it. How to help her be OK, not great. The team thinks about her "no" more than her "yes."

Or, sometimes, they prioritize the child's safety, and that's also understandable. But a mother can feel like a receptacle if her providers, friends, and family talk all about the baby without checking in with her. Or if they shame her for wanting a home birth because a hospital birth is supposedly "best for the baby." In reality, for those with low-risk pregnancies, home births are associated with fewer complications and more frequent breastfeeding.[15] Often, what's best for the parents *is* best for the baby.

A mother can also feel objectified if she's pushed into procedures like episiotomies, which are sometimes (though less and less often) done in part to maximize convenience for the provider.[16] The subtle centering of the doctor is evident in the language employed to describe such interventions. Johns Hopkins Medicine's website states that an episiotomy "aids your healthcare provider in delivering your baby."[17] The provider is the subject of "deliver," tacitly communicating that they're in charge, and how episiotomies aid parents is left unclear. In fact, those who receive them are more likely to suffer from pain during sex, along with compromised bladder and bowel control.[18]

The view of mothers as receptacles – as objects of the verbs "need" and "occupy" – is also evident in political discourse around abortion, with politicians prioritizing fetuses' lives over parents'. It's ironic that women are perhaps treated most like children when they are having children. With *Roe v. Wade* overturned, Americans will now, even more so than before, face pregnancies they don't feel an enthusiastic "yes" to. Generations will be birthed from a stifling of women's inner guidance, their "no," their desire.

From Choices to Voices

But my generation and prior generations have already been birthed this way. For years, the government has questioned the choice not just to forgo children but to have them, especially for disabled, gender-nonconforming, and BIPOC people. During the first half of the twentieth century and beyond, Black, Native American, Puerto Rican, Mexican, and disabled women faced one of the most overt denials of women's "yes": forced sterilization. State laws sanctioned government sterilization of those deemed "insane," "feeble-minded," "dependent," and "diseased," with doctors disproportionately performing these procedures in communities of color.[19]

Vestiges of this population control agenda remain. A 2014 study found that Hispanic and Native American women were more likely than white women to say that sterilization surgeries had prevented them from having kids they wanted – likely due both to economic obstacles and to biased recommendations.[20] "Those who feel pressured by others into surgical sterilization may feel more remorse due to lack of control," the authors wrote. By law, a patient must consent before such a procedure takes place. But if someone grants consent out of acquiescence rather than desire, their sense of freedom in their body may still suffer.

Trans and non-binary people constitute another population deprived of reproductive autonomy. Until around 2010, trans men in many countries had to undergo hysterectomies to be legally recognized as male, foreclosing the option of pregnancy.[21] Today, trans parents receive misinformation, with some told they can't have kids if they've been on testosterone when many can.[22] Trans activist Trystan Reese remembers healthcare providers asking him questions during his pregnancy like "have you secured a milk donor yet?" They didn't acknowledge he had a choice, as trans men can also breastfeed.[23]

Reese recalls feeling objectified when his providers overlooked his agency to shape his birth. "A naturopath told me not to 'let' the hospital induce me," he remembers, explaining that he'd asked to be induced. "The idea [was] that I am someone that is going to 'let' something medical happen to me – not 'tell me more about your induction' or 'is that something that you wanted?'" This language of "letting" is eerily reminiscent of terms like "putting out" that denote letting someone have sex with you. Yet such language captures many common reproductive experiences. Whether someone is forced to have a child, is persuaded *not* to give birth, or is told *how* to give birth, they are in the passive voice.

A patient can work with a healthcare provider and be a subject. They can ask about their options; they can advocate for their preferences; they can make choices with others' input. But the scant opportunities for such participation show how little we value birthing people's ability to be "I" in their bodies. They are often "you" and "them" to the government and the healthcare system. "My body, my choice" can only go so far if we are choosing between limited options influenced by misconceptions.

What if we could create our own choices, or co-create them with people who support us? What would it look like for a generation to be born from parents' "hell yes" – not just to whether they give birth, but to how? For every child's entrance into this world to take place in a situation their parents didn't just agree to, but fashioned? I do not just mean putting a signature on a piece of paper that a hospital printed, or nodding when a doctor recommends a labor intervention. I mean conceiving not just the child, but the path for bringing them to light. I mean parents bringing their dreams for their birth and their child to their team – the subjects of "ask," not just the answerers of others' questions.

This is something more and more parents are doing. As a doula, I help people write birth plans – documents full of preferences that they can show their doctors. Birth plans prompt parents to consider things they haven't yet been asked: Would they like to take photos of their newborn? Do they want to delay cord clamping? And, most importantly, what else do they want that is not on the templates I email them? I like to put these choices in parents' hands because I know what it's like to be treated as an object in doctors' offices. That experience is not unique to those giving birth. It happens to women, gender-diverse people, people of size, and more in many medical situations. For women, though, it especially shows up in reproductive contexts.

Attack of the Sperm

Women face reproductive objectification from the time they first learn about birth control. Even though birth control is related to women's sex lives in an obvious way, their desire tends to be absent not only from discussions with healthcare providers, but also from classroom conversations. Worldwide, sex ed curricula operate off an implicit conception of women as potential incubators, not active pleasure-seekers.

In a study of the US, UK, Japan, Sweden, and six other countries, sex ed students said their teachers "failed to discuss female pleasure, reproduced stereotypes of women as passive and lacking in desire, placed responsibility for the work of sexual relationships onto women, and cast them as sexual gatekeepers."[24] In typical sex ed lessons, men are described as experiencing erections and ejaculations. Women are taught how to accommodate erections and ejaculations without getting pregnant. Men learn about the desires they have – or are presumed to have – while women learn to manage men's desires. I remember the video I watched in sex ed stating that just seeing a pretty woman could cause a man to get an erection. The notion of a sex ed video stating that women can get wet just by looking at someone is so unlikely it sounds ludicrous – even though it's factually correct.[25]

With a blind eye turned to women's sexuality, contraceptives are often recommended without consideration for how each method might affect a girl or woman's body. It's almost as if contraception exists, not to accommodate women's desire and enable their pleasure, but to protect women from men's desire and pleasure. Even a sexy, progressive self-help book, *The Guide to Getting It On*, reads: "Knowing that men produce six billion sperm a month or three trillion sperm in a lifetime should make any woman want to have an IUD installed before she sits on the same chair that a healthy male had just been sitting on."[26] The first page encourages "all readers" not trying to get pregnant to use a "hassle-free" birth control method like an intrauterine device (IUD). These cautionary passages address men's pleasure but not women's, failing to consider whether a female reader would take well to an IUD or even

want to have intercourse with penis owners. The pressing
issue, apparently, is the onslaught of sperm women will be
subject to – or, more aptly, object to. Beware the sperm!

It's as if ejaculations are some kind of natural disaster to
guard oneself against rather than a choice made by a human.
Kids learn that sex causes pregnancy as if that is inevitable,
but sex does not cause pregnancy unless it involves ejaculation
(or, occasionally, precum) inside a vagina – something men
can prevent by using condoms, not ejaculating, or ejaculating
literally anywhere but in a vagina, as author Gabrielle Blair
points out in *Ejaculate Responsibly*.[27] If we stopped talking
about pregnancy as if women were desireless receptacles for
the unstoppable force of sperm cells, perhaps we'd realize it
makes sense for men to play their part in prevention.

Not that women can't play a role too. Birth control can
enhance a woman's pleasure; knowing she's unlikely to get
pregnant can help her relax and enjoy herself.[28] It can also
cause unpleasant side effects like depression and low libido.[29]
Whether birth control enhances or detracts from pleasure –
and what type will do which – varies from person to person,
and we can't know what's best for each individual unless we
talk about women's desire.

From Prevention to Pleasure

From ages twenty to twenty-four, I was on the pill and then
the NuvaRing. No one told me about the side effects these
medications might have for my mood or sex life – only the
possibility of blood clots. The main goal was to stop me from
getting pregnant, not to help me feel good – even though my
aim in seeking birth control was to feel good.

Seven years later, I began complaining to my gynecologist
about itchy labia. She did a "Q tip test," where she touched
different parts of my vulva with a Q tip and asked me to

report any discomfort. There was soreness in my vulvar vestibule – the area around the vaginal opening – and my bloodwork showed low levels of free testosterone (testosterone not bound to proteins). My doctor concluded that I was experiencing the lasting effects of hormonal birth control. She explained that such medications can have a long-term impact on your free testosterone, which affects the tissue of the vulvar vestibule. Some people who have taken hormonal birth control experience thinning of this tissue and consequently suffer from pain during sex, or other issues like itchiness and dryness.[30]

In other words, contraceptives – a class of drugs women go on so they can enjoy sex – can stop them from enjoying sex. Why did it take so long for us to know this? "Healthcare providers don't view women as sexual beings," said Irwin Goldstein, a gynecologist who treats vulvar pain, on the podcast *Bodies*. "They don't understand the role of women's sexuality in their life quality."[31] Just as consent education has focused on women's right *not* to have sex – and obstetric care has focused on avoiding childbirth complications – the medical establishment has focused on women's ability to forgo children, not their ability to have precisely the sex and the children they want.

The same could be said of the reproductive rights movement, which has a troubling history of putting population control before women's well-being. Planned Parenthood founder Margaret Sanger's team introduced an early version of the pill to the US even though three Puerto Rican women died from it during the clinical trial phase. She once stated that "birth control is nothing more or less than the facilitation of the process of weeding out the unfit [and] of preventing the birth of defectives."[32] She aligned with eugenicists – those seeking to reduce the population of disabled people and others deemed unwanted – and her legacy lives on. Even today, public health researchers measure reproductive health clinics' success based not on how many women are making the choices that feel best for them, but on how many are on contraceptives – a metric originally established to aid population control in developing countries.[33] The very term, "birth control," denotes the ability to stop something from happening, not to attain something wanted.

> Control (n): the act of limiting or managing something; a method of doing this.[34]

But not all reproductive activists share this focus on avoiding pregnancy. A group of Black women founded the reproductive justice movement in the 1990s, advocating not just for abortion rights but for people's right to birth and parent children as they like. "By shifting the focus to reproductive oppression – the control and exploitation of women, girls, and individuals through our bodies, sexuality, labor, and reproduction ... we are developing a more inclusive vision," wrote reproductive justice leader Loretta Ross. "The reproductive justice analysis focuses on ... better lives for women, healthier families, and sustainable communities."[35] These are things that parents are a "yes" to.

Re-birthing Our Realities

My body's "yes" leads me through life today: The "ahh" that escapes my lungs as I sink into an Epsom salt bath when I don't feel well. The "uh huh" in my hands as I open my fertility tracking app or slip my favorite condoms into my purse. Birth "control" feels more like enhancement, like a celebration of life. My life. I say yes to sex, yes to health, yes to aliveness. Yes to creating what I want to create – life-affirming sex now, a beautiful birth in the future. Nothing more and nothing less.

Even though my experiences with pregnancy and childbirth have been limited to assisting others' births, I like to think I've applied what I've learned as a doula to re-birth myself. Just as I believe children are best born from parents in settings they desire, I believe adults are best reborn through methods they desire. Even though it was pain that spawned my journey home to my body, I did everything I could to re-birth myself in pleasure. To go on a journey I desired, not acquiesced to. That was what healed me: making my own choices about how to heal myself. The rebirth occurred in the process of choosing how to be reborn.

Every day, we are all subjects and objects of "conceive," "give birth," and "bring to light." We conceive of ourselves in new manners, give birth to new ideas and ways of living, and bring lost parts of ourselves to light. When women are subjects, we are able to give birth literally and figuratively from a place we desire. And this deep understanding of our "yes" helps us say "no" to anything undesired.

Whoever or whatever we birth will also feel that – that they are born from joy and trust rather than silencing and self-doubt.

When we not only exercise options, but have the chance to create our own options, we pave the way for others to make new choices as well.

We pave the way for everyone to do what they desire – in the doctor's office, the delivery room, the bedroom, and all around the world. A world that we ourselves can re-birth each moment, through pleasure.

Chapter 7

I Want: Why Buy the Cow When You Can Both Be Free?

"**T**his is just like your eating disorder," my friend opined.

Like many of my peers, I'd engaged in a few hookups my freshman year of college. Then, before I knew it, an intervention was underway. "You're substituting one coping mechanism for another," she went on. "It's a way for you to deal with insecurities and feel better about yourself."

It wasn't just her. My therapist informed me I'd "been taken advantage of" during my first hookup that summer. Once again, I was in the passive voice. Meanwhile, my psychiatrist pontificated that it must be tricky for a young woman to decide whether to "give guys what they want," as if that question mattered more than what I wanted. As if men were the only subjects of "want." As if experiencing pleasure and connection meant giving something away. These people were trying to spare me situations where I was disempowered. The irony was, these conversations themselves were disempowering. They carried the assumption that sex was something done for men, and women just went along with it. For men.

I'd been hearing such warnings for a long time. In high school, friends cautioned me that "guys only want one thing," and my therapist told me that "boys break girls into body parts." Yet it was her who put the idea in my head that I was a bunch of disjointed body parts. And it was my female peers who made me wonder if I had just one thing to offer. When they gossiped about girls who'd engaged in casual hookups, they talked about these girls' desire for popularity or approval.

I myself started making those assumptions. When I'd see girls grinding at school dances or hear about them hooking up at parties, I'd wonder if they were pushovers for "giving in" like that. I'd wonder if they struggled to stand up for themselves or say "no." I thought that trying to stop such things from happening – to get women to value themselves more than that – counted as feminism. And now, here I was, experiencing firsthand how these efforts to save women from degradation were themselves degrading.

By assuming that women who were sexual outside relationships were being used, this thinking deemed women objects rather than subjects with their own desires. Men were the "horny bastards," as my friend in eating disorder treatment so aptly articulated, while women were emotional and love-oriented. Someone else I looked up to warned me that guys would leave once they got what they wanted – but also might leave if they didn't. I had felt like a kid in a candy store, but others' interpretations of my life made me feel like the candy getting eaten.

Consuming Women

A classic phrase came back to mind: "Why buy the cow when you can get the milk for free?" I don't remember when I first heard this, but it had long been in my consciousness: that I had something valuable to offer – my body – and I shouldn't just give it away. Women's sexuality was too precious to be free. We were to make prospective partners take us on dates, wine and dine us, and offer us commitment to "earn" sex from us, like some kind of financial exchange. And if we didn't do that – if we offered ourselves freely – no one would want to buy us, the "cows." And wouldn't that be a shame, to not be owned.

A mentor in college illustrated this concept to me with another tasty metaphor: Men want "cookies," she said, and women have power because we can decide whether to "give away the cookies." We've got men wrapped around our fingers. We can make men do chores, ask us to marry them, *anything* so they can get their cookies. Women were not just milk but also cookies. The objects of "eat" and "drink." And men were the consumers, the enjoyers. It was a heteronormative story as well as a sexist one, assuming that a relationship required two opposite genders: one seeking sex, one seeking love and money. This mentor considered herself a women's empower-ment advocate. Yet when I received messages like this, I did not feel liberated. I did not find it empowering to be food.

The depiction of a sexually empowered woman as an expensive delicacy has long been baked into pop culture, no pun intended. Ciara sang in the 2004 hit single "Goodies" that her highly sought "goodies" will "stay in the jar" until she finds someone who's "down to spend it, type that's gettin' his dough." The song's producer Lil' Jon called "Goodies" a "female empowerment" track, stating, "The female has the power."[1] The power to withhold the cookies – or the milk, as the case may be – and make the man buy the cow. Men were salivating over women, apparently, and we got to assert power by not letting them devour us right away. That wasn't the first time we heard this sentiment on the radio. Back in 1999, Christina Aguilera sang in "Genie in a Bottle" that though her love interest is "blowing kisses my way," that "don't mean I'm gonna give it away" because "if you wanna be with me, baby, there's a price to pay."

And now, a decade later, here I was, being warned that the price I was charging for my body was too low. That I should be offering intimacy in exchange for dates, in exchange for meals, in exchange for relationships – not in exchange for nothing. Yet those who doled out this advice never asked themselves why they conceived of sex as an exchange – one where a man was the purchaser and a woman was the item to be purchased. Where only the man actually wanted the sex and the woman wanted something else from it, whether that was commitment, financial support, or, as my concerned friend insinuated, the feeling of being wanted.

To me, pleasure was never a transaction at all. When I became sexual with someone, it was because I wanted to, not because the other person paid a sufficient price. I wasn't focused on what my partners were getting out of it or whether they'd "earned" those benefits. I was concerned with what I was getting out of it – the encounter itself. Not something else I'd receive in exchange. The notion that a woman would *need* something else denies us our position as desiring subjects and our ability to enjoy sex.

Sex as Currency

Whether people are looking to use women or to save them from being used, they employ similar language about men getting sex and women giving it. In the 2018 documentary *Liberated: The New Sexual Revolution*, a college man tells the camera, "Want to know how easy sex is to get in America?" He then grabs the butt of a woman dancing in front of him and says, "It's that easy."[2] Toward the opposite aim, social critic Caitlin Flanagan reminisced in a 2006 *Atlantic* essay on the days when "the notion that a girl should not give her sexuality away too freely was so solidly built into the national consciousness."[3]

This language of offering and withholding comes up in seemingly innocuous comments I still hear from women: "I don't just send a guy nudes; he has to earn them." "I don't just go down on someone; I make them work for it." I, too, don't send just anybody nudes or have oral sex with anyone out there. But to me, it's not about earning. It's not about keeping score of how much someone's given me and striving to provide the equivalent. It's about asking myself whether I feel comfortable with that activity and would enjoy it. If the thought of pleasing a partner or sending them photos turns me on – and I feel safe and respected – I'm not contemplating whether the recipient "deserves" the pleasure I'm providing. I'm doing it for *my* pleasure. And if I don't want to do something, it doesn't matter how much someone's "earned" or "worked." I still don't do it. When we're acting from desire, we don't need to keep count of how much we're "giving" and "receiving." We receive from the "giving" itself.

Transactional thinking can even be disguised as spirituality. A tantra guru once advised me to be selective about who I allowed to "plug into" me, explaining, "Your pussy is a portal to the divine, and when you sleep with someone, he gets to plug into that sacred portal. That's valuable. Not everyone deserves the chance to do that." Yet this effort to make me value myself made me feel worse about myself. It made me feel like some kind of electrical outlet, a hole waiting for someone to make use of me. Men "got to" do something to my body, got to be the subjects of desire. And I didn't get to do anything. I was there to give men that amazing opportunity – or achieve empowerment by denying it. I didn't see why it mattered how great it felt for a guy to "plug into" me, as long as he was enthusiastically consenting. It didn't make sense to withhold something I wanted just because men apparently wanted it so badly. Nor did it make sense to be selective simply because what I had was so special.

Shouldn't I be selective because I genuinely had selective taste – or be unselective because I could gain enjoyment from a variety of people or activities? Shouldn't I be focused on doing what feels great to me, not withholding or allowing what feels great to someone else? And if something feels less than great to me, shouldn't that be reason enough not to do it, regardless of how much I have to offer? Even if someone has *nothing* to offer, shouldn't they still decline what they don't want?

It seems to me that things could be much simpler than we make them. We could go after what we want and reject what we don't want without giving much thought to our "value" as people. Everyone, regardless of their "worth," could choose what feels good to them and keep out what feels bad. No calculations necessary.

Why Do We Think of Women Like Cows?

It's common today to see motivational social media posts with phrases like "you are worthy," "know your value," and "you deserve love." But applying the concept of value or worth to people implies that some are worth more than others. Such a concept would be meaningless, after all, if all values were the same. The truth is, nobody has inherent value. Nobody is worth anything. Nobody deserves anything or anyone. People can assign value to us. But assigning a value to someone is literally likening them to an object. We don't have "value" from our own perspective, as subjects, because that's a made up concept projected onto us. It's a metaphor that only makes sense within a capitalist economy.

Such an economy and philosophy originated around the time of agriculture, in line with the expression about the cow. I see it as no coincidence that during early agricultural times, people began equating women to livestock. Highly regarded in foraging societies for their contributions to hunting, gathering, building, healing, and childcare, women "were reduced to the status of possessions and domesticated animals in early agricultural societies – and remain so in many places today," Christopher Ryan, primatologist and co-author of *Sex at Dawn: The Prehistoric Origins of Modern Sexuality*, tells me.

Ryan points out that the Biblical verse reading "thou shalt not covet thy neighbor's wife" also says not to covet your neighbor's house, ox, ass, or slaves, as if all these items (and people and animals reduced to items) are equivalent.[4] Even today, brides' fathers "give" them to their grooms, as if they are indeed possessions owned by men. Virginity, too, is described as something women "give" – complete with its own food metaphor, "popping your cherry."

When people warn women not to "give themselves away" too easily, they're operating from this same idea that women can be owned and consumed. When people lament that sex workers who choose to sell an experience are "selling their bodies," they, too, are drawing from the assumption that sex entails ownership. And when people judge non-monogamous women for "settling" for partners who won't "claim" them, they're prizing women's ability to receive a high "investment" over their ability to be free. As if free is not the best thing we can be.

Stop Trying to Dip Your Chips in Me

As agriculture arose independently in various parts of the world 12,000 years ago, it also spawned the advent of trade, as well as trade-based, tit-for-tat thinking, wherein one thing can be exchanged for another. "In nomadic foraging societies, which was where almost all our ancestors lived, there was little to no private property," Ryan explained to me. "Everything was shared. There was no currency with which to express 'value.' No accumulated resources to hoard, protect, leverage, and so on." And women were not treated as goods either.

But in the days of modern capitalism, everything can be seen as exchangeable. We aim to receive what's "worth" our contributions, rather than what we actually want. We assign numbers to people by calculating their net worth, employing this as a metaphor when we tell our friends not to "settle for less than they're worth" or that they're "too good for" their partners – as if people can be ranked by "goodness." Often, these definitions of "good" are based on superficial metrics like women's conventional attractiveness and men's financial success. Such phrases are uttered to people of all genders, yet women receive their own flavor of it. Women who date men are taught to be vigilant about whether these men are paying enough for them, figuratively if not literally – because women are the ones who have been reduced to property, the objects of "own."

In addition to a new economy, agriculture brought about new family structures, as it caused people to stay in one place. In nomadic societies, childcare was shared, and children even had multiple father figures, says Ryan. This type of culture still exists among some people, like the Aché tribe in Paraguay, who believe women must sleep with multiple men to conceive a child – then they all father that child. Nobody owns these women.[5]

Flexible family structures like this existed all over the globe back when people lived in groups. But when nuclear family units and compulsory monogamy took over, people began caring who each child's father was. And so, marriages became economic exchanges whereby men financially supported women so they could own their bodies. If a woman was desirable, she was "worthy" of a man who'd provide her with shelter and sustenance in exchange for her loyalty. If she slept with other men, her worth went down. If she remained a virgin, she was valuable.

And now, today, female friends pump one another up by saying "you're worth so much more than that" or "you are a prize" – as if the best a woman can be is a trophy. We see women's underwear with "access denied" inscribed across the crotch, playfully promoting empowerment by depicting women as buildings that not just anyone can enter. We see mugs, magnets, candles, and (mostly female) shirts with sayings like "Don't let anyone treat you like free salsa. You are guac!," helping women everywhere think of themselves as $5 (or, at best, $10) appetizers rather than free ones. "You are guac, baby girl, guac," some of these items read, just to make it clear which gender is there to be dipped into. Equating women with food is supposedly a way to elevate them – but really, it's a vestige of times when women were goods and men basically bought them.

On Sluts, Whores, and Humans

A "slut" is supposedly a woman whose sexuality is cheap. If that's the case, then I'm perhaps the biggest slut of all, because mine is free. I make sexual choices based not on what a partner offers in "exchange" for the sex – or whether they're "worth" as much as me – but on what feels right in my body. I pursue the people I'm interested in, not because I think we're equally ranked and deserve each other, but because that's where my heart is leading me. I do not value myself. I am not worth anything. I do not feel I deserve anything or anyone. The whore I am.

How ironic that this synonym for "slut," "whore," denotes someone who has sex for money. When a woman uses this insult toward another woman, she implies that *she* is superior because it costs more to have sex with *her*. It costs flowers and engagement rings and a house and a promise of forever. It costs dinners and bottles of wine and romantic getaways. But even if the price is high, she's still operating within an economic mindset.

Those with this mindset like to tell women that the way to make partners care about us is to withhold sex so they'll "work for it," as if our bodies were some kind of wage. But *is* that caring? If someone cares about you, don't they want to show you generosity – whether or not there's a reward waiting for them after each act of kindness? Women are advised that being sexually coy will motivate partners to commit to them, but why would we want a relationship with someone who's not motivated to be with us from the get-go, no bribe needed?

From Calculating to Feeling

When you're led by desire, you are not quantifying your worth or anyone else's. You are going where your body leads you. If you don't like how you're treated, you leave, not because you're "worth more" but because it doesn't feel good. Because no one has to stay in a situation that doesn't feel good, no matter how they're ranked. Someone led by desire, not transactional thinking, is the sluttiest slut and the most prudish prude. Nobody can buy or earn her body. No amount of romance or praise is a high enough price. But if the person and the situation light her up, there's no such thing as too low a price. There is no price at all.

I must be a slut myself, as I do not withhold sex like a precious good or make partners "work for it." I place great importance on self-respect, self-esteem, and high standards. But not because I have a high value. I'm no more valuable than anyone else. I have high standards because those standards make me happy. At times, I've waited until someone committed to a relationship before sleeping with them, not because I was "worth it" or believed women who don't wait have low self-worth, but because I was most comfortable that way. I do not make anyone buy me – not because I "give away" my bovine milk but because I happen to be a member of the human species. Rather than thinking of sex as a transaction and charging top dollar, I consider myself valueless, invaluable.

If we all thought this way, regardless of our gender, we'd maintain healthy self-esteem and make sexual choices born neither from shame nor external pressure. We'd say "yes" to the sex we want and "no" to the sex we don't want simply because that's what feels right. We'd go after the people we want and say "no" to those we don't want simply because we trust our hearts and bodies.

Not because we "deserve more," but for no reason at all. We could care about ourselves so much that we stand up for what we want for no reason at all.

After all, we are not here to buy or sell ourselves but to be free in every sense of the word.

Chapter 8

I Touch: Feeling Myself, the Other

In a world that makes women commodities, their bodies prizes to be won, how can a woman escape her own objectification? In what circumstance can she dodge the male gaze? One may think that when she is alone, she might have the rare chance to do so. During masturbation, you are staging your own scene and catering to your own desires.

Unless, perhaps, you are a woman.

Masturbation makes us both subjects and objects. You are touching yourself. Feeling yourself, as Beyoncé and Nicki Minaj sang. You are the subject and object of "touch" and "feel." Yet it is when *female* masturbation appears in pop culture that the masturbator seems to be an object – not just of her touch, but of her gaze and her desire.

Woman, Cast as Her Own Object

To revisit the movie *American Pie*, it is anything but sexy when Jason Biggs' character Jim masturbates. The porn he's watching – particularly, the "tit" he identifies on the blurry screen – is supposed to be sexy. But he himself is alone in his room with a sock over his penis, looking rather pathetic. His plotline takes an even more pitiful, un-titillating turn when his dad catches him humping a pie. He is far from a sex object, and the film's humor relies on that.

Contrast this with the scene where his classmate Nadia masturbates. A group of guys is secretly watching her, but she doesn't need to know that to behave like the male gaze is on her. She slowly, sensually undresses, seductively smiles, plays with her breasts, and makes soft, breathy moans. Jim's masturbation is for his sake only, and when he's caught, it is embarrassing and comedic. Nadia's self-pleasure session is conducted as if it's for someone else, so when she's spotted, it only seems natural. She is putting on a performance, so of course, she has an audience.

Far from gaining freedom from objectification and simply being a subject, a woman masturbating on screen takes on the dual roles of subject and object, toucher and touched, watcher and watched. In mainstream porn's female masturbation videos, a woman's hands caress her skin the way a lover's would, tracing her shape. Just as a woman's eyes can take on the male gaze, her hands can take on a male touch when she feels herself, feels the other. In male masturbation videos, the man is more often focused on his penis, on himself. It is as if a man who masturbates in porn is pleasuring himself, while a woman is being pleasured by herself.

In music, too, a masturbating woman is an object even as she is a subject. "I know how to scream my own name," Hailee Steinfeld sings in the masturbation anthem "Love Myself." It is almost as if someone else is in the room, receiving praise for their sexual skills. Except that other person is her. The TV show *Broad City*'s protagonist Ilana caricaturizes this trope. She plays both seducer and seduced as she puts on lipstick and earrings, feeds herself an oyster, lights candles, and places a big mirror above her so she can watch herself masturbate. She is playing the traditionally masculine role by setting the mood and romancing herself. At the same time, she plays the feminine role by looking sexy for herself.

This scene is intended to be ridiculous for humor, yet it's not so different from the masturbation advice that women's magazines dole out. *Cosmo* advises readers: "Just like you would with your significant other, get yourself 'ready' for the occasion. Take yourself out to dinner or for swanky drinks, light some candles and take a bath while playing some Michael Bublé, or slip on your sexiest lingerie and just stare at yourself in the mirror."[1] Such advice imagines a woman as a "masculine," desirous subject coaxing herself into bed, and then as a "feminine" object, a reflection to be stared at. She is enacting gendered scripts all by herself. Such articles are often accompanied by seductive female faces and lingerie-covered bodies. Even when we are alone, it seems, it is our job to be hot. Not for a partner, but because this is supposedly important for *our own* arousal. Yet the meaning of "our own" somehow does not just include us. In a world where the ability to be "I" is conflated with maleness, even a woman's self-pleasure seems to involve pleasing an outside gaze.

The image of a man primping in preparation for a wank, screaming his own name, or adorning his bedroom with candles would appear cheesy and silly. Why would he be addressing himself, seducing himself, romancing himself … when he *is* himself? But a woman, apparently, is not herself. Woman does not exist. If she is afforded existence, it is as someone who is part man. Part masculine subject, part feminine object. She requires a counterpart to exist. The male gaze lurks on the periphery of the screen, if not on it. She is never alone. She is never just pleasuring herself.

Waking Sleeping Beauty

These media images don't reflect reality, but they bleed into reality. I, for one, did not grow up masturbating in a "feminine" manner, as I would venture to say many women don't. I did not pay attention to how I looked or what I wore (or stripped out of). I did not need to incorporate sexy lighting or music. I did not perform my own pleasure. Yet the more depictions of female masturbation I saw, the more I began thinking about what faces or movements I was making, or whether I should moan like the women in porn. It felt almost like there was an invisible audience in my bedroom, an announcer declaring over a loudspeaker: "Get ready for the big production, everyone! She's about to masturbate!" I wondered if my self-pleasure sessions disappointed this audience, as I did not scream or convulse or cry tears of joy. Was there enough storyline for a climactic show?

Female masturbation, I'd learned, was supposed to be not just a lovely spectacle but an emotional journey. On the rare occasion when it appeared in movies, it was not an everyday event but an awakening that moved the plot forward, from Natalie Portman's discovery of her dark side in *Black Swan* to Joan Allen literally bringing color to a greyscale world in *Pleasantville*. This image of female masturbation as an awakening did not just come from popular media, though; it came from feminist writing and talks. A common idea I began hearing during my teen years was that women should masturbate to gain empowerment or independence. *Jezebel* states that a girl who masturbates not only will feel "empowered by being able to pleasure herself" but also will "love herself."[2] The *Huffington Post* opines that "masturbation is empowering," and *Woman and Home* agrees that "getting off empowers women."[3] This trope is also present in music: "I'm gonna put my body first ... gonna love myself, no, I don't need anybody else," sings Hailee Steinfeld in "Love Myself."

While there's nothing wrong with celebrating one's self-sufficiency – it certainly makes for catchy tunes – the image of female masturbation as universally empowering was not one I related to. I didn't masturbate to awaken myself; I did it because, I don't know, I was horny. My feelings around it ranged from occasional guilt to enjoyment to ... no feelings at all because, well, women's sexual experiences aren't always emotional. And sadly, I didn't attain high self-esteem or self-love because I masturbated. The expectation that I would seemed to neglect that a wide range of women – from the fiercely independent to those chronically in toxic relationships – masturbate.

There was something, in fact, that bugged me about the masturbation-as-awakening narrative. It seemed to contain an implicit assumption that women were sexually asleep, out of touch with their own bodies and pleasure. Some female masturbation advocates attributed this asleep-ness to biology. YouTube sex educator Laci Green stated in a video that female masturbation is "not quite as intuitive," elaborating, "if you have a penis, it's just sort of like, boom, there it is! If you don't have a penis, you kind of gotta be a little more deliberate about it, get all up in there."[4] Similarly, in the book *I Love Female Orgasm*, sex educators Dorian Solot and Marshall Miller explain the gap in male and female masturbation in part by "boys' genitals" being "*way* easier for them to discover, the way they just hang down there, so easy to see and touch. Girls' genitals, by comparison, are tucked neatly away where they're less visible," they profess. "This puts women at a huge disadvantage."[5]

But our bodies do not put us at a disadvantage. Objectification, evident in the very notion that a woman would possess less independent self-knowledge or desire than a man, puts us at a disadvantage. There is nothing about being female that makes someone's own body a mystery to her, nor are men born self-aware experts. It is the male gaze that renders women's bodies mysterious and men's familiar. Yet we internalize this cultural notion that men's sexuality is out there, obvious, "boom, there it is!" – while women's is absent, hidden, and in need of coaxing.

In reality, many girls masturbate at young ages, before anyone teaches them, and continue to do so in adulthood without instruction.[6] Women are not sexual sleeping beauties in need of awakening. Rather, our desire, which is awake from the beginning, gets tamped down to the point that for some, it may need to be reawakened. This tamping-down does not only occur through overt shaming and repression. It is baked into our language. With women as sexual objects, the penetrated, the recipients of desire, the preyed-on, the unsafe, we lack a framework to imagine ourselves as subjects who seek pleasure for its own sake, for our own sake.

Women are the societal "other" – the group categorized as lacking selfhood and subjectivity, as different from the default people, men – and so we become the other to ourselves. Hence the trope of a woman finding liberation in discovering her uncharted sexual territory, uncharted even though it is hers. Hence the tone of *Wow! So empowering!* in songs and articles about female masturbation. These narratives can only exist within a culture that renders women objects. It is only if we can't imagine women living in their bodies that we deem them objects of discovery, uncovering their sexuality as if it's alien to them.

The Vulva: Invisible or Invisibilized?

The notion that a vulva is harder to see and understand than a penis may seem like a fact. Yet the view of women's sexuality as demure and in need of pursuit colors our conceptions of bodies. In Medieval times, scientists called female genitalia the "pudendum," which comes from the Latin root *pudere*, or "make ashamed." Anatomists claimed women's genitals were below their bodies, rather than in front, so they could not be seen, since they were shameful. As sexologist Emily Nagoski points out in her book *Come as You Are*, the clitoris is actually in the same spot as the penis – right in front. "Female genitals appear 'hidden' only if you look at them through the lens of cultural assumptions rather than through the eyes of biology," she writes.[7]

People of every biological sex can easily touch their genitals – and regularly come into contact with them. All varieties of genitalia have both visible and hidden parts. But beyond that, vision does not have to be the foremost way of getting to know our bodies. Feminist theorist Luce Irigaray suggested that Western society privileges vision over touch *because* we associate visibility with male anatomy. Women, she argued, are always touching themselves; their two labia are continuously in contact. Self-touch is not a discovery of a foreign body, but something intuitive and familiar for a woman. "She touches herself in and of herself without any need for mediation," she wrote.[8] For Irigaray, a woman is always in touch with herself. I'd say we all are, by virtue of our ability to feel our own bodies.

The idea that a woman who touches herself is some special, badass, self-loving kind of woman only makes sense within a linguistic system that places us outside ourselves, making us objects. There would be no big awakening awaiting us in a society with a concept of female subjectivity. There would be no *purpose* required for female masturbation in a society with a concept of female desire. It is only if women are outside their own bodies – as movies, songs, and porn position them – that female masturbation must be something other than a fulfilling of an urge. The celebratory narrative around women "discovering their bodies" obscures how peculiar it is that our bodies are unfamiliar to us in the first place.

Due to the cultural view of the penis as the most accessible sexual organ, male masturbation appears straightforward, easy, and natural. People don't think of men who masturbate as "empowering themselves," "learning to love themselves," or "becoming self-sufficient." Aren't we, as a society, beyond the idea by now that a woman who masturbates is any different?

When will a woman getting herself off be seen as the ordinary, everyday activity it is, rather than an act of seduction or badassery? When will the day come that women are not just in touch with themselves, but aware they are? When they can feel their hands drawn to their bodies, rather than passing through the mind to find a purpose for self-pleasure, to sanitize desire with reason?

Floral Vulvas and Divine Perfume: The Female Model

Although liberation via masturbation was not a relatable concept to me, it did sound enticing. I wanted to know what I was missing. And so, at age twenty-seven, I signed up for a workshop called Bodysex led by the now-deceased sex educator Betty Dodson. Dodson had gained renown for these events she'd been holding in her home since the 1970s, where women got together in the nude to talk about their sexuality, show one another their genitals, and masturbate together. Dodson believed masturbation was key to women's empowerment, writing for *Ms. Magazine* in 1974 that "when a woman masturbates, she learns to like her own body, to enjoy sex and orgasm, and to become proficient and independent about sex."[9]

As I anticipated the workshop, something about it made me uneasy. Surprisingly, it wasn't that I was about to get naked and masturbate alongside other women. Rather, it was what I'd seen on Betty's website and in her YouTube videos – particularly, her claims about women's sexuality. Terms like "female sexuality" and "female orgasm" were sprinkled throughout the pink and white pages of her website, painting a particular portrait of what being female meant. There were comparisons between vulvas and flowers, along with writing that depicted women as pretty objects of the gaze. "To see all these women moving their bodies to the music … breathing … sweating … moaning. There's nothing more beautiful in this world. And the smell in that room was hypnotic," Betty's assistant Carlin Ross wrote of a past workshop. "One woman remarked how she wished she could bottle that smell and take it home."[10]

"Each vulva was distinctively beautiful ... each woman looked so gorgeous with flushed, dewy skin and rosy cheeks," reads another account from a different Bodysex facilitator.[11] (Betty and Carlin trained other women to lead workshops around the world.) In another post, Dodson quotes sex educator Deborah Sundhal as stating that female ejaculate should be appreciated for "its lovely scent and delicate essence, for this is what the feminine – you my dear – create when aroused and feeling pleasure throughout your erotic body – a divine perfume!"[12]

These words, though coming from women intending to uplift other women, depicted female sexuality as something to be consumed by the eyes, the ears, and even the nose. Masturbation, the one sex act where women's beauty seemed irrelevant, was itself portrayed as beautiful. A female body, these descriptions suggested, was delicate and alluring, with a flower-like vulva and perfume-like scent. Where did this leave those who did not resonate with this image – or the "femininity" it represented – such as trans and non-binary people as well as non-stereotypical cis women? Where did it leave those who wanted permission *not* to look pretty when they masturbated? Did female sexual expression always have to be lovely?

Much of Betty Dodson's work defined women's sexuality in opposition to men's. "Female sexual capabilities far exceed that of the male," she wrote in a blog post.[13] In another, she expounded that women "long for slow sensuous fucking," yet companies developing drugs to enhance female arousal "want us to match the male model of fast ejaculations. ... It's time to move beyond the male model of sex to include the female model and accommodate women's ability to have many orgasms."[14]

It was another narrative I found alienating, perhaps because I didn't tend to have "many orgasms" per sitting, nor was I incapable of "fast" ones. And while I enjoyed "slow sensuous" sex, I enjoyed the opposite as well. Nevertheless, the terms "male model" and "female model" came up repeatedly in Betty's writings and videos, painting women as men's sexual opposites.[15] Women's pleasure was harder to attain but more intense, going "on and on," she wrote.[16] Her view of men as simple and women as complex extended beyond sex: She told *The New York Times* in 2020 that "men are so two-dimensional," elaborating, "if there is anything interesting about them, it's because of the women they've been with."[17]

Just Me, Myself, and I … and the Gender Binary

Betty's website evoked the same binary I'd encountered in magazines and on screen: While male masturbation was a straightforward way to keep a guy's sex drive in check, female masturbation – like women themselves – was languid, soft, wild, emotional, and, of course, totally hot to witness. Betty's videos and blog posts were created to dismantle patriarchy, yet it felt like they were ever so subtly projecting a patriarchal fantasy of my sexuality onto me. This projection was better than the social message Betty fought: that it was abnormal for women to be sexual. The idea that self-pleasure was healthy for women was radical when she started her workshops. She was a pioneer by discussing masturbation at all. Today, we can do better in *how* we discuss it.

The stereotypes still circulating about men's and women's masturbation habits reflect broader gender norms. Men are portrayed as rational, in control, linear, and efficient – while women are effusive and hysterical. Men are dominant and aggressive. Women are fragile and delicate. Men get down to business. Women are full of frills and frivolities (and vibrators and massage oils and lingerie). Men's sexuality is easy and obvious. Women's is hidden and discreet. Men are assertive. Women are coy. Men are active, desirous subjects while women are receptive, feeling objects. Yet again, we are expected to perform gender roles even with no one there to perform for.

These stereotypes are summed up in a 2015 *Men's Health* article titled "7 Secrets of Female Masturbation" (because women are *so* mysterious). "Your recipe for masturbation is pretty simple … but female masturbation is a bit more complicated," it reads. "She might see self-pleasure as more of a production, not just a quick rub-and-go activity. … Maybe she pulls out a special lubricant, lights a few candles, or draws a bath before starting."[18] It goes on to explain that, in contrast to men's "rough" technique, women touch their genitals with the care of someone brushing an eyelash off their eye. "Women … tend to be slower, gentler, and more subtle," it reads, adding: "While you pretty much have just one tool at your disposal, she likes to make masturbation a full-body activity." Then, of course, there's this: "You probably have a clear goal in mind: bust a nut or bust … [but] some women are satisfied with their self-pleasure well before orgasm occurs, or regardless of whether there's a climax."

To the extent that this is true – that female masturbation is more complex – then maybe it's true *because* of the very construct of femininity that paints it as such. If a woman looks at herself as an object, she can't fully take in the sensations her own skin is perceiving. She's too busy observing herself. She has floated outside her body to assume the male gaze, then is tasked with re-entering it. That's what's complicated. But despite this expectation, many women's masturbation sessions are uninvolved and simple – "masculine," one might say.

German sex researcher Shere Hite, who surveyed 3,000 women about their sex lives for her 1976 book *The Hite Report*, challenged the notion that women are sexually puzzling or require a big production to experience pleasure, pointing out that – despite what today's magazines suggest – this is not the case during self-pleasure.[19] "There is no great mystery about why a woman has an orgasm. It happens with the right stimulation, quickly, pleasurably, and reliably," she writes. "Women don't need 'foreplay' in masturbation." And contrary to Betty's characterization, women's masturbation sessions span around the same time frame as men's.[20] Nor are multiple orgasms the norm for either gender, though they're possible for anyone.[21]

So much is possible for us all. Our sexualities and personalities are far more expansive than the male or female model. We can all enjoy hour-long full-body pleasure sessions and masturbation breaks between meetings. We can all be simple or complicated, fast or slow, strong or gentle, narrowly or widely focused, goal-oriented or process-oriented, in sex and in life. And if we can't, that's often due to the limits of gender roles, not our capabilities. Our bodies are capable of more than we give them credit for. Yes, we should challenge the wham-bam-thank-you-ma'am "male model" – but we should also challenge the assumption that it is, by nature, male.

The Other Woman

Patriarchy divides us and disguises our similarities by assigning half of human traits to men and half to women, while erasing other (sometimes overlapping) groups, like non-binary and intersex people. When we split humanity into two groups, one is usually seen as the norm while the other is unusual or inferior. This is called "othering," a close kin to objectification that creates an "us vs. them" mentality. The "other" is not the "us," the subject, but the "them" or, in this case, the "she." The societal subject is deemed relatable and normal – and the other is less self-like, less human.

I didn't see it at the time, but this was what Betty Dodson's platform made me feel: the sense of being squished onto one side of a line dividing humanity. A line that passes through verbs, slicing sentences into subjects and objects. And I was on the side of the object, the other, the not-me. How empowering can that be? How radical can a message or movement be when it maintains a split between a masculine subject and feminine other? How many boundaries can we break when we are naturalizing that "femininity" by attributing it to the body?

> Naturalize (v): regard as or cause to appear natural.[22]

To naturalize means to depict something as human nature, overlooking the oppression that went into its making. We do this when we talk about cultural predicaments – like women's sexuality being more appearance-based or complicated – as if they're our innate inclinations. When we bond over these traits, we are bonding over a shared oppression-based identity. When we describe these qualities as present during solo sex, they come to appear even more natural, as if no one else is influencing them.

Even if we see women as equal, we instill a view of them as inferior whenever we reinforce the gender binary. This binary is built on hierarchy. And that was why it made me uneasy to hear how my body was so different from men's. I was being defined as an other, a non-man, half a human. Before I even stepped through Betty's door, I was fed a specific version of what female sexuality was – of who I was.

Are You My Sister?

It was an old feeling. I often did not feel like I met others' expectations of how women were. Different environments I spent time in all seemed to define "girl" and "woman" differently, but they all excluded at least someone – often, me. In junior high and high school, a girl seemed to be someone who was relationship-oriented, enjoyed elaborate beauty routines, was emotionally effusive, was obsessed with boys, and loved children. I was not all this. And so I didn't feel like a proper girl, nor did the girls in school consider me part of their circle.

And in Betty Dodson's circle – her literal circle of women – a woman seemed to be someone who was sexually "feminine," men's opposite. Someone who felt empowered and awakened when she touched herself. Someone who felt a connection with other women. Who felt sisterly toward them. The word "sisterhood" appeared throughout Betty's website in statements like "the sisterhood will always carry us through when we are in the sacred circle"[23] and "I love looking around the circle and seeing all the different body types. They're all beautiful … it builds sisterhood."[24] Was it physical beauty that tied women together and made us women? What constituted sisterhood?

The belief in an innate femininity that makes someone a woman and unites all women is called gender essentialism. The notion of "sisterhood" has essentialist undertones, as it implies that all women possess a common core while playing into stereotypes of women as relational while men are independent. And when sisterhood is described in terms of our sexuality, the message is even stronger. This kind of sisterhood is not just social but biological. It is naturalized. Down to the very cells of our bodies, supposedly, there's something universal about femininity. There is nothing wrong with having chosen family, or even considering all women your sisters. But people carry assumptions about what it means to be a sister, what it means to be a woman, and these assumptions can leave some feeling like they're doing womanhood wrong.

Another word that frequently points toward gender essentialism is "goddess." To some, the common thread that ties women together is not just biological; it's spiritual. Women's bodies are an expression of a grand, immutable force. One Bodysex facilitator describes the event as a "gathering of goddesses." "We are all goddesses," she recalls thinking as she witnessed "the unique beauty of every vulva."[25] Once again, our divinity, our connectedness, our power is defined in terms of beauty.

I don't mean to disrespect women who identify with these terms – especially those being vulnerable enough to share their stories. They're entitled to use whatever language resonates with their identities and experiences. If identifying as a goddess makes a woman (or anyone) feel good about themselves, they should. But when such generalizations are made about entire communities, I wonder: What about those who don't identify with the image of a "goddess" or "sister" that's endorsed? As I read more and more posts describing the Bodysex women as feminine creatures, I wondered if I was a woman by their definition. Was I part of the sisterhood? Was I one of the goddesses? This was a place for all women, wasn't it? If that was the case, I'd find a way to fit in at the workshop.

Time to Rock and Roll

On a Saturday morning, about a dozen women trickled into Betty's New York apartment, removing their clothes in the doorway. As I stripped down, I wondered if my body would be seen as a symbol of femininity or an object of admiration. Pillows were placed in a circle around the living room floor, and each participant sat on one. In the center of the room were glowing white candles, conjuring up magazine articles about pre-masturbation mood-setting.

The first day's activities were fairly unthreatening. We went around the circle and discussed how we felt about our bodies and sex lives. Then, it was time for "genital show and tell," where each woman got up in front of the others and spread her legs. Betty classified participants' vulvas based on art terms like "classic" and "gothic," helping each woman give her genitals a name. When it came my turn, I gave my own vulva a gender-neutral moniker, Storm, subverting the expectation to project femininity onto it. Nor did I refer to it as "she," as some did. It would be going by the pronoun "it," as it was not a girl. It was just an organ with a whole lot of gendered qualities assigned to it. Thankfully, nobody objected.

It was the following day, during "erotic recess" – the group masturbation portion of the weekend – when things got challenging. Recordings of tribal drums played as we lay in our respective spots in the circle, Hitachi Magic Wand vibrators in hand, and Betty demonstrated her "rock and roll technique," which involved rocking back and forth on your spine with a Hitachi on your clitoris and a barbell-shaped toy in your vagina. Some of the women appeared engrossed in juicy build-ups full of moans and profound emotions – what one might call "feminine." I remained quiet, unmoved, and in my head, became overstimulated after an orgasm (thank you, Hitachi), and sat up to survey the room.

"You have to keep going. You're just getting your juices warmed up," Betty told me. And that was all it took to trigger the pressure I already felt to possess a more "feminine" sexuality. Between the lines of her words, I sensed I should be masturbating more like a woman.

"I can't do it," I said. "I feel like I'm missing something. It's not as great for me as it is for everyone else." The other women seemed to be having some kind of transcendent experience. I wanted to have that. I wanted to be a goddess. I wanted to be part of the sisterhood.

"What do you mean?" Carlin asked.

"I mean, everyone seems like they're experiencing something so beautiful and meaningful. I'm not. I don't have the urge to cry or laugh or even moan. I only experienced a simple physical release."

"You know, me too," one other woman said. "Masturbation is just a physical release for me. But that's great. I enjoy it. It doesn't have to mean anything more." It occurred to me that maybe, the sisterhood I was missing out on was mythical. Maybe other women were "masculine," too. Maybe I didn't have to be "feminine" to belong to this group – or the larger group known as womankind.

Embracing My Inner Grumpy Vampire

After erotic recess, we broke into small groups, where each woman took turns getting a massage from the others. Carlin described how massaging one another would solidify the sisterhood. That familiar feeling of alienation crept back in. I was expected to feel bonded to these women. But besides that comforting interaction I'd had with one other participant, I still felt separate from the group and from women in general. The touch I was supposed to deliver to my fellow attendees felt like an enmeshment with an ideal of womanhood I could not embody. I knew my resistance was shaped by past experiences. Perhaps I was replaying early feelings of exclusion from various female groups. I did my best to move past this feeling and gently massaged other participants' hands, sitting a bit off to the side.

Betty, who had been lounging next to me in the circle, was now on a chair surveying the little massage groups. She looked over at me and began talking to Carlin. "There's one woman here – she was sitting next to me, and she's a vampire," she said. "She just takes and doesn't give." My body stiffened and I bowed my head, pretending not to hear. But I could tell she was talking about me. I was the only one who had been next to her, besides Carlin herself. I had wanted to give. I had wanted to be part of the group. But given that I felt like the odd one out, I struggled to do that. I sensed that I was simultaneously forced into and barred from the sisterhood – that I had to be part of it, but that I had to be feminine to be part of it.

This was how I felt about womanhood in general. I wanted to be one of the girls. I wanted to experience camaraderie among women. But they didn't seem to want me. I wasn't really a woman in their eyes – eyes unknowingly emitting the male gaze's piercing beam as they split humanity in two and cut me off. These forms of exclusion are subtle. They happen when we make generalizations about how "women are natural helpers," "women are neat and clean," or "women are emotional creatures." These statements are often uttered to bond women together. They are said by women to women to signify, "You're like me. I get you." Yet if you don't fit a given woman's description of what a woman is, these statements convey the opposite: "You're not like me. You're not one of us."

I've seen this happen in many other settings intended to unite women. When I trained as a doula, one of my instructors said that doulas are important because "we're women and women have the right hormones to empathize." She elaborated that women naturally "tend and befriend" others, forming warm connections in situations where men go into "fight or flight." I thought in that moment that I would not be a great doula, as I did not consider myself especially social or empathetic. I felt left out of a female tradition. Eventually, I realized I can be a great doula and a great friend without being feminine in every way. I now see my "masculine" qualities, including my logical mind and independence, as important assets. But I was not yet at that point on the day Betty Dodson called me a vampire. I was desperate to be a better sister.

With that goal in mind, I went to another Bodysex workshop a year later. Betty had forgotten about me by then, but she did give me a new name: "Grumpy." She didn't explain why this time; she simply said, "come over here, Grumpy." While I was getting better at letting loose in this group – yes, even during erotic recess – perhaps Betty sensed that I still wasn't jumping into the weekend's activities with the same enthusiasm as others. And for once, I was cool with that. Maybe I would never fully fit into the sisterhood – the Bodysex sisterhood and the supposedly universal sisterhood that everyone with a vagina belonged to.

Maybe that was OK. Maybe it wasn't my fault if I didn't fit into groups of women. Maybe it was the fault of those who defined "woman" in narrow ways. Maybe it wasn't such a bad thing to be grumpy. Maybe the enforcement of gender norms by women themselves was something to be grumpy about. So, I decided to embrace my grumpiness – and oddly enough, since then, I have not felt so grumpy anymore. Today, I laugh about my time with the late Betty Dodson, including the creative names she called me. I hope if she can read this from wherever she is, she is laughing with me.

The New Siblinghood

Over the next few years, I went to several more Bodysex-style workshops run by different educators. To my luck, I did not earn any nicknames. I didn't have trouble fitting in because I didn't try to. If an activity made me uncomfortable or just didn't jive with me, I sat it out. I stopped accepting invitations to women's circles that used language like "delicious feminine energy" and "hottest meeting on Earth." It was OK, I realized, not to be feminine, hot, or mouth-wateringly delicious – so why put myself in situations where that was expected? I no longer assumed something was wrong with me just because there was something wrong with how women related to one another.

Today, I aim to create wide, open spaces for people's full selves to expand into. When I teach or coach people on sexuality, I embrace everyone's capacity to be "feminine" and "masculine" – and neither is superior. But I don't use those terms. Instead of male and female sexuality, I talk about *sexualities*, plural. Masculinity and femininity are not rooms with locked doors but vast fields we can move into, out of, through, or away from as we like.

I do strive to treat people as if we are all part of some siblinghood. Except it's just the siblinghood of humanity. None do not belong, and all are welcome.

The members of the Bodysex community are my siblings. So are all the people who don't feel like they fit in.

However you look, however you behave, however you identify, you still belong in this family.

You still belong in this world.

Chapter 9

I Define: Embody Your Divine Self

I sat amid a crowd in a San Francisco warehouse as a teacher drew two lines on big white sheets of paper: a straight line progressing diagonally from the bottom left to the top right, then a squiggly, twisty line that curved up and down and up and down all over the page. "Masculine energy is straightforward and simple, like a line," she explained as she pointed to the first drawing, then the second. "Feminine energy is all over the place, like a rollercoaster, which is why women are insane."

It turned out Bodysex was just a doorway into a much vaster and more offensive world of gender essentialism masquerading as progressiveness. The gender binary implicit in Betty Dodson's online presence was explicit in a practice I was learning around the same time called orgasmic meditation, or OM. As the OM teacher uttered the above words about "masculine" and "feminine" energy, my fellow students gave a knowing chuckle. Ha ha, women are crazy. Everyone knew that.

This class, run by a company called OneTaste, was teaching us this tired, ableist stereotype through the lens of a specific sexual act. During an orgasmic meditation session, a man strokes the upper left quadrant of a woman's clitoris, moving his finger ever so gently, "as if he were touching an eyeball," the teacher explained. The woman lies back and feels, without any goal, as "feminine" sexuality is "non-linear" and "goal-less." This all takes place within a "nest" of pillows that a man sets up for a woman to lay her head and legs on. He is also responsible for setting a timer, which goes off after thirteen minutes. Once it hits that thirteen-minute mark, he presses on her legs to "ground" her back to reality, and after fifteen minutes, the OM comes to a close.

In an OM session, there is a "stroker" who's touching the clitoris and a "strokee" who's being touched. OM practitioners say that a woman can be a stroker, but, in practice, it is almost always a man. They say it's the man's job to "keep the container," to be a rock, to provide some structure and stability for the woman to fall into as she goes wild and lets out her many feelings. The strong masculine is there to tame the unruly feminine. OM teachers and coaches tend to use gendered language, glossing over the prospect that someone with a clitoris may not be a woman, let alone not be "feminine."

My OM teacher went on to explain that we've been thinking about orgasms all wrong. We typically think of orgasm as a climax, she said, which is a sharp peak and release of tension. However, women's orgasms did not work this way. Women's orgasms, like their energy, were rollercoasters, including many peaks and troughs of pleasure but no clear beginning or end. "Orgasm," she elaborated, was the "activation of the involuntary systems in the body." It included processes such as flushing of the face, shaking of the legs, and sweating. In other words, a "feminine" orgasm spanned the whole arousal process and could go on indefinitely. Men typically had climaxes, while women had "expansive orgasms," which could be elicited through this ritualized stroking of the clitoris's upper left quadrant. Most people saw orgasm as equivalent to climax because of patriarchy's male-centered mentality, but OM was here to shine light on the feminine form of pleasure.

While I had never heard anything quite like this before, I had heard the same basic argument about gender many times over. It goes something like this: "We've been applying standards based on men to women! It's time for us to create a new, female standard." I had heard this said about men's and women's supposedly differing work styles, relationship values, and so on. Sometimes, it had merit. For instance, differences between male and female bodies render some health research done on men inapplicable to women. Mostly, though, the argument devolves very quickly into gender essentialism backed more by social norms than science.

OneTaste's version of this argument was also one I'd heard before from the likes of Betty Dodson: that we've been expecting everyone to possess a male sexuality, and female sexuality deserved its time in the spotlight. Yet when people make this claim, their concept of female sexuality is often so divorced from women's actual experiences, it feels more like a male-gazey projection than any real woman's sexuality. "Female sexuality," in these definitions, is something exotic, something mysterious: a rollercoaster, "crazy," nonsensical, directionless, hard to understand or relate to. Often, this very perspective is more male-centered than the one it critiques, defining female sexuality as that which is foreign to the self: the other.

When the OM teacher discussed the "feminine" form of pleasure, I did not feel the least bit seen, even though I was supposedly a feminine being. In fact, I had no clue what she was talking about. But maybe I'd just been so brainwashed by patriarchy that I'd fallen out of touch with my feminine nature.

Uncovering the Mysteries of the Feminine

I'm not being sarcastic. This was a real concern of mine. It sounded so enchanting to orgasm for minutes on end. Even though the experience they were calling "orgasm" did not, to me, sound like an orgasm. OneTaste's founder Nicole Daedone had a charisma that made me see why OM had been described as cult-y.[1] While she was not present at the "Intro to OM" class I took in San Francisco, I interviewed her one-on-one several times. Listening to her speak was like a psychedelic trip. "Climax is the point where we check out," she once told me, while the feminine orgasm was "the point where we check in," allowing full presence and surrender to the moment. In her TED Talk, "Orgasm: The Cure for Hunger in the Western Woman," she explains:

> We have a pleasure deficit disorder in this country. ... There is a cure, and that cure is orgasm. But it's going to be a very different definition of orgasm than we know. It's not going to be that fleeting moment of climax that seems to take the whole rest of the act hostage. It's going to be a definition of orgasm that actually works with a woman's body, so that rather than trying to stuff a woman's body into an ill-fitting definition, we have the definition work with what the woman's body does.[2]

She goes on to quote the Dalai Lama: "The Dalai Lama has said that it will be Western woman who changes the world." He is another figure, albeit a very different one, who believes we need to prize and honor femininity. "The female biologically [has] more potential to show affection ... and compassion," he once said.[3] The notion that women deserve rights and influence because we are kinder, gentler, and more feminine is sometimes called benevolent sexism. This idea stems from a romanticized concept of femininity that puts women on pedestals. It holds women to a high, narrow standard, fosters assumptions that treat women as the other, and implies that more "masculine" women don't merit as much respect or power. This implication was evident when the Dalai Lama stated that a female Dalai Lama "must be very attractive," or else there's "not much use" for her.[4]

Daedone puts her own spin on the Dalai Lama's ideas in her TED talk, declaring: "It will be turned-on women and those who dare to stroke us who actually change the world by feeding this desire for connection that we all have." I grew enraptured by this prospect of a turned on, connected life. And so, I continued investigating the peculiar world of orgasmic meditation. I attended an OM "turn-on" – a OneTaste-sponsored meetup where people play "connection games" – the following year. There, I told the group that I wanted to be more "in my feminine." I was coming to understand this meant to be relaxed, in the flow of life, and able to attract my desires effortlessly. Who wouldn't want that?

After the meetup, a OneTaste staff member gave me information about a retreat the company was hosting, telling me it was all about being in your feminine. She also encouraged me to sign up for OneTaste's $12,000 "orgasmic meditation coach" training program – something the company was known for pushing.[5] I didn't go for either, but I was almost tempted.

A Cure for Female Masculinity

The way that OMers described "the feminine" sounded so seductive: to be so engrossed in the moment that you stopped thinking. To be aware of your heart and body rather than caught in your mind. To be so receptive that, rather than striving or fighting, you simply magnetized what you wanted. To be in the "orgasm state," as they called it, your entire life. It was tantalizing. I had a problem for which OMers offered a simple diagnosis: an excess of "masculine energy." I was overworked, often in a rush, and stuck in my head a lot of the time. Their practice promised to help me slow down, enjoy life, and follow my intuition.

For several months, I worked with an "OM coach" who had completed OneTaste's training. One day, I mentioned to her that I was booking flights for a trip with my boyfriend, and she asked, "Do you feel like you do most of the work in your relationship?"

"Overall, no," I said. "Just when it comes to planning and logistics, because I'm very organized and enjoy that stuff."

"You poor bitch," she exclaimed over the phone. "You must not feel like a woman." Organization and structure were "masculine," she said, while the "feminine" role was to surrender into "the masculine container" and be "held."

In that one conversation, the alluring aspiration of femininity turned into a shame game. Maybe, I started to think, I'd be happier if I were less "masculine." Maybe my tendency to think and plan made me less womanly, less sexy. Maybe I needed to immerse myself in OM so that I'd act less like a man. I didn't realize then that nobody else got to define what a woman was or who *I* was for me – that I could be the subject of "define."

I already had a feeling there was nothing about femaleness that would make someone more magnetic or "in the flow," as OMers professed. Anyone who's always working and rushing could benefit from relaxing and letting things come to them, regardless of their gender. Yet equating these qualities with femininity gave them extra oomph – the kind of oomph that persuades people to shell out thousands of dollars on courses and retreats. Associating your company's promises with female sexuality, after all, makes them sexy. Filtering them through the male gaze and its mystical fantasy of women's sexuality makes them even sexier.

Fast forward a couple years, and OneTaste is the subject of a *Bloomberg* article stating that its managers ordered staff to sleep with customers,[6] a podcast called *The Orgasm Cult* that details the story of a woman repeatedly pressured into sex she didn't want by the company's leadership,[7] and a Netflix documentary called *Orgasm Inc.* revealing cult-like business practices.[8] OneTaste came under FBI investigation in 2018 for sex trafficking and violations of labor law, and Daedone was indicted on forced labor charges in 2023.[9] It's one more piece of proof that the division of people along "masculine" and "feminine" lines leads to objectification. When we view women as more yielding, more emotional, and altogether alien from men, it is only a short leap from there to treat women as objects. And once women take on the object role, it is but another short leap to justify their commodification.

Objectification, but Make It Spiritual

I'd soon learn that the qualities OMers ascribed to women were known throughout New Age circles as the "divine feminine." There was a world of coaches, speakers, authors, and social media influencers teaching women to embody the divine feminine, and men the divine masculine. The "divine feminine" was radiant, attractive, magnetic, and receptive. The "divine masculine" was a rock – rational, strong, and powerful. Many proponents of these concepts saw themselves as liberating women from patriarchy by helping them do things the female way in a world that prizes the male way. Yet their beliefs about what constituted the male and female way sounded awfully patriarchal themselves.

Somehow, when ideas about masculinity and femininity are dressed up in spirituality, it becomes acceptable to say things that would never be OK to say in other contexts. David Deida, a men's coach who popularized many of these ideas, wrote in his 1997 book *The Way of the Superior Man* that "the feminine always seems chaotic and complicated from the perspective of the masculine."[10] This is a flowery way of expressing that women will always be the other. That men are unable to understand women as fellow subjects. Women are not "I." Women are "them." Just to drive home the point that women are irrational and incomprehensible, Deida writes in another chapter, "a person with a feminine essence may not keep her word, yet it is not exactly 'lying.' In the feminine reality, words and facts take a second place to emotions and the shifting moods of relationships."

An ex of mine who was an avid David Deida reader interpreted my actions through this othering lens. One night, he called to say he'd be half an hour late for a date, and I expressed frustration that he'd been late for our past few dates as well. He apologized, so when he picked me up, I put it behind me and greeted him with a smile. "Women's moods change so quickly," he observed. "The feminine is like a wild ocean; it's all over the place." Apparently, my decision to forgive him was evidence of this. Rather than put himself in my position and ask himself why *he* might act the way I did – because, I don't know, I just wanted to enjoy the date – it was all about this wild feminine force filtered through the male gaze.

Deida's not the worst of it, though. When masculine/feminine coaching combines with the assignment of "value" to people, we get philosophies like those of former kickboxer and media personality Andrew Tate, who promoted the concepts of "high-value men" and "high-value women" on YouTube. For men, he said, value stems from "capability," the ability to "kill somebody," and being "rich with a nice car," whereas being a "high-value female" is all about being "hot ... female beauty is extremely valuable."[11] Tate was recently indicted on rape and human trafficking charges after being accused of luring women to his Romanian properties and forcing them to make porn.[12] It seems once again that advocating a "feminine" ideal that objectifies women sets the stage for literally treating them like commodities.

The language of women-as-possessions exists throughout the coaching world, with many speaking of women's desire to be "claimed" by men. Women's coach Anna Rova, who teaches a women's course called "Claimed," writes on her Instagram that women seeking relationships with men should not have male friends, lest said friends' masculinity rub off on them. The post describes a time in her life when she was hanging out with guys platonically: "No wonder all these great masculine men were ending up dating my more feminine girlfriends and ending up in relationships with them, leaving me to Netflix and chill with premium pizza and a tub of vegan ice cream."[13] And she ends with a kicker: Being friends exclusively with women was "how I attracted my husband and you can do too" (by purchasing her course).

There is almost a formula in these coaches' and companies' marketing: Shame people's gender expression, imply it's why they're single while other, more "feminine" or "masculine" people have partners, then offer to help them embody their gender role – their "divine" one, of course – for a price. Except don't call it a gender role; call it a spiritual path. But if it's really the natural order of things for women to be feminine, how is femininity so fragile that a woman can't even have male friends without turning masculine? Why would we need to be schooled and shamed into being what we innately are? These coaches seem adamant that masculinity and femininity are immutable essences ... yet terribly anxious that people can lose their gender at the drop of a hat.

The Fragility of Femininity

When I moved to LA in my late twenties and got involved in spiritual activities – ecstatic dance, kundalini yoga, sound baths – I heard it more and more: "Embody the divine feminine." Gurus taught workshops on how to unleash that wild feminine energy within us women and how to hold the sturdy masculine container as a man. One "feminine embodiment coach" told me not to ask for a love interest's number because then I wouldn't "be in my feminine," which meant "total surrender." Many of these people drew on tantra to argue for the need for "polarity" – the existence of two opposing masculine and feminine forces – in relationships. Yet almost all of them were white.

The truth is, tantra has little to do with these teachings. If you look at tantra's origins, it looks very different from this. Archeological evidence suggests that tantra originated with people of African heritage around 10,000 years ago in Northern India's Indus Valley, according to Devi Ward Erickson, founder of the Institute of Authentic Tantra Education in Canada. Now, there are many tantra lineages in many places including India, Southeast Asia, and Tibet. Most white tantra teachers who talk about "masculine" and "feminine" are really teaching neotantra, which resulted from British colonialism in India around the turn of the twentieth century. "Traditional tantra is focused on enlightenment, and every part of human existence functions as a tool for that: food, sex, sleep, pooping, pain, sorrow, joy, everything," Ward Erickson told me. "Neotantra focuses on sex games, polarity, and the dynamics of 'men and women' as they are understood through a white, cis, heteronormative lens."

Neotantra teachers like David Deida like to qualify their teachings by stating that we *all* have masculine and feminine sides. Yet they are almost always focused on teaching women to be "in their feminine" and men to be "in their masculine," not the other way around. Embedded in their philosophy is an assumption that men are naturally *more* masculine and women are more feminine – combined with a confusing simultaneous belief that women and men must *learn* how to be feminine and masculine, often through expensive services. The polarity coaching business both naturalizes gender and unwittingly acknowledges how constructed it is. So constructed, apparently, that one must spend thousands of dollars to embody it.

It's often politically progressive people who bring up the masculine and feminine in this way. Yet the same pseudo-spirituality gets employed by conservatives. Fox News commentator Keith Ablow responded to a J.Crew ad where a woman paints a boy's nails by writing: "These folks are hostile to the gender distinctions that actually are part of the magnificent synergy that creates and sustains the human race. They respect their own creative notions a whole lot more than any creative Force in the universe."[14]

There's that familiar contradiction: If being male makes you masculine, why would a boy stop being masculine just because his mom painted his nails? If femininity really is an inherent quality of women, how could a woman become less feminine just because she asked for someone's number? How can a woman's actions be unwomanly when they authentically came from her, a woman? If something feels natural to us, who is anyone to tell us it's unnatural? And if this capital-F Force is so powerful, why must we police others' actions to protect it?

Divine Gender Is Too Much Work. I Give Up

A friend of mine I'll call Tom, a fan of neotantra retreats, used to school me on masculine/feminine dynamics. A few years back, I told him over brunch about a man I'd recently dated, whom I'll call Scott. When Scott met up with his ex to gain closure soon after we started dating, I told him I wouldn't feel comfortable dating him if there were lingering feelings between them. He said he had no interest in his ex – so I trusted him and kept seeing him, only to find out a month later that they'd not just stayed in touch but hooked up.

"You weren't in your feminine when you had that conversation," said Tom. "The woman doesn't tell the man what to do. The masculine is dominant. When you told him not to get back with his ex, you were dominating him. And that made him want to defy you – because he was like, 'who are you to give commands? That's my job.'"

"I was asserting a boundary," I replied, confused. "Is that really so domineering?"

"When you set a boundary like that, it puts you in the masculine role," Tom explained (or, some might say, mansplained). "The feminine way to do it would be to show your emotions. If he had seen you cry, he might have acted differently." He went on to tell me I had been too "reasonable," as "the feminine isn't reasonable," and "if Scott wanted someone reasonable, he'd date a dude."

"He actually said he liked that I'm level-headed and not emotionally reactive," I replied. Tom rolled his eyes and told me, "That's like a woman saying, 'I want a nice guy.' Men like women *because* they're emotionally reactive. It sounds like that's how his ex was: super emotional. If a man is straight, he's looking for someone feminine."

These concepts of femininity and masculinity were perhaps intended to empower people. But in that moment, I felt the opposite of empowered. I felt awful about myself for not being "feminine" enough. I imagined it was my lack of softness, sensitivity, and emotional lability – the fact that I wasn't a rollercoaster, as OneTaste claimed women are – that caused Scott to choose someone more womanly than me. A truly empowering message would have sounded more like this: "It's amazing that you are level-headed even amid stress. It's amazing that you are organized and a good planner. It's amazing that you know and express your boundaries. What wonderful qualities to bring to a relationship. Those traits have nothing to do with gender, and they have nothing to do with anyone dishonoring or neglecting you."

It didn't hit me until several days later that if a man needs a woman to act "feminine," maybe that's because he doesn't feel masculine. A man who is confident that he himself is logical, powerful, and successful won't feel threatened by a woman who embodies those traits. She won't "out-masculine" him – or perhaps she will and he won't care, because he doesn't need to feel masculine. He feels confident that he's a man, and that's enough. I also realized Tom was operating off a very specific idea of femininity: a heteronormative, monogamy-centered ideal that assumes the "feminine" and "masculine" complete each other, as if each member of a couple must be half a person. The neotantric notion that attraction requires masculine-feminine "polarity" implies that everyone must either be straight or mimic heterosexual dynamics.

The irony is, if I were to take Tom's advice and try to be more feminine, that itself would not be "feminine." Femininity, according to the whitewashed tantric view, was all about *not* trying. It was about being at ease and just letting things happen. "The feminine doesn't chase," I had been told; women were meant to be the objects of "chase." Yet performing femininity to win a love interest's favor *is* a form of chasing – even when that performance involves waiting to be pursued.

There Is No "Should"

The good news is that actual tantric concepts offer us a more liberating paradigm. Every tantra lineage has a different definition of "masculine" and "feminine," says Ward Erickson, a Black biracial woman trained in Tibetan Buddhist tantra. Some of these concepts are completely different and even opposing. For instance, in one lineage, the moon is "masculine" and the sun is "feminine," and in another, it's the opposite. But what different tantric lineages have in common is that they are not prescriptive. The "masculine" and "feminine" are abstract metaphors drawn poetically from male and female bodies, not literal ideas about how men and women should behave.

"There's not a 'should' in there," says Ward Erickson. "The focus of this tradition is not on cultivating more duality. The masculine and feminine are going to arise ideally in perfect balance within each of us." This balance looks different for everyone, she says, and is achieved not by trying to act more "masculine" or "feminine" but simply by devoting yourself to tantric practices. "I'm a very fierce and fiery woman; I would be described as 'being in my masculine' by [neotantric] groups," Ward Erickson says. "I would be shamed ... I would be told there's something wrong with me for being who I am." But in her tantric lineage, the feminine is connected to the fire element and is perfectly in line with her personality – not that it needs to be. "The practices within tantric Buddhism are all focused on balance, regardless of your sexual anatomy," she says. "In fact, we often visualize ourselves as Buddhas of all genders."

To me, it seems that if masculinity or femininity is part of someone's identity, then that person can just be themselves, and they're automatically being masculine or feminine. If I'm a feminine person and I'm being true to myself, then I'm still being feminine when I'm asking for someone's number, planning a trip, expressing a boundary, or doing other "masculine" things (which, to me, don't sound masculine at all). But, of course, this message won't persuade people to shell out thousands of bucks.

Tell Me Your Pronouns So I Know What Box to Put You In

The masculine/feminine coaching industry has made surface-level attempts to include the LGBTQ+ community. It seems that in these circles, gender essentialism is fine as long as you're stereotyping people of all genders and sexualities. When describing same-sex couples, white tantra gurus still talk about the "masculine" and "feminine partner," as if they're not basically telling them to act straight. When they try to include gender diversity, the contradictions are even more glaring.

"The School of Womanly Arts is a place for all women," reads the website of Mama Gena, founder of this institute focused on women's sexual empowerment. "Students ... are cisgender, transgender, and still trying to find the words."[15] She uttered this same line to over 1,000 women in the daily Zoom calls I joined for her 2021 "Morning Pleasure Ritual Challenge," where we learned how to add pleasure to our lives. She then went right on to talk about how women just want to have fun and can't work all the time like men, as evidenced by the clitoris's 8,000 nerve endings (a statistic based on a study of cows).[16] She added that we women are natural mothers, always wanting to care for others, so we need to learn to balance that with self-care. Afterward, she sent us emails calling us "goddesses."

Echoing the Dalai Lama's sentiments, Mama Gena writes on her website that "violence flourishes without the feminine" and we must "reclaim the values of the feminine," like "intuition," "community," "sisterhood," "receiving," and "surrender."[17] In case there's any doubt as to whether she's equating those qualities with genitalia, her book *Pussy* calls the vulva the "seat of our divine feminine power," claiming that it "turns on when the rules of the feminine are being observed."[18] But she perhaps reaches peak gender essentialism with this line: "If you want to learn how a woman operates, just learn how a pussy operates. It is one and the same."[19]

It seems to me that if someone wants to be a trans ally, which involves challenging the notion that having a vulva makes you a woman, they should also challenge the notion that having a vulva – or identifying as a woman – makes you a feminine goddess. But what do I know? I'm just another woman who's "trying to find the words" in a world where the definition of "woman" seems increasingly narrow, even – no, somehow especially – in communities striving to unite *all* women.

In social media posts by sex-positive professionals, I hear the same generalizations that have long been made about women and their sexuality. It's just that now, they're made about "people with vulvas." I hear people ask for others' pronouns, then make assumptions based on them. Instead of fitting all people assigned female at birth into a box of "femininity," we're now doing the same thing to anyone who uses "she/her" pronouns. Too many people are following the letter of the law but not the spirit of it – the spirit of rejecting essentialism. They're paying lip service to LGBTQ+ inclusion yet failing to challenge stereotypes that hurt LGBTQ+ people and straight, cis people alike. They're fixating on whether people go by "he," "she," or "they" without really allowing them to be "I," to be subjects defining themselves.

Declaring Our Divinity

The sex-positive spaces that have felt most feminist to me have, ironically, been ones that were not specifically for women. That's probably because, when people try to appeal to women, they often operate off exclusionary definitions of what a woman is. The same way that clothing-optional resorts trying to cater to women end up promoting objectification, communities striving to celebrate "femininity" end up promoting stereotypes.

In fact, the group where I felt most comfortable in the female gender role was a college sexuality workshop that shunned gender roles entirely. We were instructed to use the gender-neutral pronoun "phe" for everyone in the group and to speak for ourselves instead of making assumptions about others. Hippie-dippie, I know – yet there was no talk of goddesses, yonis, or feminine energy. We simply strove to understand one another as individuals. Instead of having an identity imposed on me, I was free to embody the range of human qualities within me. And many of these qualities *were* "feminine" – but that felt completely different when I was not assumed to possess these traits due to my genitals.

Women's groups like Betty Dodson's and Mama Gena's can serve a purpose. They can help women feel safe expressing themselves free from sexist expectations. But they can enforce these expectations too. Women can look at other women through the male gaze and objectify them just as much as men. In fact, the idea that women are gathering in women-only spaces to let their true feminine nature shine, free from patriarchal influence, is itself patriarchal. As long as we are labeling women "feminine," rather than letting them define themselves, the male gaze is still present; it's just hidden. The cycle of naturalization and exclusion will continue until we ask ourselves: What do we believe it means to be a woman? And who does that definition leave out?

There's nothing wrong with teaching people to value nurturing, gentleness, or receptivity. Nor is there anything wrong with teaching strength, reliability, or logic. All these attributes are beautiful to possess if they arise organically within you. And that's why we should teach *all* people to appreciate those traits within themselves. Calling qualities "masculine" and "feminine" makes people feel inadequate if they don't live up to their gender. Telling people to embody the "divine feminine" or "divine masculine" implies that they are less divine if they don't perform gender roles. Yet there is nothing spiritual about splitting humanity in two. When virtues get distilled into rules, they become constricting rather than liberating.

True spirituality means throwing away preconceived notions and smiling at all the sparkly colors of humanity. It means freeing people from boxes, not closing them in.

If we simply teach people to connect to their authentic selves and make decisions in the moment – from that place of self-knowledge – there will be no need for masculinity or femininity how-tos.

There will be no need to try to embody the divine feminine or masculine.

All there is to do is to embody your divine self. Your divinity is already within you.

Chapter 10

I Bleed: A Girl Becomes an Object Becomes a Subject

When is it that we are indoctrinated into this unspoken yet ever-important group known as "women"? It happens in little ways throughout our lives, from the moment our parents buy us pink baby clothes and into old age. But it is perhaps during someone's first period that they are explicitly declared a woman and assigned the traits, values, and expectations associated with female objects. When girls reach this milestone, they are often told, "You're a woman now." And for some, that's a scary thing to be.

Before that, you're a girl. That comes with its own connotations. You are sugar and spice and everything nice. You play dolls and dress-up while boys learn about dinosaurs and get lost in video games. Yet the category of "girl" is somewhat looser than "woman." You can be a normal girl and play outside and get dirty. You can start your morning with a simple routine – no makeup, hairstyling, body hair removal, or bras. And you do not typically have to worry about catering to the male gaze or escaping it. It is when we are women that we're asked to step up – or, really, down – and perform femininity in a new way.

"Woman," unlike "girl," carries the connotation of "receptacle": a sexual receptacle for men and a reproductive receptacle for children. When we get our first periods, these parallel constructions of womanhood converge to coax us into objecthood. Because we are technically fertile and headed toward becoming sexually eligible, the notion that we are there to be penetrated looms larger. And menstrual blood, cushioning the womb, serves as a symbol of the softness and selflessness we are expected to offer children – and everyone. Perhaps that's why, when people said "you're becoming a woman," I heard, "you're becoming an object."

Welcome to Womanhood, Leave Your Subjectivity at the Door

I remember grieving when I got my first period, grieving something I could not name: the lost innocence of being a subject. I had gone from "I" to "her." I felt smacked in the face with what mature womanhood represented: being sexualized. Being a self-sacrificing mother. I was now defined in terms of others.

Sigmund Freud once wrote that as girls matured, they were tasked with shifting their source of pleasure from the clitoris to the vagina. Contrary to popular belief, he didn't see this as a natural developmental stage. He saw it as a social expectation – and a hard one to meet.[1] He spoke of how challenging it was for girls to redirect their sexuality away from the sensitive clitoris – the first place they turned to for self-stimulation – and toward the less richly innervated vagina, a body part valued for the pleasure it brings men. Puberty in girls is marked by "a fresh wave of repression, which particularly affects clitoral sexuality," he wrote.[2] "What thus succumbs to repression is a piece of masculine sexual life."

I read this transition as a metaphor for what girls experience when they go from living their own lives to lives centered on others, as prospective partners or mothers. Sometimes this transition is literal: In parts of India, girls are taken out of school and married off during menarche.[3] In other places like the US, the change may not be outwardly acknowledged, but it is felt within our clenching uteruses, our leaking blood, as we mourn our prior selves. To exist within a culture that defines sex based on reproduction and female passivity, women are expected to suppress what the clitoris symbolizes: desire and pleasure for one's own sake. Suddenly defined by our vaginas – what goes in, what comes out – we go from simply feeling desire to receiving it.

The word "vagina" stems from the Latin word for "sheath," as in, "for a sword."[4] In the patriarchal imagination, it is there for men to insert themselves into. For women to be objects of "penetrate." In relation to children, our bodies are conceived of as objects of "inhabit" and "feed off." "Mother" is from the Latin root "mater," the same word behind "matter" and "material."[5] We represent the material world, the earth, the inert soil that men sow their seed in. The Latin root "man" means "hand," the appendage that separates us from animals.[6] Men are the humans inhabiting Mother Earth, venturing through Mother Nature. Men are marked by mind, women by matter. Men are marked by subjectivity, women by objecthood.

Around seventy years after Freud put forth his theories on clitoral and vaginal sexuality, feminist theorist Carla Lonzi stated that to be "clitoridean" – in touch with your clitoris – means "thinking in the first person."[7] The clitoris is not defined in relation to anything, while the vagina is seen as a container for a penis and a portal for a child. This distinction is merely symbolic, as the vagina can be a source of pleasure, but it's powerful. We are subjects when our lives are governed not by the symbolism of the vagina, there for others to fill, but by what the clitoris represents: living for ourselves.

Bleeding the Same Color

I lost my period almost completely for two years. Dieting and weight loss erased this bodily reminder of vaginal modes of relating. I reversed the Freudian trajectory and remained clitoridean, avoiding all thoughts of my reproductive capacities and what they symbolized. Then, at seventeen, in eating disorder treatment, it came back. And I felt a fear I couldn't articulate. I told the center's dance therapist I felt uncomfortable with this bodily function.

She replied that menstruation was beautiful. "It naturally marks your entry into womanhood," she said. "Men have elaborate rituals and hazing processes to mark their entry into manhood. But women don't need that. Their body does it for them." That did not sound comforting to me. I did not want my body – or others' interpretations of it – to determine if and when I became a woman. I wanted to say what I was. The dance therapist's theory implied that men define themselves while women's selves are defined for them, in the passive voice. It was another of those "truths" about the body that only seems true because of how we interpret bodies. One could find aspects of male puberty to mark the entrance into manhood: the growth of facial hair, the Adam's apple, vocal changes. And people do have rituals around female puberty: bra shopping, leg-shaving, and ironically, conversations with elders about menarche "making you a woman." These rituals' existence calls into question how natural this transition really is.

Yet many view the femininity associated with menstruation as a universal force. That same summer, I spotted a poem on the treatment center's wall: "we need a god who bleeds now" by feminist writer Ntozake Shange.[8] The poem states that we need a god "whose wounds are not some small male vengeance" – one who "spreads her lunar vulva & showers us in shades of scarlet," like "our mothers tearing to let us in." A god "whose wounds are not the end of anything."

Such evocative words suggest that, if we worshiped a menstruating deity, we might value feminine traits like caring and nurturing. The poem implies that having men in charge leads to violence and that elevating those with uteruses would lessen the vengeance and bloodshed on Earth. Rather than affirming that we all bleed the same color, such imagery emphasizes how differently we bleed: Contrary to men, with their self-serving brutality, women serve others. Men are the sword; we are the sheath. Even our blood is a gentle shower. Our vulvas are "lunar"; we are like the moon, cyclical and fluid.

This thinking is seductive, as we do need more compassion and less violence. We do need more respect for culturally feminine values like caring and connection. But deeming these qualities women's domain neglects that we all benefit from them, carry the capacity for them, and have equal responsibility to create change. Calling vengeance "male" makes it sound like a product of biology and naturalizes unkind male behavior. Equating gendered traits with biology also implies that gender-nonconforming people are abnormal or unnatural.

I Get to Say What I Am

We are all so much bigger than these boxes. Yes, I am compassionate, I am caring. But I am also angry, self-serving, and vengeful at times. I am soft, I am hard, I am active, I am receptive. I am an earth mama, a friend to animals and plants, and a dreamer with my head up in the clouds. I bring about both beginnings and ends, openings and closures. I cannot be defined. And I don't think anyone can really know themselves unless they can embrace all these qualities, all the "feminine" and "masculine" within us, because none of these traits are really masculine or feminine at all. They are human.

As a teen girl peering up at Shange's words about how a god with periods would behave differently, such ideas did not help me embrace myself. They only added to the discomfort I felt around regaining my health and maturing. These were the expectations placed on me. Because of the body I was developing, I'd be expected to nourish humanity. To be peaceful, calm, soft, unobtrusive, nature-bound. To be emotionally labile like the ever-changing moon. To be feminine simply because blood came out of my vagina. To be a soft, warm sheath designed to soothe a sword.

That poem lingered in the back of my mind as I noticed red on my underwear and felt like a lower being for reasons I could not understand at the time. I now see it was not the blood that bothered me, but the sense that just by bleeding, I was part of a metaphorical human sacrifice. Each month, I'd bleed for my species. Each day, I'd devote myself to my children, mankind. I would be the god who bled, held up high on a pedestal away from the rest of humanity, separate from the self, the "I," the subject. I would be the other, someone outside the world, with its wars and its religions, not a participant but a victim.

Selling Sisterhood

Ideas about menstruation equaling womanhood – a specific version of womanhood – are all around us. Since I've written about menstruation, I receive PR pitches from menstrual companies playing on stereotypes about periods – often from an "empowerment" angle, as if products are needed to free women from their own physiology. In a winky-winky tone, they allude to the supposedly universal experience of female suffering – so that we can all bond over having a terrible time stuck in these awful bodies.

A pitch for a period-delaying drug promises to prevent "your period from ruining your plans." Another one, from a menstrual cup brand, reads: "It's kind of an old, outdated joke to hope you don't get your period on Valentine's Day, but we all know no one wants it." And perhaps the most creative: "If you're anything like me, this is you once a month," begins an email promoting a period pain relief device, accompanied by a GIF of a woman collapsing in agony.

"We all know." "This is you." Some of the most objectifying phrases out there, defining people for themselves. It's what philosopher Louis Althusser called interpellation: speaking someone into existence.[9] Shaping who they are by *telling* them who they are. Declaring them, in this case, a woman, someone defined by pain. Such interpellating phrases are, on the surface, descriptive, making observations about what is. Yet they can become prescriptive, conveying, "This is what's normal" and, by implication, "This is how you should be."

Such statements can be self-fulfilling: If someone gets told they're "feminine" again and again, they just might perform that role. If someone gets told they're emotional, they may become emotional due to that stereotype and the stress of being subjected to it. And, perhaps most insidiously, if someone gets told they're meant to suffer, they may suffer for it. They may not get help for things like cramps or PMS because this is, supposedly, just how women are. It is the monthly child support they pay to mother humanity. Severe menstrual pain and mood disturbances tend to point toward larger health issues. But brands would rather naturalize period problems – and laud their Band-Aid solutions as the answer to women's suffering – than question whether it is normal for women to suffer in the first place.[10] Painting pain as part of some universal sisterhood is not sisterly at all. And it has real consequences: People end up accepting misery.

When we make assumptions about how others experience their bodies, we do the same thing spiritual coaches do when they school women on "the feminine." We treat women as representations of capital-W Woman rather than multifaceted

people. Even when we make seemingly positive assumptions – believing that women are portals to the divine during
menstruation – we are still defining others for them. We are
still reinforcing a binary wherein those with uteruses have
certain qualities that people without them lack.

I remember sitting in a Starbucks shortly after a breakup
years ago and hearing a song my ex used to play for me.
"Our song is playing and I'm crying," I texted a friend. "Ugh,
periods," she replied, as if that explained my sadness. She'd just
seen me buy tampons, which apparently told her all she had
to know about my emotional state. It's a way women convey
to one another: "I get you. I see you. I am like you." Except if
you're *not* like the person saying these things, you feel either
alienated from the category of "woman" or pressured into
it. Or both. If someone wants to bond with other women,
it would be more empowering to bond not as capital-W
Women but as individuals. We could learn what we actually
have in common with someone, rather than use our mutual
membership in a gendered group as a proxy for getting to
know them. We could let that person be who they are – and
appreciate them for who they are.

The Body Has No Destiny

One-dimensional portrayals of menstruation and womanhood
come out even in feminist efforts to celebrate periods, efforts
sometimes classified as "period positivity." The period-positive
movement aims to destigmatize and normalize menstruation.
Yet much of its rhetoric fits the narrative of periods existing
to nurture humanity. This kind of rhetoric has its place; words
like period-positive activist Rupi Kaur's "I bleed each month
to help make humankind a possibility" call out the absurdity
of shaming a bodily function no one would exist without.[11] Yet
this singular depiction left me wondering how I, not just my

progeny, could benefit from my body. Humanity was relying on me to propagate its species, to carry its burden. Where was I in that?

The narrative that those with wombs are made to have children exists within childbirth empowerment movements too. Trystan Reese, the trans man I spoke with about his childbirth experience, recalls hearing natural birth advocates call childbirth "what our bodies were made to do." This insinuates that if you have a uterus, parenthood – and, specifically, motherhood – is your biological destiny. But what if the body has no destiny? What if our bodies weren't "made to" do anything? What if we're the ones who give them purpose? What if, regardless of *why* our bodies are the way they are, what they are there *for* is up to us? What if we can utilize and enjoy them for whatever purposes work best for us?

"Gender essentialism [is] the idea that you're born one thing and it always means you will follow these steps in your life," Reese explains. "If you're assigned female at birth, you'll be a girl, you'll be beautiful, you'll be feminine, you'll have kids, you'll put your kids first forever, and you'll die. That's not great for women, that's not great for men, and that's not great for trans folks." Saying that menstruation "makes you" anything puts someone in the object role, being defined. What makes it especially objectifying is that they're being defined by their genitals.

Must We All Be Moon Goddesses?

Another common period-positive narrative associates women with Mother Earth and the femininity it symbolizes. "Our periods connect us to the moon and to the sea," reads the online publication *Everyday Feminism*. "We are creatures of the Earth, and we are gifted with a beautiful reminder of that each time we bleed."[12] The blog for the menstrual cup brand Diva similarly speaks of menstruation's "connection to the natural world, earth, and moon," while the menstrual health brand Funk It Wellness gives "a quick intro into why you are in fact a Moon Goddess."[13] A post on the women's site *Girls Globe* states: "Menstruation is an experience that unifies women across the world. It reminds us of our great feminine abilities."[14]

Do periods unify us all, though? Not only do experiences of menstruation vary, but menstruation is not a universal female experience. Between post-menopausal women, young girls, trans women, pregnant women, those on continuous birth control, those with health conditions affecting menstruation, those who have had hysterectomies, athletes with low body fat, and more, menstruators actually constitute a minority of women, as only about half the world's female population is even of reproductive age.[15] It is almost as if healthy, reproductive aged, cisgender women – women considered appropriate objects – have a monopoly on "femininity."

The tendency for women's cycles to sync up when they spend time together is also sometimes presented as proof of a natural sisterhood. But a number of studies have failed to find evidence for this phenomenon.[16] And not only do few menstrual cycles actually line up with lunar phases, but the evidence for any lunar influence on periods is flimsy: Some findings suggest no connection and others show there might be one, but only for those with minimal exposure to artificial light.[17] Either way, I don't think these phenomena say much about how earthly, moon-like, or goddess-like menstruators are. The sun and moon affect us all; they influence our sleep, moods, and more.[18] If menstruation turns out to be impacted by the moon, I see that as one more piece of evidence that all our bodies are part of nature. If such a connection makes a biological process magical, then all biological processes are magical. All bodies are.

The gendered meanings drawn from celestial bodies – like those drawn from human bodies – are subjective, universal as they seem. Different tantra lineages' differing concepts of "masculine" and "feminine" illustrate this. Devi Ward Erickson, the tantra practitioner I interviewed, is part of the Shangpa Kagyu lineage, which views the moon as masculine and the sun as feminine due to the corresponding colors of semen (white) and menstrual blood (red). It's not that differences between bodies don't exist in objective reality, but the meaning we make of them is not objective. We can come up with reasons why something is feminine or masculine, and some people may even find these associations validating. But others will look at the same bodies and see the opposite. Neither interpretation is wrong. What's important is that we can choose the symbolism and language that resonate with us.

Seeing Myself (Period) Positively

Because I didn't find many period-positive efforts empowering, I had to find a way to empower myself – and that meant to define myself. To strip my body of all the symbolism imposed on it and decide who I was. For me, period positivity didn't mean celebrating the femininity that menstruation represented. It meant decoupling menstruation – and my body itself – from femininity. The more I've been able to separate my period from the essentialist ideas that undermine my self-determination, the more at ease I've felt with it. I used to think I disliked the body I was born in, when really, I disliked the meanings others made of it. My body was perfect all along.

I love getting my period now. Every time I do, I get to redefine what it means to have a period – and to be female. I define it in ways that others never defined it for me, ways that center my own body and what I choose to do with it. I relish the sexual sensitivity I gain from the extra pelvic blood flow, something I definitely didn't learn about in school. I celebrate the sense of wellness I feel each time I see evidence that my body is healthy enough to menstruate, something it has not always been.

But menstruation means something different to me every month (or more like every six weeks – sorry, moon). I've had periods where I lie in the bathtub for hours and type poetry on my phone, where I break personal records at the gym, and where literally nothing is different because it's just a bodily function, for god's sake. I discovered all these meanings myself, and I redefine them for myself each month. I let each cycle be different, each moment be different, and that is also how I live my life.

I allow being a woman, like having a period, to mean something different every day. I wear floral dresses with sneakers. I read and write about childbirth and astrophysics. I lift weights and make chocolates in a pink checkered apron. I cry and I lead. And I will not tone down or apologize for any part of me. I take pride in my body, not because it's feminine, not because it's masculine, but because it is my home.

Making Meaning of Our Own Bodies

I used to feel compelled to reject all aspects of womanhood because I didn't like the version of it that was sold to me. But as I came to realize I could take the aspects I liked and leave the rest, I embraced many elements of cultural femininity, including some facets of essentialist period positivity. Sometimes, I search YouTube for "moon time" yoga sequences, dancing through a twisty, bendy ode to my cycle. I wash my sheets and tidy my room at the end of my menstrual phase, then lie in the fresh bedding excited to turn over a new leaf. Is this really a new start? It is because I believe it is. Some ideas become self-fulfilling prophecies, and that can be empowering when we're the ones thinking those thoughts for ourselves, contemplating ourselves into being.

If someone else tells us what our bodies mean, we are objects. But if we make meaning of our bodies and honor that meaning in how we organize our lives, we are subjects creating experiences that fit who we are. I don't know if menstruation is especially sacred, but I celebrate it as one part of having a sacred body. It may not make me feminine, but it adds to the richness of the colorful being I am. It may not make me a woman, but it gave me the opportunity to reclaim womanhood. In redefining my body, I realized I could redefine being female. I could make it mean everything I am, no more and no less.

Today, I'm so glad to be a woman. I cannot think of a better thing to be. I cannot think of a better place to reside than my own body. And I love to connect with the moon. Sometimes, I walk down to the beach at night, look up at it, and say, "Thank you for being there for me." I listen to the ocean waves crash and feel the lunar light pulling the sea, pulling me. I love feeling connected to the Earth too, and to my feet as they are planted in the sand. The difference? I now know I don't have to be "feminine" in this way or any way just because I have a womb. I'm expressing an authentic side of myself, not as a symbol of Woman, but as me. As exactly who I want to be.

"Be" is among the most powerful verbs. We are subjects whenever we say "I am."

Nobody can take that away from us. Even when they say "you are," we get to say whether they're right.

We get to write about ourselves in the first person. To tell the winding stories of our bodies. To weave our muscles and bones into poetry, to form a narrative from nerves and blood cells.

We get to say what it means for us to bleed and to be.

Chapter 11

I Grow: The Politics of Pubes

"Sorry, I'm not used to there being hair there."

These words came from a partner who had announced just seconds earlier, "I love eating pussy" – which seemed like a fit because, well, I had one. But apparently, this partner's idea of a pussy was different from mine, and the fact that mine had hair was a deal-breaker. Even as I was learning to see my body through my own eyes, others had their own views of it.

At age twenty, it had never occurred to me to do anything with my pubic hair. It hadn't posed a problem for me or anyone else. My vulva was the one body part, in fact, that had somehow escaped self-objectification. After all, barely anyone saw it. And in situations where someone did, there was so much happening down there, on the inside, subjectively, that my mind was on how it felt, not how it looked. I hadn't really wondered whether it was attractive. I didn't think it was supposed to be. It was there to feel pleasure, not to please somebody else.

But as I lay there, the encounter reaching an abrupt and awkward end, it hit me that my vulva was not just the subject of words like "sense," "desire," and "enjoy." It was an object of verbs like "see" and "evaluate." And now, it was becoming the object of my own scrutiny. I wondered whether there was something wrong with my pubic hair. Did it make me less desirable? *Should* I be doing something to it? It was a grim realization that no part of my body could avert the male gaze. No part really was just there to feel. At least not in the world where I lived. Everything was being looked at. Even the seat of my subjectivity was objectified.

The Genitals as Object

Not used to there being hair there? I thought to myself. *Doesn't everyone have hair there?* Apparently not. A 2016 survey found that 83.8 percent of American women removed at least some pubic hair, with those under forty-five especially likely to groom.[1] Between the 1990s and the early 2010s, the portion of *Playboy* centerfold models with little to no pubic hair increased from 11.4 to 78.5 percent.[2] The rise of online porn and its trend of hairless vulvas likely contributed to this change in personal grooming choices, though some scholars link it to the 2000 *Sex and the City* episode where Carrie gets a Brazilian wax.[3]

Today, even a search for "full bush" on porn sites yields videos featuring partially removed bushes, and online galleries celebrating vulva diversity tend to feature images with at least some pubic hair missing.[4] These websites use nature imagery to describe female genitals; Betty Dodson's site, which includes a page of mostly groomed female genitalia,[5] calls the vulva a "genital flower" and uses a tulip-shaped logo.[6] Even images aimed at displaying women's natural beauty depict a version of nature that's not natural at all. Supposedly, we are so pretty, pristine, and ladylike that our genitals look like flowers. And also, we must spend money and go through pain to make them look that way; I have never seen a flower with hair.

With female hairlessness so naturalized, it's no wonder that hair might look surprising on a vulva. Sociologist Roger Friedland wrote in a 2011 paper of an eighth-grade boy who was shocked to learn that women grew pubic hair.[7] It was also in 2011 that I received the "I'm not used to hair there" comment from my significant other, who kept promising to go down on me if I would just wax my genitals. Eventually, I caved. I got a DIY waxing kit from CVS and locked myself in my college dorm bathroom – but the sensation was so painful, I couldn't get past the first strip.

I didn't want to give up that quickly, so I took a stab at shaving … pun not intended but unfortunately appropriate. Since my labia were covered in stubble, they scraped together when I walked, scratching each other. It felt like my genitals were made of sandpaper. The trooper I am, I then trialed the hair-removal cream Nair, thinking perhaps it would leave less stubble. But alas, the sandpaper labia returned.

Visually, I did get a certain pleasure out of seeing myself so exposed, so naked, so sexually accessible. Everything was … out there on display. Was I looking through my eyes, though, or through the male gaze? If I had never seen myself through the male gaze, would I have wanted an exposed vulva? I didn't think so. I wouldn't have been looking there in the first place. If female hairlessness were not idealized, I wouldn't have viewed my genitals more positively in their bald state. And if no one had ever noticed or criticized my styling choices – or women's generally – I would not have even thought about my genitals' appearance, positively or negatively.

Beating Around the Bush

Operation Bombshell Pussy was short-lived, and my relationship ended soon after anyway. My next few partners didn't have much to say about my pubic hair, so I forgot about it again. As I had from the beginning, I immersed myself in the sensations my genitals were feeling during sex rather than thinking about how they looked. It was when I began going to clothing-optional resorts, sex parties, and other nude events that my gaze was directed toward my nether regions once more.

"So, how does it feel to be the only woman with … you know," asked the man next to me at lunch one afternoon at Jamaica's Hedonism resort. I didn't know; I was as blissfully unaware of the other women's looks as mine. He had to spell it out for me that literally all the other female guests had bald genitals. Still, I didn't feel insecure. If anything, I found it strange that so many women would engage in a practice that was such a hassle. By the trip's end, however, so many people had gone out of their way to let me know my self-presentation was atypical that the insecurities began to creep in. One man called it a "lobster trap." Another said it made me look like a "hippy" and asked if I smoked weed. Later that year, at the couples' resort Desire, a random man walked up to me, told my boyfriend he "just had to do something," then gave my bush a pat. When it wasn't denigrated, it was fetishized.

It was funny how, even when I wasn't thinking about how my genitals looked at all, people still saw them as if they were styled for others' eyes. Just tweeting about the unfair expectations placed on women's pubic hair elicited replies like "bush is sexy." Many construed my pubic hair as some kind of statement. A statement such as: "I would like to bring back the 70s" (if I were to believe articles on the topic or replies to my tweets). Or, apparently: "I am a hippy." I experienced that familiar objectification that comes from people making meaning of your body for you. But my vulva was not an announcement of how much I loved disco or the Beatles. It was not announcing anything. It was just sitting there being what it had been since puberty, before I was aware of these cultural associations or had a sense of myself as an object.

Fun Little Beauty Things

The comments piled up. "What is *that*?" a date gasped when he reached into my underwear. Another man told me, "I wouldn't expect someone who likes oral sex to have pubic hair," elaborating that it was "hard to go down on" someone with hair there. I started to wonder if I was selfish to expect pleasure. "What made you decide to keep your pussy so hairy?" yet another guy asked – a line of questioning that confounds me. Such inquiries presume that having a hairless vulva – something that requires lots of time, money, and discomfort to maintain – is the default while having hair is a deliberate decision. In reality, hair is the body's default, and it's the burdensome removal process that's a conscious choice.

Still, it was a choice many women were making. Women were doing all kinds of things to their genitals, sometimes in the name of empowerment. Actress Jennifer Love Hewitt announced in her 2010 book that she was a fan of vajazzling – a term she coined for putting jewels and decals on otherwise drab genitalia. "The fun part of being a girl is that there are little beauty things you can do to make yourself feel special," she told *Maxim*.[8] She elaborated on the talk show *Conan*, "It's really for the girl to do for herself."[9] *For herself*, I thought. *That's fascinating*. Which part of themselves, exactly, were women adorning their bodies for? Unless you spend a good chunk of your day peering down at your genitals, what difference does it make to you, yourself, how sparkly they are?

But the truth is, many of us are spending more than a chunk of our days mentally, if not visually, surveying our bodies. Women have become their own spectators, both the lookers and the looked-at. We play subject and object to ourselves, working to please our own eyes, drinking in the sight of our reflections. Experiencing ourselves as other. We do fun "little beauty things," things that are enjoyable because we are outside ourselves, looking in. Often, the "female" gaze we are peering through is really an internalized male gaze. But we've internalized it so deeply, it feels like ours. We gain pleasure from our own self-othering.

That's not always a bad thing. People of all genders gain pleasure from self-gazing and body modifications, from haircuts to tattoos. But I don't think it's completely coincidental that women are disproportionately the ones gazing at their bodies, particularly their body hair. I doubt that personal preference accounts entirely for the fact that over four in five American women groom their pubic hair while only about half of men do.[10] Most people care how they look to some extent, but the question is how much we care and at what cost. The level of care and cost often seem higher for women, who spend an average of $10,000 on shaving or $23,000+ on waxing over the course of their lives.[11]

It's not like there's something about female biology that makes us want to style our genitals. We didn't always. Women in the US rarely got rid of any body hair until razor companies began promoting shaving to women in the early 1900s. Their previous customers were mostly men who shaved their beards, but, of course, they wanted a larger clientele. Gillette launched its first women's razor in 1915, promising in an ad to solve "an embarrassing personal problem" – the problem being women's underarm hair.[12] Just as I didn't think at all about my pubic hair until others told me it was abnormal, most women didn't think about their body hair until companies began pushing products on them.

It was not just marketing but stereotypes that contributed to the norm of hairless female bodies. Because the trend of pubic hair removal began around the 1980s, soon after the rise of second-wave feminism, Friedland considers the disparagement of female body hair a form of anti-feminist backlash, infantilizing women and discrediting feminists for being "hairy."[13] Pubic hair, his paper suggests, symbolizes a woman's sexual maturity and desire. Dictating that women remove it, therefore, is a way to strip women of their subjectivity and make them fully visible as objects. "Shaving it away stamps it as a mere organ, a passage where anyone can linger pleasantly, where something is done, not somebody known," he writes.

Whatever its origin, body hair shaming turns up the hyper-vigilance many women already experience around their looks. We are constantly aware of how we're perceived. Those of us who conform to beauty standards such as hairlessness may receive admiration instead of denigration. Yet sexualization does the same thing as shaming: It positions us outside ourselves. We hold our bodies in our minds' eyes, gaining pleasure or displeasure through our own self-image, an image filtered through the eyes of others who have seen us.

As long as my gaze was focused outward, how I looked did not matter for my pleasure; it mattered how I felt. And I felt better when I was not subjected to hair removal processes that irritated my genitals. Engaging in beauty rituals that detracted from my enjoyment so that someone else could enjoy my body seemed like the epitome of objectification. I would not compromise my tactile pleasure for anyone's visual pleasure.

The Pleasure of Being an Object

Then, at age thirty-one, over a decade after my initial experiment with intimate grooming, I came across an intriguing research finding: Women with bald vulvas reported better sexual functioning and a more positive genital self-image.[14] I began to wonder if I was missing something. I imagined what it would feel like to once again have everything bare, completely on display, accessible to the gaze. And this thought began to turn me on.

Yes, I had come to the conclusion that the hints of pleasure I'd experienced with shaving stemmed from looking through the male gaze. Yet knowing that made it, somehow, hotter. The fact that this sexist standard made me angry made the thought of caving in to it a turn-on. It was so forbidden, so taboo. It was as if, through my fantasies of being the perfect object, my mind was granting me permission to do something I wouldn't let myself do in reality. It was, in essence, a submission fantasy. I imagined submitting to the male gaze – and liking it. Maybe that was what other women were getting off on: being looked at.

This remained a fantasy until one Saturday afternoon, when I was video chatting with a Bumble match. He declared over FaceTime that he'd like to make me a "pillow princess" – someone who lays back and relaxes on the pillow while a partner pleasures her.

"Oh, and what would that entail?" I asked.

"I'm in the mood to spoil you," he said. "I can come over, massage you, and eat your pussy. No need for anything in return."

I considered his proposal. "Maybe we can go for a walk first just so I can make sure you're not a serial killer. But … well, it's a good offer. I'm intrigued."

We texted as he prepared to come over. I sent him photos of my massage oils along with instructions for how I'd like him to use them. "I'll massage you wherever you want," he replied before adding, "My only request is that it's cleanly shaven."

"Wait, that what is cleanly shaven?"

"Your vagina." Oh.

An opportunity had presented itself. I knew I didn't have to do anything to my body. I could've just ended the encounter, or we could've worked around it. But … that curiosity I'd been sitting on for the past few months crept back in. This was my chance.

"Fair enough," I replied, realizing I had just about an hour to somehow get all my pubic hair off. I speed-walked to CVS to buy a good razor and shaving cream. At that point in my life, all I shaved were my armpits, which I could tackle with a very basic razor and soap. My pubes would require something more heavy duty.

As I strode down my block like a woman on a mission, I googled "how to shave your vulva," forgetting what exactly I'd done in college, and came across a *Teen Vogue* article titled "How to Shave Pubic Hair If You Have a Vagina." I fumed as I read that although doctors caution against hair removal, as the hair protects you from infections, you shouldn't "let that stop you from stripping away unwanted follicles."[15] I had read research showing that those with pubic hair have a lower risk for sexually transmitted infections and genital pain.[16] Pubic hair serves as a barrier, and removing it can cause skin abrasions that let unwanted microbes in. I was livid that a teen magazine would gloss over that. So livid, in fact, that I got even more turned on.

I know. How could someone so against objectification get turned on by being an object? Doesn't that ruin my whole argument? I've asked myself that question many times, and I've come to believe that what I do in the privacy of my bedroom is not an argument for or against anything. I do not vote with my orgasms. And apparently, performing the opposite role in the bedroom that you assume in other parts of your life, like your work, is a common desire. "We are subconsciously or unconsciously always seeking balance within ourselves," professional dominatrix and BDSM educator Colette Pervette told me later on, in an interview for this book. "For myself, as a dom, as someone who is kind of alpha and in control in most of my life, there are moments when I do have the fantasies to be submissive, to be objectified."

Smashing the patriarchy for a living had created a similar desire in me. I was going to, for one brief evening, *be* the thing I was mad about. I was going to let go of my anger over women's objectification and see the positive in it: It was great fuel for fantasy. It felt good to explore a side of myself I'd been rejecting. To stop fighting sexist double standards for just a moment and find enjoyment in them where I could.

I arrived back home, mission accomplished, razor and shaving cream in hand, with half an hour to spare. The *Teen Vogue* article suggested trimming the hair before shaving it. I skittered around my apartment searching for scissors. Of course, just when I needed them, I couldn't locate them. I'd have to make do with the razor and shaving cream I'd just purchased for $24. (I know they were $24 because I saved the receipt as a tax expense. This was an experiment for my work!) I lay in the bathtub and chipped away at the hair. And chipped away.

My phone buzzed. "Did I lose you?"

"Nope, just getting some things done!" I typed back with sudsy fingers. Little did he know how much I was accomplishing. I emerged from the bathtub with red and bumpy but hairless labia, then threw on a sundress and got the door just as he rang the bell.

I'm terrible at keeping secrets, so pretty much the moment he arrived, I blurted out, "I have a confession."

"Oh?"

"I just shaved for the first time in eleven years."

"My god, eleven years? You didn't have to do that." That was true. I knew I didn't. But I'd done it … for me? Well, yes, but not entirely. I'd done it for him for me. I'd done it to be seen. To get off on being an object. The fact that it was for someone else's gaze was what made it hot. I was exploring a whole new side of myself. I relished the excitement of exciting someone else.

Some flirtatious banter and an orgasm later, I politely excused him so I could make myself dinner. But before I reached the kitchen, I made a beeline back to my bedroom, got out my hand mirror, and stared at myself through what I knew was an internalized male gaze … taking a surprising pleasure in that submission, that objecthood.

Sugarcoating Hair Removal

But the next day, when I tried to walk … well, what was I expecting? You guessed it: the return of the sandpaper labia. I complained to my roommate and, at her recommendation, booked an appointment at a sugaring salon – where they use wax made of sugar and lemon to rip out body hair – for three weeks later, when the hair would grow out. She told me this would last longer and help me avoid the bumps and stubble associated with shaving. I was feeling that familiar anger toward societal beauty standards and the discomfort women go through to meet them – but I didn't want to stop at anger this time. I wanted to truly understand why women did this, to see the other side of the equation.

During the sugaring session, I yelped as the "sugarist" yanked the hairs out. "This can't damage anything, can it?" I asked nervously between squeals.

"Well actually," she smiled, "one added benefit is that it damages your follicles, so the hair will grow back less and less. Especially if you keep coming back and are consistent with your routine."

I froze as I processed what she was saying. This person was damaging my genitals and telling me it was a bonus – without giving me the chance to consent to that? I recognized that damage to hair follicles was not particularly dangerous. But if a treatment were to thin out a socially desirable form of hair, like the hair on my head or eyelashes, I probably would have had to sign a waiver. Yet even though pubic hair has a protective function, this was not deemed worthy of a warning. The salon seemed to care more about making sure I stayed "consistent" and kept paying them.

"It won't make much of a difference after just one or two sessions," she reassured me, adding, "If you don't want your hair to thin out, you can just shave it instead" – as if, either way, I had to do *something*. When I checked out, I felt uneasy to see the other customers, all women, lined up as if this were just a routine activity: go to the salon, get your genitals painfully pulled and possibly damaged, get dressed, pay the tip. It felt like some kind of post-apocalyptic movie.

The salon's website, of course, contained socially conscious-sounding phrases like "our mission is to inspire every body, mind, and spirit. We do that with the transparent way we treat each customer." They went on to describe themselves as "intentional" and "harm-free." But they were not transparent with me about everything this process entailed – nor did it feel very intentional how the sugarist assumed everyone coming in would want thinner and less healthy pubic hair.

Profiting off Pubic Hair

They were by no means the biggest culprits. Lots of businesses now "empower" women by giving them cheaper or more effective ways to remove hair. The razor brand Billie aims to fight the pink tax – the higher price for women's personal care products compared to men's – by offering free shipping on subscriptions and coupons for customers who refer friends.[17] Nood, an at-home hair removal device, makes similar promises about sparing women time and funds, with a website comparing Nood to other methods that "cost an arm and a leg."[18] Playing on the feminist trope of liberation through renouncing shaving, an ad on Nood's Instagram reads: "In as little as 8 weeks, you can kiss shaving goodbye for good!"[19] An Instagram ad for the lasering salon LaserAway similarly says: "Raise your hand if you didn't shave today."[20]

Hair removal solutions like these may indeed save women who already shave time and money – but on something they don't need to spend any time or money on in the first place. By implying that women need such a service – and it's just a matter of choosing the cheapest one – brands are contributing to the beauty ideals that ultimately drain women's wallets and time, all under the guise of empowerment. But it's hard to feel empowered when you look at Instagram pages like Nood's, which calls "coochies" with hair "werewolves" and depicts the female bush as a monster that's "out to get you."[21] RoseSkinCo, the brand behind a similar device, put an ad on its own Instagram reading: "Because you'll still notice. Don't let body hair bug you all winter long."[22]

This is when the notion of "doing it for yourself" becomes insidious: Women are taught not just to cater to others who may observe and judge them, but to observe and judge themselves. Such ads might as well say: "Because even when nobody's looking, the male gaze is still lurking around the corner." Brands are teaching women to work awfully hard to please "themselves" – selves molded by patriarchy and consumerism. With these forces coloring our very vision, can we ever just do anything in private?

Yay, Choices

When hair removal brands want to pay lip service to feminism, they need only pull out one magic word: "choice." If a woman has options, the thinking goes, then she's empowered. Billie's website reads: "Yep, we sell razors. That doesn't mean we think everyone *has* to shave – quite the opposite. We want to release womankind (and the next gen) from outdated and unfair expectations to be hairless, and let them decide whatever's best for them that day. No pressure, just options."[23] But what good are options in a world that punishes you for choosing certain options and rewards you for choosing others? And are brands really contributing to women's sense of choice when they push their products, even – no, especially – if they associate those products with empowerment?

In search of an alternative to sugaring and CVS razors, I bought a Billie subscription that same summer. When I canceled it several months later, tired of competing in an endless race against the growth of my pubes, they asked me to type in a reason. I wrote, "stopped shaving." Over the next few months, I nevertheless received emails from Billie with subject lines like "it's been a while" and "let's get back together." Inside the emails were messages such as "we haven't heard from you in a bit … say the word and we can get you shaving again!" and "does your skin miss feeling velvety-smooth and buttery-soft?" Ironically, I found my skin smoother and softer when I let the hair grow, no bumps or stubble. But Billie begged to differ. It goes to show that no brand is really there to offer "no pressure, just options."

This disingenuous celebration of choice is even more glaring in larger brands' marketing. In a 2021 Gillette Venus video promoting a pubic hair removal product line, an animated hair belts out: "I'm just a pube and it's not fair. All I ever wished to be was just another hair. But when they got one look at me, the ruling from society was 'ew, not you!' Oh, what's a curl to do?"[24] The little pube then urges the listener to "take care of us, your pubic hair – if you trim, or you shave, or you're bare down there. Whichever way's your way, it's all OK." Except, um, there's one option missing: Just leaving it. Which is clearly *not* what this ad is advocating, despite the language about body acceptance.

In another ad for the same line, Princess Nokia sings that "it's your choice" what to do with your pubic hair, grooming down there is "self-care," and "Venus has the tools so you can do you." The accompanying website states that this "#SayPubic" campaign aims to "normalize the conversation around pubic hair" – though that seems limited to normalizing the conversation around getting rid of it.[25] Anything you do to your body, apparently, is "self-care," as long as it involves buying a product. That's businesses' ultimate goal – to get you to buy their products – no matter how much they defend your right *not* to. An advertisement is, by definition, promoting the item it features.

A Whole Other Ball of Wax

About a month after my first sugaring experience, I decided to try it again, but in a more relaxed setting to minimize pain, both physical and emotional. I wanted to try everything, really give it a go, before knocking it once and for all.

Around that time, I'd been writing about orgasmic births – childbirth experiences that include pleasure and/or orgasm. One expert I'd interviewed said the key to preparing for an orgasmic birth was to get comfortable with intense sensations and learn to enjoy them. She suggested ice baths for this exercise, but I had another idea. Since I thought it would be cool to have an orgasmic birth one day, I decided to bring that intention to my next sugaring session: to breathe through and relish the intensity. I texted my friend Nicole Ambrosia, an embodiment coach and aesthetician, and asked if she could steward this experience.

"OK ... BDSM sugaring in preparation for childbirth. I gotchu!" she wrote back. I came to her apartment on a Thursday morning, and before getting started, we discussed pubic hair preferences and why she personally goes hairless.

"I like how it feels on my fingers," she said. "The smoothness, and how a cock can slip on it for a frictionless experience." I smirked. This felt different from my last sugaring appointment. Partly because I already knew her, I trusted that she cared about women's well-being. She really did it for herself – and wanted me to. And, at that point, I was. It was not just a sexual turn-on but an adventure, like getting a new haircut. I was trying on a new persona.

When we do something novel to our appearances, we get to play a new character. New looks get us in tune with different parts of our personalities. It felt as if I became someone different when my pubes were freshly shorn. After being something of an outcast much of my life, conforming to beauty norms gave me the rare experience of being conventional. I decided to go all out and start shaving my legs too – something I hadn't done since college – indulging this inner girly-girl I didn't know existed within me. It was freeing to allow myself to sport whatever look I wanted and not restrict anything due to patriarchal rules *or* feminist rules. There were no rules.

My friend spread the wax over my pubic area and lay a piece of fabric covered in puppies on top of it, which was oddly comforting. She guided me to breathe as she tore off little strips one by one, when I said I was ready. Strangely, it didn't hurt this time – maybe because I wasn't feeling the pain of being preyed on by the hair removal industry.

Doing It for Yourself

As I had more and more conversations, I realized people removed their pubic hair for all sorts of reasons. A male acquaintance told me sugaring made him feel "a whole new level of naked." A female friend said she could feel more sexual sensation after getting lasered. A trans friend told me shaving was part of her transition process, a way to express her identity. Still, I think there's a difference between doing a BDSM sugaring session in preparation for childbirth – or shaving as part of gender transition, or lasering to enhance pleasure – and removing your pubic hair because that's, in your mind, just what women do. I also see a difference between catering to the male gaze because it feels enticingly naughty and doing so because you've never learned any other way.

In simplified terms, you could boil the difference down to whether or not you're "doing it for yourself," as popular feminist wisdom goes. But it's also worth asking yourself: Who's the "you" that you're doing it for? If the "you" is the internalized gaze of others who might judge or desire you, that's understandable and, in many ways, practical. I would not wish the comments I received about my pubic hair on anyone. I just wish businesses would stop pressuring women to cater to others' gazes and calling it empowerment. I wish more women truly felt empowered enough to weigh their desire to be alluring objects against how they feel as subjects, including how their hair or lack thereof affects their comfort, pleasure, and health.

Many girls and women are now paying attention to how their genitals look before knowing much about how they feel. In a 2019 study, 98 percent of Australian women aged seventeen to twenty-five said they'd engaged in pubic hair removal, and over half had completely hairless genitals.[26] Not only that, but participants considered women without pubic hair more "normal" and "clean." In another study, 88 percent of Belgian women ages fifteen to twenty groomed their pubic hair.[27] Meanwhile, many women don't have their first orgasms until they're in this age group.[28] We are learning how to be sexy before we learn how to be sexual, thanks largely to businesses that conflate women's sexiness with their sexuality.

Before making decisions about how to style their genitals, women should know their vulvas look fine as they are – but what matters more is what they feel and do. They should know that unshaven, un-vajazzled genitals can be sexy, but women don't *need* to be sexy to be sexual. Rather than teach women to look a certain way "for themselves" – for their own pleasure – we should decouple their pleasure from their looks. Then, once someone knows what feels good to her, she can select a pubic hair style that's in line with that. I believe I had a positive experience with pubic hair removal in my thirties, but not my twenties, because I understood my sexual proclivities and how my grooming choices fit with them. Someone can't do that if they don't yet know what their own desires and fantasies are. Someone can only be empowered in the object role if they're a subject stepping into that role – not if they've been an object by default all their lives.

A lot of young women are already full of self-knowledge and agency, but for those still developing these qualities, uncritical advice about shaving like *Teen Vogue*'s "don't let that stop you" isn't super helpful. A number of sites geared toward teens gloss over the potential downsides of pubic hair removal, along with the societal pressures around it. Columbia University's Go Ask Alice! advice column responded to a series of questions about what to do with pubic hair by stating: "On average, women tend to report preferring a partner with at least some pubic hair intact, while men are more likely to report wanting a pube-free partner" – not acknowledging how misogyny, exploitive advertising, and unrealistic porn fuel those preferences.[29]

Playing With Pubes

My twenty-year-old self wasn't wrong. The societal expectation of hairless vulvas is objectifying – and the personal choice to remove hair sometimes, though not always, stems from self-objectification, even when it's "for yourself." But today, I see a fuller picture. I see that if we make the deliberate choice to be objects in ways that please us, we can still retain our subjecthood. I also see the many reasons people modify their bodies, all of which can be empowering if they stem from a deep understanding of our own drives and pleasure.

I truly am not for or against women removing their body hair. But I hope that if they do, they can do it from the place I eventually got to: a place of playfulness, lightness, and experimentation. I hope they can feel good about their genitals whether the hair is grown or shorn, and maybe even relish the variety. And I hope that even if they enjoy being objectified, they're still comfortable being sexual whether or not they look like culturally palatable objects. Many people like being objects of the gaze. The important thing is that we're creating the scenario where we're looked at – the objects of "look," but the subjects of "create." The choices we make around grooming and styling are rarely just for us, and it is rarely just us making them. Even when we alter our bodies "for ourselves," that's usually because we're looking at ourselves, probably in ways shaped by others. That's OK. It's inevitable. There is no "self" outside of others.

It would be naive of me to think the pleasure I gained from removing my pubic hair was unrelated to the scorn I faced for having it. I think we can all agree that reducing your chances of being mocked and harassed feels amazing – liberating, even! – not because it constitutes empowerment but because it provides a sense of safety in an unsafe world.[30] The best we can do is consider our own feelings and desires as we navigate this world – and not judge ourselves for wanting to fit into it. Or hold ourselves to the expectation that we make all our choices "just for ourselves." There's no such thing. We don't live in a vacuum. The world is full of appearance-related judgments and perceptions, and it's damn near impossible *not* to think about them as we get dressed every morning.

Still, we can find ways to play with how we're perceived. We can push back against cultural tropes, make art with them, and get off to them. We can defy them or utilize them to be seen as we wish. Hopefully, whatever we do, it'll bring us some enjoyment. That's what I aim for. I may not regain the innocence I had when I'd never considered how a partner might perceive my genitals. But I can find ways to enjoy being seen. And to enjoy myself regardless of how I'm seen.

Did the pleasure I experienced through pubic hair removal stem from the male gaze? Oh, absolutely. Does that mean I should deprive myself of that pleasure? Hell no. The fact that my appearance became such a focus – for my society, my partners, then me – may be unfair, but just because something is unfair doesn't mean we should make ourselves miserable just to prove how unfair it is. Patriarchy makes us miserable enough already. If we can find joy in something as joy-sucking as patriarchy, bless us. May we bask in all the joy that we can find. May we relish the fun little beauty things we do for ourselves – or whoever we're doing them for.

The Volition of the Vulva

After my sexy summer of shaving and sugaring, I got too caught up in life to maintain the look, so I let it grow out. But, to my surprise, it took forever. I twiddled my thumbs for months, trying to will the follicles to sprout new strands. My first sugarist's words came back to me, and I feared I'd permanently altered my body. I was suddenly sad. I felt bad for the poor hairs. I missed them. All they were trying to do was grow into their fullest expression, faithfully guarding my vaginal microbiome. They were looking out for me. They loved me. And I loved them back.

Then, at last, a few hairs sprung up. And a few more. And I realized how glad I was to see them again. To see they were still there, still thriving, despite society's efforts to hinder their growth. As I write this now, I'm happy to report that my bush has fully grown back, and while I'll probably experiment with shaving again at some point, I don't think I'll resume sugaring with any regularity. While some like that it damages their follicles and causes less hair to grow back, it's important to me to be able to have it if I want to. It would be sad to lose the hairs. They seem to want to be there.

It seems, in fact, like the strands have a subjectivity of their own. They grow. They reach. They feel; body hairs have touch receptors.[31] They do not seem to like being removed, as evidenced by the discomfort, redness, and bumps left over. Rather than position myself outside my hairs – visualizing them, styling them – I position myself deep in the follicles, feeling the desire for blossoming and the bliss of being touched.

Subjectification means subjectifying every part of you, feeling into each little hair and seeing what it wants, how it feels, what it senses. I take comfort in the fact that my hairs aren't aware of the oppression imposed on them. Even after being torn out, they continue to grow back.

The body is a reminder of what continues to exist when it's supposed to give up, what continues to grow when it's supposed to shrink, what continues to heal when it's damaged. What retains its subjectivity when it's objectified.

Descartes said, "I think, therefore I am." Audre Lorde said, "I feel, therefore I can be free."[32] I say, I have a body; therefore, I am a subject. My subjecthood is indestructible.

I let my body grow, so I am reminded of its subjectivity – and mine – every day, inch by inch.

Chapter 12

I Care: Sexual Empowerment Sells

Why are women sold such a cheap version of empowerment, one characterized by hair removal solutions and gimmicky menstrual products? The answer is already in the question. It is almost always about money. The PR pitches flooding my email inbox daily are a testament to the price brands place on sexual liberation, with a confusing combination of feminist language and good old fashioned body shaming.

Exhibit A: Lorals vanilla-scented "oral sex underwear," which launched in 2018 with the promise to block women's "tastes and fluids" so they can "feel fresh" and be "empowered" to "get more oral." Exhibit B: DeoDoc's scented vaginal wipes and washes, "empowering women" by reminding them, "armpits are not the only body parts that sweat." Exhibit C: the Ziggy Cup, a device to give women "self-confidence and total freedom" by holding period blood in during sex because "maybe a certain someone thinks it's gross" and "life is too short to not have sex 12 weeks out of the year, am I right?!" Exhibit D: VSPOT, a "vaginal rejuvenation spa" offering "treatments for vag empowerment" such as a "V-lift" that "plumps and smooths out wrinkles" in the vulva. Exhibit

E: It Just Works, a supplement that eliminates "all types of odors (including vaginal) and has helped people feel overall more confident in the bedroom."

I will spare you the rest.

The Self-Love Industry, Making Money off Self-Hatred

Such companies present a paradox: They're profiting off the shame and insecurities they claim to alleviate. They're literally invested in women's continued oppression. To get people to buy their products, businesses must claim to solve a problem – which means they must convince their target audience they have one. And if a company aims to convince women they have a problem, they're not exactly in the business of helping women love themselves just as they are.

There is no such business. If self-love were a business, it wouldn't generate much profit, because it would help people realize they don't need all these products. Still, that hasn't stopped brands from marketing their items as avenues to self-love – often via self-love's close cousin, self-worth. It's a convenient opportunity to promote a product while appearing to promote empowerment: Just draw upon the capitalistic assignment of worth to women. L'Oréal pioneered this tactic with its faux-feminist "because you're worth it" slogan, conveying to women that they can increase their value by having expensive hair.

Nowadays, even more than self-worth, you hear about self-care. Self-care, if we believe brands' marketing, means covering your skin in anti-aging creams and, apparently, putting scented stuff on your genitals. It means making yourself a better object. The object of "care," in this case, which seems like a good thing – except that brands often conflate caring about yourself with caring about your looks. Whether by promising to make your face firmer, make your hair less frizzy, or give you that nebulous thing called "glow," they appeal to the patriarchal gaze. Even spas offering Botox and fillers are now marketing their services as self-care.

"It's time to broaden our wellness boundaries beyond salt scrubs and sweat sessions to include anything that we do that makes us feel better about ourselves – including injectable appointments," reads an article on the website *Well + Good*.[1] Yet such procedures only make us feel better about ourselves due to misogynistic norms and predatory marketing – like the marketing of these very services. If we weren't made to feel bad about ourselves in the first place, we wouldn't have to be the objects of "feel better about." We'd be too busy being subjects. We'd be looking through our eyes, not looking *at* them so closely we felt the need to cover them in wrinkle cream, under-eye masks, eyelash serum, and god knows how many other products.

"After a filler appointment, many patients say they're a better spouse, they're a better mother, they're a better worker because they're holding their shoulders back and have a little confidence," a dermatologist who provides fillers told *Well + Good*.[2] This is how deeply we've internalized the male gaze, how closely our sense of self is tied to our looks: Whether or not a woman has youth-enhancing chemicals in her face affects how good a partner, mother, and worker she is. Would this be the case in a world that did not define women by their looks, then tell them their looks were never good enough?

Well + Good also quotes a psychologist's observation that "when we feel good, we look good" and "vice versa." Yet the "vice versa" – feeling good because we look good – seems to disproportionately apply to women, as women are the ones taught to constantly look at themselves. If we looked more at the world around us, maybe we could feel good on days when we looked bad. Instead of celebrating how profoundly a woman's appearance affects her life, we should question why those two things are so connected.

The Quest for Tight, Vanilla-Flavored Vajayjays

The promotion of this inverted consciousness – this tendency to gaze at ourselves and define how we feel by how we look – is especially insidious when it comes to our genitals. To reach our full capacity for pleasure, we need to focus on our own sensory experience. Yet you would not get that impression from the companies claiming to improve women's sex lives by enhancing how they look, smell, taste, and feel to the touch.

A PR pitch for ELITONE, a device that promises a "tighter vijayjay," reads: "ELITONE is exactly what women need to tighten up, so they can loosen up and enjoy the moment(s)" – as if the way to make sex better for a woman is to create a tighter fit for her partner. So that she can feel more confident, for "herself." For the male gaze within her own eyes. This pitch implies that women are too worried about their "loose" genitals to relax in the bedroom. Yet pushing a product that tightens the vagina contributes to that very worry.

It's circular logic: The same brands professing to help us feel better about ourselves make us feel bad about ourselves, creating the very need to feel better. Companies claiming to fight female shame profit off it – which means they benefit from us feeling ashamed. Outside that shame, there's little use for their products. A tight "vijayjay" isn't necessary for a woman to enjoy penetration. Our ability to enjoy oral sex has nothing to do with whether our vulvas taste like vanilla, as Lorals' early marketing suggested; we're not the ones tasting them.[3] Nor must we "not have sex 12 weeks out of the year" in the absence of a device like the Ziggy menstrual cup, unless we have a "certain someone" who "thinks it's gross" – in which case the issue is not our bodies but others' attitudes toward them. Attitudes encouraged by PR like this.

Another Ziggy Cup pitch exclaims that period sex "should not be taboo!" Vaginal deodorant maker DeoDoc's website similarly claims that it's "breaking taboos."[4] It's a common claim companies make: They're smashing stigma! They're starting a conversation! They're not afraid to talk about vaginas! The Gillette pubic hair line's site uses the same lingo: "People still get a little weird about the phrase 'pubic hair.' But the more we say it (or sing it), the more we'll think to take care of it."[5] As if pubic hair requires *any* "care." As if talking or singing about removing it is of any use to feminism. The equation of care with removal, of stigma-smashing with product-pushing, shows how superficial, watered down, and objectifying the concept of self-care has become.

I don't blame women who buy products or undergo treatments to increase their self-esteem. I've done it myself – and there's even joy to be found in it. But let's stop calling it empowerment and call it what it is: a way to be seen more favorably in a misogynistic, ageist, racist, classist, fatphobic society. We may be doing these things for ourselves, but that's not really progress when doing something for yourself means doing it to hate yourself less.

Self-Care or Self-Criticism?

This marks a diversion from the original concept of self-care, which was – like many diluted, barely recognizable motions toward women's empowerment today – pioneered by Black women. Black Panther Party leaders Angela Davis and Ericka Huggins advocated yoga and meditation as ways to care for oneself while navigating oppression and doing activist work.[6]

Given that self-care was formulated for fighting oppression, it's ironic that the self-care industry often promotes oppressive beauty standards. Calling Botox "self-care" overlooks the role of ageism in the trend of trying to appear younger. Calling hair products that "tame" and straighten "unruly" locks "self-care" ignores their racist undertones. Calling slimming spa treatments and weight-loss plans "self-care" obscures the fat-shaming they encourage, which doesn't improve anyone's well-being. Not to mention, equating self-care with buying stuff is already classist. How is it helpful to "start a conversation" that extends the same conversation we've been having for decades – one that boils down to "your body isn't good enough" or "your body should resemble thin, white, young bodies" or, at best, "your body would benefit from improvement"? Once again, the same companies claiming to solve a problem are creating it. The same companies claiming to dispel shame are encouraging it.

It's almost as if some brands view women's bodies themselves as shameful, then offer to reduce that shame by changing them. "We're trying to eliminate the shame of having a vagina!" former reality TV star Lo Bosworth told *New York Magazine* in 2016 after launching Love Wellness, a company that sells vaginal wipes, cleansers, and moisturizers.[7] She perhaps meant she was trying to eliminate the cultural shame imposed on vaginas. Yet it's hard not to feel like a company views vaginas themselves as shameful when its website describes a suppository that "manages odor" and wipes that "keep you fresh post-gym, post-sex, post-whatever."[8]

"There's no reason why you should have fifteen products for your face and zero products for your vagina," Bosworth added in her *New York Magazine* interview – almost making a valid point, except the real point is that maybe you don't need fifteen products for your face either.

Penis Envy, Repackaged

Even companies focused on women's pleasure seem to view their bodies as problems to solve. The promise to close the orgasm gap – the tendency for men to report more frequent orgasms than women – is prevalent in sex brands' marketing.

Yet rather than look at why this gap exists – and why it seems particular to heterosexual intercourse[9] – brands frequently assume that, as usual, women are missing something – and should shop to make up for their lack.

"Two out of three women do not orgasm regularly during sex. We've got the answers now with this range that is coming out in March," a Durex representative assured *Marketing Week* while announcing a new condom, toy, and gel collection.[10] A 2016 K-Y press release promoting a sensitivity-boosting gel that "aims to close the notorious orgasm gap" claims that "women typically take up to three times longer than men to climax, which can lead to less sexual satisfaction and more faked orgasms."[11] Women's bodies are supposedly not set up for the sex lives they want, so these products profess to fill in the gaps.

"Men are able to have three orgasms in the time a woman can achieve one," echoes an email I received from the VSPOT "vag empowerment" spa about the O Shot, a vaginal shot that purports to increase women's sensitivity. I'm unsure where this statistic came from, as women can orgasm as efficiently as men when they receive clitoral stimulation – and are *more* likely to have multiple orgasms within a short time frame.[12] Sex brands do not need to provide physical solutions to the orgasm gap because there is no biological gap to solve. On the O Shot's website, VSPOT founder Cindy Barshop states that women who get this shot are "having orgasms just like a man does."[13] As if there's something masculine about having orgasms. As if the penis functions optimally without assistance, while the vulva is an incomplete organ.

The view of women's genitals as incomplete is a specter that has followed us through history. Sigmund Freud posited that upon first seeing the opposite sex, children deduce that boys have something girls don't: a penis. This is the basis for the infamous concept of "penis envy." It is not the penis itself that the girl is after, though; it's the power that it represents.

In Western culture, the penis is equated with presence and wholeness – it is *there* – while the vagina is seen as absent, a not-penis, something missing. Penis envy is really a desire for what psychoanalysts call the *phallus* – the penis as a symbol of power and presence.[14]

As feminist theorist Luce Irigaray observed, Western culture defines women by their lack, as the negative of men. The vulva is seen as an absent penis, the woman as an absent subject. "Woman's erogenous zones never amount to anything but a clitoris-sex that is not comparable to the noble phallic organ, or a hole-envelope that serves to sheathe and massage the penis in intercourse: a non-sex, or a masculine organ turned back upon itself," she wrote.[15] But this is not objective reality. The problem is not that women are lacking, but that they're made to feel they are. If we saw women as subjects, we'd see them as possessing a complete clitoridean sexuality unto themselves.

Femaleness as Lack

Many products give off the impression that women's genitals are missing something, whether it is pleasure, cleanliness, health, a lovely scent, or shiny adornments. Not only are there vaginal jewels sold online for "vajazzling," but there are also glitter bombs available to keep the vaginal canal looking festive.[16] And in case that's not enough, Etsy offers ground wasp nests that supposedly tighten the vagina.[17] Meanwhile, salons provide vajacials – facials for the vulva.[18] What are they good for, exactly? Try asking Khloé Kardashian, who just might boast the world's most hydrated pussy, between regular vajacials, vitamin E oil to bolster the vaginal lining, and an eight-step skin care routine just for her genitals.[19]

Unlike products and treatments promising to "close the orgasm gap" by making women more sexually masculine, the above offerings are more about making us extra feminine. But both suppositions – that we lack masculinity and that we lack femininity – stem from the same place: lack. Exaggerated expressions of femininity are dubbed "masquerade" in psychoanalysis.[20] Some read masquerade as compensating for women's supposed lack: Media theorist Mary Ann Doane calls it "the decorative layer which conceals a non-identity."[21] Perhaps, in the same vein, vaginal products provide a decorative layer to conceal women's non-penis. They capitalize on women's sense of lack by providing a means for masquerade. They offer additions to women's genitalia, which are seen as subtractions, inversions, negatives. Our sexuality is not afforded the ability to exist on its own, so businesses step in to fill our emptiness.

When we aren't made to feel we're not enough and must add something to our bodies, we're made to feel like we're too much and must subtract something. One pitch I received from a women's health clinic lists "benefits of labiaplasty," including "increased performance in athletics," "hygiene," and "sexual pleasure," as supposedly, such a procedure will "leave the vulva more exposed." As if women are so poorly designed, our very genitals interfere with our mobility, cleanliness, and enjoyment.

I received this kind of message myself from VSPOT, which offered me a complimentary O Shot when I was twenty-five, alleging it would alleviate my struggles to orgasm with partners and allow me to orgasm through intercourse. Their gynecologist told me that if the shot didn't work, I might want a "clitoral dehooding" to make my clitoris more accessible, as its hood was purportedly too big for optimal pleasure. Rather than gain the sexual confidence promised by the "vag empowerment spa" – or the increased genital sensitivity – I left with a sense of my own deficiency.

Whether we're told to add to or subtract from our genitals, these recommendations draw upon the same presumption of women's incompleteness. It took me years to unwind the sources of my own sexual struggles and realize I wasn't broken. The biggest turning point was that epiphany: I didn't need to change my body, but simply to appreciate it and fully feel it. I came to see my physical design as the awesome asset it is, not an obstacle to overcome. Since then, I've approached sex with a sense of myself as equal to my partners, not as someone who needs to purchase something to attain equality. When I do make sex-related purchases like toys, it's not to compensate for my body's lack but to explore all the astounding things it can do.

Food, Water, Shelter, and Vibrators

Not all companies are so pernicious. Sex toy startups, for instance, help destigmatize pleasure as something that enhances well-being. Yet as more sex brands claim to promote "wellness," the same way beauty companies profess to offer "self-care," the illusion of a physical female deficiency grows stronger. Toys are not just fun or spicy additions anymore. They are medical aids, necessities. Sex toy brand Maude, for instance, describes itself as a "sexual wellness brand" selling "essentials like vibrators."[22]

When a product associates itself with health or describes itself as essential, we are made to believe we need it in order to be well. Sexual pleasure is beneficial for health, but pleasure doesn't depend on a product. Such marketing implies "that women's bodies are incapable of being healthy without mechanical intervention," sociologist Lisa Wade tells me. "It's suggesting that their bodies are pathological or broken. There's no question in our culture that men can masturbate and have orgasms without a device."

A number of feminist sex toy startups also claim to level the playing field during sex and make women more sexually independent. These are worthy goals, but such marketing implies that only those who can afford these products – or care to buy them – can be sexually empowered. Promoting a product as a pathway to equality insinuates that we are unequal without it. But the issue is broader than that: Companies that use feminism to sell products trivialize empowerment – and trivialize womanhood in the process. It's one of many ways capitalism commodifies feminism by replacing societal change with shopping. As if what women really care about is not respect or rights but obtaining a shiny, new, preferably pink item. As if women buying sex toys – while men go about their days as usual – will rectify gender inequality.

Thanks to sex brands' social media presence, it's now cool to talk about your vibrator like it's your best friend and savior. While this can help reduce sexual shame and sex toy stigma, it puts women's liberation and fulfillment in the hands of a device – and the company that sells it. The Instagram for Bellesa, a brand with over 500,000 followers that sells sex toys and woman-centered porn, reposts tweets by women full of glowing words about vibrators, such as "just used a vibrator that changed the trajectory of my entire life ... I understand human existence now."[23] The page also reposts tweets by Bellesa's Twitter account like "can't stop ordering sweaters and vibrators."[24] The posts address followers as "bbs" ("babes"), "girlies," and "besties" as they discuss being a "hot girl" with a "gorilla grip coochie and gorgeous gorgeous tits" and collecting sex toys like there's no tomorrow.[25] These words paint a stereotypical feminine persona that's centered on the products more than anything else, tying toys to a sexually attractive and empowered identity, interpellating followers as customers.

When brands post over-the-top praise for the very products they sell, it's worth remembering that their primary goal is probably not to advance women's rights but to encourage us to buy something. If a company implies you need a vibrator to reach peak empowerment, they're perpetuating the assumption of female lack. Sex toy brands like to play off the trope of vibrators replacing men, claiming to liberate women from selfish lovers by offering them toys. "Before you text them ask yourself this: could it be solved with a weighted blanket and a vibrator?" tweets Bellesa.[26] But if a woman needs a product rather than a person – if her independence hinges on her vibrator – she's still lacking. It's as if the toy assumes the position of the missing phallus, providing a woman with power. Or rather, a commercialized sense of it.

But subjectivity cannot be found in a box that arrives in the mail. It cannot be offered in an Instagram giveaway. The good news is that it's free. It comes from realizing how little you need in the first place. Instead of telling women they'll achieve equality once they buy something, we should teach them they're inherently equal. After all, we already have the best pleasure device in the world: a body.

In the meantime, we can choose what we buy and – more importantly – what we buy into. That is self-care: refusing to buy into the myth that you are incomplete. Refusing to buy things just to fill a nonexistent empty hole. And realizing that most things you can buy for your bedroom or your body are just for fun. It's once you realize this that they can actually be fun.

As long as we're trying to address our absence, we will not be present. As long as we're trying to compensate for our lack, we won't feel full – because we will not have questioned the lie that we are empty.

Self-care is not about resolving a deficit we suffer due to our femaleness, but becoming aware of the wholeness we already possess. It is not about fixing how we look so we can function better, or fixing how we function.

We don't need to take the shame out of having a vagina, or whatever body we have. We only need to realize that there is none.

Chapter 13

I Receive: Sex Work as Play

One sunny April afternoon in 2021, I lay on my couch and checked my Twitter. "OMG why can't I find a way to fuck Suzannah?" read a tweet from one of my followers. "Probably because I don't know her IRL. ... Why can't I find a way to cyber-fuck Suzannah??" I began to wonder how many of my followers were wishing to cyber-fuck me. Then another question popped into my head: What would they pay for it?

This question had entered my mind before. A few months prior, a friend had suggested I sell sexy photos and videos on the cam site OnlyFans, pointing out that many people were camming to make money during the pandemic. Indeed, OnlyFans usage surged from 120,000 creators in 2019 to a million by the end of 2020, along with 90 million subscribers.[1] Plus, I already had a platform to promote myself.

At that time in my life, I'd developed an interest in new age spirituality. And so, when I was feeling indecisive, I used angel cards – cards with illustrations of angels and little tidbits of advice purportedly from these divine beings. When my friend first mentioned OnlyFans to me, I'd pulled an angel card. It read: "Let yourself receive." Quite progressive of the angels, I thought. I took this card to mean there were people who were happy to compensate me for my charm and radiance, and I should accept that opportunity.

My Body Is Priceless

The word "receive" resounded in my ears. It would be nice, I thought, to take a break from giving, from working hard. To surrender to what my body enjoyed, to receive pleasure and praise *and* money. But the thought of taking payment for images of my body gave me pause. I had worked hard to be seen for my mind and heart, as had many women before me. I thought about it again and again over the next few months, but each time, I shot it down. Who was I, someone who railed against the objectification of women, to make money as a sex object?

Yet another friend told me about her OnlyFans and encouraged me to make one. "I don't know how I feel about putting a dollar amount on my body," I told her. "I'm priceless."

"The Grand Canyon is priceless," she replied. "But you can take a photo of it and pick a number."

Though she was likening me to a vista – an objectifying comparison on the surface – I understood the crux of her argument. She was drawing the distinction between doing sex work and selling *oneself*, two things sometimes conflated in anti-sex-work rhetoric. I'd heard people indignantly refer to "women selling their bodies," yet this phrase itself seemed to objectify sex workers. Describing sex workers' bodies as for sale seemed to only perpetuate a culture where their bodies – and women's bodies in general – are viewed as literally up for grabs.

Having interviewed sex trafficking survivors for articles, I understood there were situations where someone might justifiably feel they were being sold, such as if a trafficker denied their will and rights. I was also aware of the societal problem of weakly consented-to or acquiesced-to sex work and its connection to the objectification of women. I wanted to use my platform to fight objectification, not encourage it. Would it promote objectification to put my body out there for (mostly male) attention? Or would it be a statement against objectifying sex workers and all women? Would it show the world that no matter how erotically someone presents themselves, they can still be a subject with desires and boundaries? Decision paralysis. Maybe the only way to find out was to try. Plus, the opportunity felt too thrilling to pass up.

Paid for Pleasure

"To my Twitter followers who secretly (or openly) are sexually interested in me: I will engage you in a sexting conversation, NSFW photos included, for a price," I tweeted from my blue velvet couch. "DM me with the best offer you can make and we'll take it from there." To my surprise, the offers flooded in. $50. $100. $300. I accepted them all. After all, lying in bed with my favorite sex toys while receiving others' praise was something I'd probably have enjoyed doing for free.

Over the course of that day, I made $700. The sessions continued over the next few weeks, some over text, some over video, as admiring clients – primarily men, but a few women – complimented the photos, texts, and voice recordings I shared. Some had me enact elaborate role-plays over text. Some asked me what I liked, then strove to deliver it virtually. Some craved non-sexual chit-chat. Others wanted to get right down to business. Some were attractive to me, but even when they were not, I was attracted to the situation. My exhibitionist side had found an outlet. And as I lay there giggling and twiddling my rose quartz dildo, a seismic shift took place.

Each orgasm I experienced for money shattered three decades
of conditioning regarding the meaning of work and play.

Growing up, hard work was valued in my household and
community. From childhood, it was drilled into me: Study
hard. Get good grades. Don't watch TV until you're done with
your homework. Get into a good college. Study more. Get
a good job. Work hard. Make money. Work now. Play later.
Stress and strive. You need to be successful.

Nope, I didn't, at least not now. Climax by climax, I exposed
this as a lie. Here I was, simply doing what my body wished
to do. Playing. Playing harder. And making money for it. For
relaxing and shining my light into the world. Another cam
session, another myth shattered. The myth that I had to prove
myself. The myth of "no pain, no gain." The myth that I had to
earn my right to have fun. That I could only receive as much
as I sacrificed. That I had to do things I didn't want to do or be
someone other than me to get my needs met. That I, as I was,
right here, right now, was not enough.

Work (n):
1. Activity involving mental or physical effort done in
order to achieve a purpose or result.
2. A task or tasks to be undertaken; something a person
or thing has to do.[2]

Contrary to the commonly accepted definition, this work was
effortless – and not obligatory but desired. I was letting myself
receive, just as those silly cards predicted. I was also giving
something; my clients got enough out of it to pay for it. But
that "giving" itself felt like receiving. It felt natural and not a
lot like work.

Nor did I feel like an item for purchase. I was neither the
cow nor the free milk. I was neither complimentary salsa nor
expensive guac, neither the bride whose father "gives her away"

nor the sex worker "selling herself" – because my sexuality was not me. It was a part of me that I was sharing freely, even as I charged for it. I was a human enjoying experiences with fellow humans. Although I was an object of my clients' desire, I was a subject in staging that very scene.

Let me pause to acknowledge that this is just about the most privileged description of sex work someone could write. I was in a rare position: in a profession where I wouldn't lose my job for doing sex work – though I did lose hundreds of Twitter followers – and the income was merely supplemental. And, of course, as a white, feminine-presenting woman, I was not judged as harshly or mistreated as often as many sex workers. My experience does not represent most sex work by a long shot, but it does represent the type of experience all sex workers should have access to: one they can have if and only if it brings them pleasure.

Sex Work Is Work

I thought back to this slogan used by sex worker advocates, making it clear that this job should be taken seriously. That it was as respectable as any other job. "Sex work is first and foremost an income-generating activity," reads a Global Network of Sex Work Projects policy brief titled "Sex Work as Work."[3] I understood why it was important to emphasize this point: Sex workers deserve the same protections and rights as any workers. But personally, I did not experience sex work as work in the traditional sense. I experienced it as a chance to listen to my body and give it what it wanted. I was making money off my pleasure more than my sweat, blood, and tears. Sex work was play.

Other sex workers have described their jobs similarly. In a study of cam models, one used the same language that came to me: "I get paid to have orgasms. That's fuckin legit."[4] "The data suggest that the erotic and affectual pleasures are what keep models in the business," wrote study author Angela Jones, elaborating in another paper that "the motivation for choosing to perform erotic labor for a living is not just about access to wages, but it is also about the acquisition of pleasure and satisfying sexual desires."[5] Kaytlin Bailey, host of the podcast *The Oldest Profession* and director of communications at Decriminalize Sex Work, tells me that lots of sex workers love bringing "erotic energy" to their jobs. "It's not appropriate to bring that energy to most other workplaces," she says. "I know many sex workers that actually no longer need to engage in sex work out of financial need, but it's something that they don't want to stop doing."

I didn't want to stop either. I wanted to expand my new endeavor. At customers' and followers' urging, I started an OnlyFans page combining seduction with education. I posted photos and videos illustrating sex advice: breast massage instructions, clit-stroking tips, and squirting facts as demonstrated by me on my own body. I got to exercise my creativity, explore my favorite topics, and get off to it.

Still, elements of the job were beginning to feel more like work. Every day, I was responsible for putting out content to please an audience. Sensitive content. Content that required me to face body insecurities, fears of leaked photos, and judgment from strangers as well as people I knew. Some subscribers got triggered and outraged by my page. Some sent frequent and annoying DMs without tipping. Past sexting clients tried to sext with me for free. When I had to set a boundary and say, "please don't message me unless you're willing to pay," I felt bad for them as well as me. They wanted to feel desired for who they were, not their money. I wished I could have helped them feel that way.

Later that year, as I confronted a heartbreak and a health crisis, I shut down my OnlyFans. I was at capacity in terms of life stressors, and I couldn't handle the added stress of knowing there were X-rated images of me online. That's the part of sex work that was the most work: facing the stigma of being a sex worker.

The Cost of Getting Paid for Sex

Still, here and there, someone would find old social media posts advertising my sexting and camming and request a session. One such request arrived via an iMessage to my email address as I ate breakfast on a December morning. Initially, the man asked me about sex and love coaching, another service I offered. I let him know the price of an initial consultation, as well as my availability. "Do you have a min now? Just to go over how all this works. I'll Venmo even for a min," he replied, then called me. Looking back, I see it was a rookie move for me to pick up. If he really wanted to pay me for the call, he should have done so in advance. But at the time, I was naive enough to pick up the phone, thinking we'd chat for five minutes, then he'd pay and book a session.

Once he had me on the line, it become clear he was looking not just for sexual guidance but for virtual intimacy. I told him I was open to a hybrid coaching/camming agreement. I'd done that with one client who was shy around women and wanted real-life practice. It had helped him, and he'd remained respectful. The new potential client was excited about this prospect and told me he'd like to book our first full session for that evening. He then asked if he could have a "preview," promising to "tip generously."

Another rookie move. I should have stopped and collected the money before proceeding. Instead, I got on camera, stood back, and let him see me, as he requested. I told him I wouldn't get naked before receiving payment, but he talked me into spinning around and lifting up my shirt as he commented on my form from different angles. Even as his pushiness made me uneasy, I remembered his promise of a generous tip and continued for that sole reason. It was the first time I'd engaged in sex work just for the money, without a "hell yes."

As the evening approached, I reminded him of the fee for that night's session, which was due in advance as a general policy. Instead of paying that *or* the promised compensation for the first call, he sent me a series of texts such as "I just hate being lonely. I really do and I have a lot to offer. I have good genes," "I'm deprived of sex," and "you would be a good friend for free." When it came time for the call I'd blocked out the evening for, he disappeared, only to text me in the middle of the night: "Hi I know what you want but is there a way? If only you heard me." My body shook with rage when I woke up in the morning to this text. The incident was a sexual violation. I'd consider it abuse. I'd consented to a financial transaction. I'd consented on the condition that he pay me. I did not consent to a free cam show.

I let him know I wasn't open to further communication and blocked him – but not before adding, "If you would like my professional advice, I feel you would have more success with dating if you were to focus on respecting women, appreciating what they do for you, honoring their boundaries, making sure you're giving as much as you're receiving, and not being pushy." Block. This is what sex workers are exposing themselves to. This is why sex work is more work than it ever should be.

After that, I deleted old Twitter and Instagram posts advertising my sexual services so nobody would request a session again. I also revised my coaching contract to include strict clauses addressing advance payment, no-shows, and sexual advances. I did not want to put myself at risk for another violation. I understood that such boundary breaches might be avoided with fewer rookie moves, but I'd also seen how easily they could happen. I didn't know if I could ever prevent them entirely.

My "Yes" Cannot Be Bought

A year later, another man contacted me on Instagram, requesting a hybrid coaching/cam session to help him feel confident naked and overcome erectile difficulties. "Are you able to walk me through getting naked and masturbating in front of you?" he asked. I was only advertising regular sex coaching at this point, so he was taking a risk by requesting this – but I wasn't opposed to it. Guiding someone through a masturbation session was something I'd done before and enjoyed. And though I'd sworn off sex work, the truth was that I missed it.

"Yes, I'd be able to guide you through that," I wrote. I collected the payment. As we got on video, I relished that familiar rush of endorphins. I remembered what I'd missed about camming: feeling free, spontaneous, and present in my body. Making pleasure my work.

Then, immediately after we got off the call, he flooded my Instagram inbox: Could we meet in person? Could he tell me a secret? Could I lower my price? Pretty please, what if the call was just ten minutes? I asked him to reserve his questions for our sessions. But of course, he just had to send me more confessions, including that he didn't struggle with arousal issues – he'd just said that to trick me into a cam session. "Can I ask you what makes you keep your pussy so hairy?" he added. That was my breaking point. My patience stopped at deception and pubic hair fetishization. Too many digital boundaries had been trampled on. Block. I had no tolerance for sex work that was this much work.

He contacted me over email hoping to book another session, trying to negotiate some more, letting me know he was just giving me a compliment. Block. Then, he created a new Instagram account, pretending to be someone else to reach me. Block. I thought I'd be able to spot red flags at this point.

But I still couldn't seem to spot them soon enough to avoid these violating interactions. That's when a hard truth about sex work settled into my previously naive mind: It opened up the potential for me to have sex with people with bad intentions. People who were looking to use me. Cybersex was a form of sex. And since my client base consisted of random people approaching me on social media, it was damn near impossible to weed out all ill-intentioned people.

My clients were paying me to cater to their desires, which was great when their desires matched mine. But sometimes, I was discovering, they didn't. I could set limits, I could express wishes, but customers' desires took priority. They were the ones paying. Money had created the temptation to say "yes" to things I was OK with but did not desire. And even to things I was not OK with – like interacting with questionable people in the first place. Money made it tricky to really hear and honor my "hell yes." I had to practice what I preached, and I preached, "if it's not a hell yes, it's a no." I did not want to put my body through anything it was not a "yes" to. At one point, sex work was a "hell yes" to me. Now, it was more like a mix of "yes"es and "hell to the no"s. That was a no. There was no price someone could pay to override my body's voice.

And so I stopped doing the one type of work that felt to me like play – for good this time. Because the truth was, I did not live in a world where sex work could be play. I did not want to have sex that felt laborious in any circumstance.

No Pleasure, No Gain

It's not that I expected sex work to be easy. One reason I'd avoided it for so long was that I expected it to involve vulnerability, courage, and dealings with difficult people. It was nevertheless sad to get a taste of what it could be for work to be pure pleasure, then have that pleasure ripped away, inevitable as it may have been.

Sex workers' rights advocates have pointed out that many problems people identify with sex work apply to other kinds of work. "When we focus so much on sex work as a symbol of exploitation, it blinds us to what we're really talking about," says Kaytlin Bailey. "There are horrific examples of exploitation in agriculture and domestic labor." I agree. I think we could stand to raise our standards for all jobs – and to raise them beyond combating horrific exploitation. Ironically, it was sex work that showed me what those higher standards could look like. They look like allowing your body rest, joy, and social interaction, feeling nourished at the end of the workday rather than drained, and having your desires and boundaries heard.

These standards defy the capitalist values that pervade the US and much of the world. The values that say the harder you work, the more admirable you are. The values that say gain, particularly monetary gain, requires pain. These values objectify us all by undermining our enthusiastic consent. They cause us to put our passions, relationships, and mental health on the backburner. They may even lead us to see others as commodities, resources to drain rather than beings to honor. Instead of this, I dream of a world where all work can feel like play, including sex work. Where all sex work is in line with sex workers' desire, not just their acquiescence. The same goes for all sex and all work.

Doing the Dirty Work

The usual pro-sex-work adages don't always hold these ideals in mind. It's the oldest profession, proponents sometimes say, as it's a biological imperative to accommodate men's need for release. "It is often asserted that prostitution provides an outlet for sexual impulses which might otherwise be expressed in rape," criminologists Norval Morris and Gordon J. Hawkins have written.[6] Sex work allows men to unleash their urges on consenting sex workers instead of raping, the thinking goes – as if rape is a physical urge.[7] As if most sex workers *want* would-be rapists as customers. A sex worker's desire is nowhere in there; just male clients'. This argument perpetuates a view of women as commodities rather than challenging it.

The view of sex work as a necessary evil to curb men's sex drives has ancient and puritanical origins. Saint Augustine wrote in 386 AD that even though "commercial women" are "ignoble," we must allow sex work, as "if one suppresses prostitutes, the passions will convulse society."[8] You hear similar arguments in pro-sex-work writing today: "Most men want, even need, sexual outlets," reads a 2014 letter defending sex work as "at worst, a necessary evil" in the *Montreal Gazette*. "Lacking those, some will pay prostitutes. Like it or not, this is a fact of human existence."[9] It is perhaps a more palatable defense to make sex work a supply-and-demand issue, pointing toward the same supposed pussy deficit referenced by incels, than to praise its potential for pleasure. It is more accepted to deem sex work a necessary evil than to deem it not evil at all. Or to work toward a society where it contains no "evil" – no gender inequality, no begrudging consent.

The suggestion that sex work could be rewarding for all involved – and include a variety of gender dynamics – is too taboo to garner mainstream attention. So, advocates fit it into our cultural definition of work. They present it as an obligatory service to prevent male aggression – or to increase a country's GDP, as the Global Network of Sex Work Projects emphasizes.[10] Pleasure is absent from these discussions. Yet subjectifying sex workers means advocating for their right to do work that pleases them. Not work that feels like a mere obligation or a source of violation. Not work that's just another way to meet a demand. Not work under its dehumanizing capitalist definition.

From Jobs to (Blow) Joys

Women already receive enough messages about sex being work. Women's sexuality is already treated like a service, especially if we sleep with men. We get taught it is our wifely duty to please our husbands, to keep them from straying. We learn terms like "handjob" and "blowjob" that suggest sex is a job for us; the terms for the female equivalents don't contain "job." My friend, embodiment coach Nicole Ambrosia, coined the term "blowjoy" to convey that when we please our partners, it should be because that pleases us, too. We should cease normalizing sex that's a job and normalize sex that's a joy for all involved. And while we're at it, we can cease normalizing work that's a job and normalize work that's a joy.

Why is the grueling job full of sacrifice and intellectual feats on such a pedestal in the first place? Perhaps because it's associated with men. The professions we equate with success – doctors, lawyers, CEOs, stockbrokers – are stereotypically held by white, upper-class men. Rather than emphasize that sex work is similarly strenuous, we can challenge whether work should feel this way. Rather than seek acceptance by adhering to patriarchal, capitalist, puritanical values, we can celebrate sex work's potential to challenge these values. Sex work that is not just fully consented to but actively desired implodes these values. And by fighting for acceptance on the grounds that sex work enables connection and happiness, we can contribute to that implosion.

If we don't look beyond our cultural prizing of "no pain, no gain," we'll end up trying to fit sex work into oppressive ideals of work, rather than allow the light ignited by enthusiastic sex workers to illuminate a path out of this mentality. If we don't acknowledge sex work's potential for enjoyment, we'll continue to normalize situations where sex workers' desire is absent. Sex work will continue to appear as an inevitable or necessary evil. And although there certainly is evil within the sex industry, the way to fight this exploitation is not to deem sex work inherently exploitive. It is when we look beyond this stereotype that we can imagine something better. The more we recognize sex work as something that can be entered into consensually and even enthusiastically, the more we'll spot, condemn, and prevent situations devoid of consent.

Some scholars have suggested we replace the standard of enthusiastic consent with "authentic consent" to accommodate sex workers.[11] While there's merit to the idea that sex need not always be motivated by raging horniness, we should be careful about undermining the importance of sex workers' enthusiasm. Sex work is hard enough when you *are* enthusiastic. While economic constraints may lead some to do sex work they're not thrilled about – and these people shouldn't be punished – we should keep sight of the vision for a society where no one feels compelled to have sex that doesn't excite them. Sex devoid of enthusiastic consent holds just as much potential for harm whether it's paid or unpaid.

Nice and Cute and Fun

Ever since my foray into sex work, a conversation I had with a therapist years ago has run on repeat through my head. I was complaining to her that my boyfriend at the time didn't fully see or get me. "When I ask him what he likes about me, he just says I'm nice and cute and fun," I lamented. "He doesn't realize how smart and accomplished I am."

"Being nice and cute and fun is a virtue," she replied. "Few people retain those qualities as adults. They're not inferior to intelligence or success."

I hadn't seen that at the time. Nor had I unpacked the fact that "nice and cute and fun" are deemed "girly" attributes, while intelligence and success are deemed manly – and maybe that was why they were hierarchized this way. I'd been too busy fighting the notion that, as a woman, my body was the most important part of me. I'd embraced a feminism that appreciated women for their brains over their beauty.

But sex work opened my eyes to the empowerment of being acknowledged for being nice, cute, and fun. It helped me realize that prizing the brains our culture deems masculine over the beauty more commonly deemed feminine was not the way to fight patriarchy. It *was* patriarchal – and elitist, as those who make money off their bodies are often of lower economic status, as Victoria Bateman points out in her book *Naked Feminism*.[12] Why is, say, developing an app considered a better accomplishment than bringing yourself and others joy through your smile and spontaneity? Why is mental intelligence deemed superior to sensual or somatic intelligence? Why is work more impressive than play? Why is improving your mind a noble pursuit, while improving your body gets labeled as petty and self-involved?

Yes, we should challenge the double standard that renders women's looks more important than men's. Yes, we should prioritize how our bodies feel above how others see them. Yes, the size of our hearts is more important than the size of our breasts. Yes. But if we must denounce all things superficial in order to be seen as subjects, we will find ourselves in a trap, afraid to be too "feminine" lest we come off as objects. It's OK to care about your looks and want praise for them. It's OK to devote your career to adding beauty to the world. In a culture that has prized the mind over the body for millennia, it's actually radical.

I am certainly not here to tell anyone what to do with their bodies, or to tell them they *must* enjoy their work. But I am hoping to question our values around work – and maybe, as a consequence, how we treat others. And, more actionably, how we treat ourselves. If we can admire sex workers as much as scientists and praise stay-at-home parents as much as surgeons, maybe we'll treat others with more dignity and less judgment. And if we can challenge the notion that our productivity is what makes us important – if we can feel just as proud of ourselves for caring for our pets as we do for getting promotions – then maybe, we'll be easier on ourselves. We'll allow ourselves a little more play.

On the Subject of Sex Workers

Can a sex worker be a subject? The answer is evidently "yes." If sex workers were predominantly men, we would not even be asking this question. A man's choice to get paid by jerking off all day would be more likely met with high fives than grumbles about low self-worth.

But if even I, with all the privileges a sex worker could have, found myself unable to escape objectification in this industry, it's clear the world today is not set up to subjectify sex workers. Most have it much harder than I did. While I was unable to report harassment to Instagram out of fear of punishment for doing sex work on the platform, many sex workers –especially those of color – are scared to call the police on abusive clients out of fear they'll be arrested. Again, anti-sex-work stigma – and its codification in law – is often what encourages objectification in this line of work.[13] The view of sex work as inherently oppressive leads to more oppression.

Still, in a world hell-bent on objectifying sex workers, many manage to retain their subjectivity. Though they're paid to cater to clients' desires, they find work that matches their desires, too. Most encounter boundary-pushers like I did, but they've become experts on asserting boundaries, and their job's joys outweigh the travails. I asked Colette Pervette, the dominatrix I quoted earlier, how she does this. "Check in with how you feel in these experiences with these clients," she says. "It's OK to let go of what doesn't feel good, what feels draining."

I'd add to be guided by what *does* feel good, if possible – to ask yourself if you feel a calling toward this work. My own rule of thumb is that before engaging in any sexual interaction, free or paid, I need to feel a full "yes": my body feels aroused, my heart feels connected, and my mind feels at ease.

Subjectification 101: You Get to Be All of Who You Are

Unfortunately, financial inequalities prevent many from holding these sexual standards, whether sex is their work or not. Yet another common, covertly objectifying pro-sex-work argument is that women already trade sex for money anyway. As actress Raven-Symoné said in a discussion of paid sex on *The View*: "Women who get bags, women who get cars, women who get apartments, women who get shoes, women who get a house and alimony … you're getting paid."[14] Such bartering might be enjoyable and even sexy for some women, but it's too often accepted as women's natural role or necessitated by income disparities. Marriage itself has been seen for too long as an exchange of women's bodies for men's money.

I'd like us to break out of this convention altogether, rather than draw upon it to illustrate that sex workers are just like the rest of us. Instead of women bonding over *all* having sex we're kind of "meh" about for money, we should stand up for women's right to have sex they're glad to have, whether they're paid or not. Stating that typical relationships between men and women are transactional normalizes sex devoid of female desire. Instead, we should work toward a society where anyone who chooses to get paid for sex, formally or informally, enjoys both the sex and the money. Where the payment contributes to a "yes" rather than causing someone to push past a "no."

The old system that renders beauty women's primary asset, while men's is money, still shapes what sex work looks like, even in its modern digital forms. Eighty-seven percent of OnlyFans subscribers are men, and 70 percent of creators are women.[15] But sex workers are not just here to please the male gaze. Many are educators and healers, and in a world where everyone was subjectified, people of all genders would feel free to seek this education and healing. The position of sex worker, too, would be occupied by people of all genders who have a passion for it, enough of a passion to make the challenges worth it. And a lot of people doing sex work today would *not* be doing it. It would be limited to those who freely chose it – but it's more than that.

Some feminists say the important question to determine whether sex work – or shaving, or anything – is empowering is whether it was chosen. But I think the important question is why we're choosing what we're choosing. An empowering choice is one made from a deep understanding of ourselves, our desires, and our feelings – with the financial and social freedom to act from that place. I hope that one day, that's how all sex work will be entered into.

In the meantime, I am not concerned about women's choices as long as they stem from self-knowledge, self-love, and self-trust. I am concerned about the forces pushing us not to know, love, and trust ourselves. If subjectification means you can't make money by flirting and rubbing your clit, then I don't want to be subjectified. A true subject gets to switch between subjecthood and objecthood as they please. It is in fully expressing all our seemingly contradictory aspects that we can be unified and whole.

Fun, Passion, Inspiration: A Labor of Love

Soon after I began doing sex work, I asked a good friend who's a life coach what she thought of it. "No career choice is wrong as long as you're connected to love," she told me. "Love is fun, passion, and inspiration. If you're experiencing those things, you can trust where you feel led." To me, that is the highest form of work someone can do. Work that produces passion, fun, and inspiration. Work that connects you to love.

Sex work is not a typical job, and that's a good thing. Sex workers who love their jobs can inspire us all to build careers and lives where we listen to our bodies rather than fight them. Yes, what they do is work. And sex work in its enthusiastic form is play, as all our work should be. Maybe not 100 percent play, but enough play to connect us to love. Sex work is a legitimate profession – and legitimacy doesn't hang on stress or cerebral strain.

Even though I've stepped back from sex work, I still strive to play my way through the workday. To give to the world by receiving. To provide for myself by simply enjoying my body and the pleasure it brings me.

I strive to make each task I undertake feel juicy and embodied, thrilling and mischievous. I take calls in the sand while eating chocolate, insert sex jokes into emails when it won't get me in trouble, invite my cats to Zoom meetings, take breaks to massage myself, and do my taxes in pink lingerie. I strive to live with calculated irreverence, with a reverence for the spirit of play.

And if I must wear a scarlet letter on my forehead, let it be the letter I. Let it be a declaration of our right to enter whoredom at the service of our own passion, fun, and inspiration.

And if anyone tries to judge us for the pleasure we take in our play, let these words stick with us: If you're connected to love, you cannot go wrong. You cannot be wrong.

And if the best you can say for yourself is that you're nice and cute and fun, you can say you've made it.

Chapter 14

I Like: You're Just Not That Into Them

"My body doesn't look the way it did before," a new mom told me during a sex coaching session. "When I get naked in front of my partner, I think about that now: my drooping breasts, my belly, my vagina. I don't know how to feel confident in bed anymore."

She was searching for a way to see and evaluate herself more positively during sex. While I had a feeling this was possible for her, I wanted to first offer an alternative: to stop looking at and evaluating herself altogether.

"Instead of thinking about your body, have you tried thinking about your partner's body?" I asked.

"What do you mean?"

"Well, I assume you're attracted to him?"

"Right."

"So, the next time you start thinking about what you look like, look at him and focus on what he looks like. Focus on what you like about him, not what you dislike about yourself."

"That's so simple but makes sense," she laughed. "I'd never thought of it that way."

It's not how women are taught to think: to direct their attention toward others, particularly in a sexual manner. Especially if that means making a man the object of the gaze.

Sexy Is Not a Feeling

Advice geared toward increasing women's sexual confidence typically teaches us how to appreciate our looks – and, ironically, how to make our looks worthy of appreciation, often by altering them. "Soft lighting is flattering ... Switch your regular lightbulbs for peach-colored ones or group several candles in various areas," reads a 2010 *Cosmo* article titled "How to Feel Sexy All the Time."[1] It continues: "Whether you're with your guy or solo, staying in with a DVD should be relaxing ... but there's no need for it to be schlumpy ... Watching a hot actress like Angelina or Scarlett while you're wearing baggy sweats and a tee isn't going to do your ego any favors. Get into the sexiest mood possible by stripping down to your underwear."

Other *Cosmo*-approved ways to "feel sexy"? "Going to sleep in boxers and an old tee shirt may be comfy, but it won't give you confidence as you walk from your closet to bed. Pick up a pair of PJs that make you feel hot." And one more thing before you turn out the lights: "Taking one last second to primp can make you feel great. Keep a bottle of your favorite perfume on your nightstand, and spritz your body once before you crawl under the covers." God forbid women spend the "last second" of their day feeling less than fuckable. For themselves, of course – for the ever-present male gaze peering at them from their empty bed.

The unspoken assumption in women's magazines is that "sexy" is a feeling – one to strive for. By 2019, *Cosmo* had also published an experiment where a writer wears lacy underwear to "feel sexy and more confident" and a series of interviews with women and non-binary people on "when they feel their sexiest."[2] Back in eating disorder recovery, I learned that "fat" is not a feeling. Saying you "feel fat" is a stand-in for saying you feel depressed, angry, lonely, or bad about yourself. I think "sexy" is similar. When someone says they want to feel sexy, they usually mean they want to feel confident, self-assured, energetic, or sexual.

As I've already discussed, businesses profit off women's desire to feel sexy. They ignore what's behind this desire and offer clothing, makeup, accessories, or body modifications as solutions. They equate feeling sexual with feeling sexy – and equate feeling sexy with looking sexy. The result? Women start to believe that feeling sexual requires looking sexy. That in order to be sexual beings, they must look hot. Not even for a partner, but for themselves. So that they can feel presentable, whether alone or with company. So that their looks can be pleasing even when there is no one there to please.

The New Beauty Myth

In the classic 1990 book *The Beauty Myth*, feminist author Naomi Wolf exposed the lie that women must be beautiful to attain the lives they want.[3] Today, fewer women buy into the idea that they need to be beautiful to be happy. So, advertisers and magazines tell women a slightly different beauty myth, which is actually the same: that they need to *feel* beautiful to be happy. It's not about the superficial, they insist; it's feeling beautiful that matters. Then, of course, they tell women how to feel beautiful: by acquiring conventionally attractive bodies and faces. The end goal is still visual beauty.

Modern-day women don't have to be sexy all the time. We just have to "feel sexy all the time," even when that involves "hot" pajamas, flattering lightbulbs, sexy underwear, bedtime primping ... and a bunch of other things traditionally done to help women *look* sexy. Even women's empowerment gurus embrace such advice; Mama Gena writes in her book *Pussy* that as women, "it is our sacred responsibility to look and feel as beautiful as possible."[4]

The tendency to treat "sexy" and "beautiful" as feelings illustrates the cultural conflation of women's sexuality with their sexiness and, more broadly, their identity with their image. We've confused women's subjectivity with their ability to be objects, all because we still lack a concept of real female subjectivity. Woman, her soul, her inner self, does not exist. So, we dress it up. We identify sights to stand in for her. Her hair, her skin, her nails … is that what a woman is? What about her clothing, is that her? Is that the place from which she can derive her sense of self? Sexy, is that her inner state?

We still don't know how to define a woman. But that's OK. A woman does not need to be defined. She is undefinable. Her identity need not be visible. We need not glide our gaze across a woman's skin to see who she is, or stare at our own reflections to know who we are. We can direct our attention outward.

A Woman's Place Is in Her Body

This does not mean we can never attend to ourselves. I did give my client, the new mom, some tips on how to see herself more positively, which included wearing things she looks good in. We may always gaze upon ourselves, so we can aim to do so in a more loving light. But we must remember: We are the ones looking out our eyes, not the reflections in the mirror. We can acknowledge ourselves as physical beings, but we must enjoy this physicality as subjects inside our bodies, not observers peering in from the outside.

Popular sex advice still gives off the impression that a woman's natural place is outside herself. When I was hired to revise and modernize *Glamour*'s sex position articles, I deleted lines about "giving him a great view" and snuck in a line I'd never read before: "You get a good view!" Even when the guidance is geared toward women's empowerment, the message still promotes an inverted consciousness, a turning of the gaze back on oneself. A woman's pleasure is made out to be about her partner's pleasure. *Women's Health* offers an article called "8 Reasons Guys Love It When You Orgasm," where a male writer lists motivations like "we get a private show" and "your voice sounds amazing at that volume."[5] In a *Cosmo* article similarly titled "8 Reasons He Really Wants to Make You Orgasm – Nay, Needs to Make You Orgasm," another man writes, "it is a testament to our manhood" and "we just want to be the best."[6] Get your orgasms, ladies ... it's *hot*!

The irony is, 32 percent of *Cosmo*'s readers reported in a 2015 survey that when they could not orgasm, it was because they were in their heads or focused on their looks.[7] Articles about how attractive women are in bed probably aim to combat such insecurities. Yet the way out of this self-consciousness is inward, not further outward. The way to feel more pleasure is to focus on your own sensations, not your partner's arousal and ego.

I Love You, I Love You Not

Popular advice encourages women to assume others' perspectives – usually men's – in dating as well as sex. Women are supposed to be empowered by ditching romantic prospects who are "just not that into them," per the 2004 book *He's Just Not That Into You*.[8] But teaching women to ask themselves whether someone's into them, rather than what they're into, encourages them to think of themselves as objects – the objects of "like." Or "dislike."

I've heard many versions of this phrase in everyday conversations and on social media. "If a man really likes you, he'll pursue you." "If he wanted to, he would." "If a man wants you, you will know, and if he doesn't, you will feel confused."[9] Never mind that not all men subscribe to the traditional role of pursuer – especially in an era when many men are conscious of women's boundaries. Never mind that not all women's love interests are men. Never mind that someone can have many possible reasons for not pursuing you – poor timing, self-doubt, difficulty navigating the nuances of dating, the idea just not occurring to them – and you may not understand why until you stop speculating and pursue them yourself.

This kind of advice puts women in the backseat, monitoring love interests' actions rather than taking action themselves. It's a maddening game that causes much more trouble than directly asking someone if they're interested. Almost all my own relationships began with me boldly pursuing someone. Everyone I pursued had feelings for me – and had their reasons for not acting on them right away: They weren't sure if *I* was into *them*. They were afraid it wouldn't work out. They wanted to take things slow. If I had gotten caught up in whether they were "into me," rather than trusting that I was into them for a good reason, none of these connections would have formed. Good thing that each time, I followed my intuition before anyone else confirmed it. Good thing there was a fire in me before anyone else was there to start it, and I let it light the way.

Breaking the supposed hard news to a friend that someone's "just not that into them" is now considered tough love. But it rarely accomplishes much beyond making women doubt themselves and second-guess their own perspectives. A few years ago, a Bumble match ghosted me just as we started making plans. I'd assumed he was just flakey or afraid of intimacy – until a friend told me, "Sounds like he wasn't into you." It was her who caused me to worry that something about me was unappealing. It was that conversation that led me to wonder how he saw me, to make myself the object of his gaze.

"You deserve to be chased," my friend said. "You deserve to be caught. You're the woman, and it's the man's job to go after you." It's an idea that often goes along with "he's just not that into you," encouraging women to hold out for relationships where they're valued. Yet the notion that we should be chased and caught undermines our enthusiastic consent. Where is a woman's will when she is running and being chased? Why need there be a runner and a chaser? Why can't both people, whatever their gender, move toward each other, both as subjects of "pursue"?

Upon considering another dating prospect, my well-intentioned friend told me to just give him a chance, and I admitted I didn't really like him. "Go with who likes you," she replied. Women are often told this: to go with who likes them. To picture themselves as the objects of "like," not the subjects. What we like or dislike comes second to our ability to be liked. If the person who likes us is a man we're not attracted to, we're told "he'll grow on you" or "he's such a nice guy." Less often are straight men told "but she's so nice, give her a chance" or "she might have a great personality!" It's women's attraction, or lack thereof, that's under constant questioning, because we are seen as recipients – not subjects – of desire.

What Are *You* Into?

Another friend gave me a piece of advice years ago: "Don't think so much about whether someone likes you. Think about whether you like them." She was not saying to violate a person's boundaries or try to turn their "no" into a "yes." She was saying that before you worry about whether someone likes you, gain clarity on what *you* like. Figure out whether you really like them or just want to be liked *by* them.

That is what it looks like to navigate relationships – and life – as a subject: to make decisions based on what you like.

It's not that whether someone likes you back is irrelevant. The reason you don't like them might be that they're not showing enough interest. But rather than fixate on their perspective, you can focus on their actions and their impact on you. You can ask yourself, not whether they're into you, but whether they can co-create the relationship you envision. Encouraging a woman to decode *why* someone isn't showing up for her – or how "into her" they are – decenters her desire. Telling a woman "if he wanted to, he would" puts the question of whether a man wants a woman above whether he can deliver what *she* wants. Instead of "if he wanted to, he would," we can say: "Whether or not they wanted to, they didn't – and that's useful information."

Puzzling over whether love interests are "into you" is also a recipe for taking things personally. You can hear this subtly personalizing tone in the book *He's Just Not That Into You*. Funny, helpful advice about not settling is sullied with lines like "if a guy truly likes you … he won't keep you guessing" and "men are never too busy to get what they want."[10] This suggests that men are assertive go-getters who always have their act together, so if a man says he's too busy to see you, he must not want or like you. The truth is, there are many reasons someone may say they're busy. There are many reasons someone may be a poor communicator and "keep you guessing." There are many reasons someone may not ask you out or text you back. But what matters less than the reason is whether *your* desires are being met.

When you're focused on someone else's perspective, you distance yourself from your feelings, getting caught up in self-consciousness rather than enjoying the relationship. That's what my client was experiencing: She was focused on whether her partner was into her, instead of enjoying the fact that she was into him. It's not that his desires didn't matter. But we can best honor others' subjectivity when we are fully present in our own lives, as subjects.

Self-Love Through Other-Love

Relating to others from the inside out is easier when you refrain from assigning a "value" to yourself or others. When you go after what you want, not what you think you deserve. You don't have to convince yourself you're "worthy" of a love interest. You need only determine whether you're both a "hell yes."

It's a subtle but transformative difference. It's the difference between asking yourself "am I enough?" and asking "does this feel right?" It's the difference between figuring out what you're worth and figuring out what you're a match for. It's the difference between needing to find yourself attractive and realizing that even if you don't, someone else might: attraction is subjective. So, you might as well stop worrying about what you see in the mirror. We get stuck in our heads when we impose an obligation on ourselves to view ourselves as worthy objects. Or when we believe we must love ourselves before anyone else can love us.

"No one else can love you until you love yourself." Another common but counterproductive piece of dating advice. Deeming yourself incapable of a relationship because you don't love yourself only hinders self-love. Struggling with self-love doesn't make you unlovable; it makes you relatable. You need not wait for a future time when you love yourself to find a relationship. You need not be the object of your own affections; be the subject of your affections toward your partner(s). Instead of trying to feel more positively about yourself, take the focus off yourself and enjoy your positive feelings toward others. That *is* a form of self-love. Loving yourself doesn't mean staring at your reflection, attempting to find yourself beautiful. It means being the subject of loving verbs. It means behaving in ways that facilitate your fulfilment.

Focusing on your own sense of "I" is not self-centered. It doesn't undermine the "I"-ness of the "you"s around you. It makes you more attentive to them. It makes you more compassionate. Being a subject leaves you available to make others the objects of your care. By making myself the subject of "like," I am able to put others before me. Instead of focusing on my own discomfort around people, I consider how to help them feel at ease. Instead of thinking about how others see me, I think about how I see them. That's the message I hope all my clients and readers take from me.

If you're feeling insecure, bring your attention outward. If you're afraid someone won't like you, focus on whether and why you like them. If you're worried about whether you are bringing someone pleasure, become aware of what pleases you.

Instead of chasing that elusive feeling of "sexiness," strive for the feelings that label represents, like comfort, aliveness, and joy.

You can have those no matter how sexy you look. Or how sexy you feel.

Chapter 15

I Write: Inhabiting
the Active Voice

For my Intro to Gender and Sexuality Studies class in my freshman spring of college, I read the essay "This Sex Which Is Not One" by feminist philosopher Luce Irigaray. In it, she describes how the vulva's two lips are always touching. These lips make up one body part, yet they are two: one left, one right. They are different but the same. They each exist in their own space, yet they pleasantly caress each other, neither overtaking the other. There is no subject–object dichotomy, no "possibility of distinguishing what is touching from what is touched." This image illuminates how, not just different genders, but opposing concepts can coexist, neither one dominating or erasing its counterpart.[1]

Western culture instead views bodies through a hierarchical framework: The penis is considered the superior organ, representing power and desire, while the vulva signifies nothingness. And so a woman, despite having these two lips, despite being two, is counted as zero. A hole rather than whole. As my professor brought attention to Irigaray's description of the vagina as an "envelope," she posed the question: "Why do we say 'man fucks woman' or 'man penetrates woman' when we could say 'woman envelops man'?"[2]

I ~~Get Penetrated~~ Engulf

"Man fucks woman." I contemplated the sentence. The woman was the object of "fuck." In the way people typically described heterosexual sex, she "got fucked." In other uses of the phrase, "getting fucked" was not generally a good thing. It was a misfortune to get fucked, to get screwed, to get screwed over.

> Fuck (v):
> 1. have sex with (someone).
> 2. ruin or damage (something).[3]

Sex and exploitation were so synonymous in the English language, a phrase for having sex also meant being harmed. The object of "fuck" was "someone" yet also "something." No wonder it had been upsetting when my body turned into something "womanly." I was turning into an object to get fucked. Language reflected the violent way my culture thought about sex.

> Penetrate (v): succeed in forcing a way into or through (a thing).[4]

The role of a woman was to be penetrated. To be forced. To be ruined, violated, intruded upon, broken into. A thing.

I had not yet had penetrative sex, but this was how I'd heard it described. Someone had to pop my cherry, deflower me, take my innocence. Damage me to make me into a mature female. A woman, marked by emptiness. For that pivotal night, I was to surrender to my role as object and accept my own passivity. For sex to degrade and devalue a woman ... I feared this was inevitable. I feared it was nature. A woman, after all, was the one getting penetrated, getting fucked. She was in the passive voice, built to be an object. The man's desire was for her, and she was to acquiesce to it. It seemed that was what our bodies were made for.

Yet this simple flip of a sentence opened up new possibilities: "Woman envelops man." Or, really, "woman envelops person." "Woman envelops world." If I were to envelop, to take in, to fulfill my desire, then maybe sex – and relationships – could be just as rewarding for me as for a partner. Maybe it would not be a splitting-open, but an opening-up. I had always had a feeling that my body was more than a hole to be occupied by men or children, a vehicle to be used for others' purposes, a means to an end. Now I saw this feeling wasn't wishful thinking. It was a wise inner knowing. It was real. The problem was not with my body but with the language used to describe it, language that painted women as destined to be damaged.

The phrase itself, "penetrative sex," made the penis the subject and the vagina the object. It centered a straight cis male perspective, as did "vaginal sex." From the perspective of a vagina-owner being pleased, *all* sex is vaginal or at least vulvar. From a female subject's perspective, PIV intercourse might be called "VAP (vagina around penis)" or "penile sex." Instead, we name sex acts based on what the penis enters, from its perspective: oral, anal, vaginal.

Even the word "envelop" did not sound quite right. It sounded too delicate and fragile. Another student in my class used the word "engulf," which sounded more powerful. I also came up with my own term, "penvelop," a portmanteau for penetrating and enveloping that makes both people subjects: "We penveloped." This still left a lot out – like how sex can happen without a phallus and an orifice. A verb like "touch" or "contact" or "commune," which could be used for any act or body parts, might be more widely applicable. After all, physically and symbolically, people can relate to one another without any penetration *or* enveloping.

There were endless options, but it was "woman engulfs" that stuck with me when thinking about intercourse – something I had not felt ready for. Even if I hadn't put it in these terms, I wanted to be sure that before I took that step, I knew how to engulf. To be centered in myself and take someone into my body, not simply allow them to take me. I hadn't realized that was what I had been waiting for. Not a knight in shining armor to carry me off into womanhood. Not a sword to pierce and open me. Just myself, in all my selfhood. In a world that relegated me to the second and third person – to "you" and "she" and "them" – I had to find my I-ness.

The Nature of Words

For another class the following year, I read the essay "The Egg and the Sperm" by Emily Martin.[5] It points out how biology textbooks describe sperm as shooting and swimming toward an egg, like little armored knights rushing to puncture the passive single-cell damsel. But really, the sperm mostly move sideways, not forward. It is the egg that pulls them in using sticky molecules on its outer surface. Sticky molecules on the sperm, in turn, make them adhere to the egg. They are both subjects and objects of the same verb, the egg and sperm. I saw myself as that egg, able to reach out to a partner and rejoice as we moved toward each other to create something new. I had a new way of thinking about my body, about myself. I was an engulfer, an enveloper, a puller-in. My body was a source and site of pleasure and desire. A penis was there not to break into me for its own pleasure, but to please us both.

Once I could speak of myself in the active voice, I could imagine myself in an active role – and claim that role. Nothing about my first "penetrative sex" experience felt like "forcing a way into or through a thing." There was no force, no discomfort. I had no walls, physical or emotional, to push up against or get through. Both of us moved toward each other. A penetration and an engulfing. Both and neither. A mutual joining. Every step of the way, I was an active participant. Before it even happened, I got to know myself using my own fingers and toys, for my own pleasure. I knew how I liked to engulf. I asked for what I wanted without hesitation. I did not accept that it could be less than enjoyable for me. This was for my satisfaction just as much as my partner's. I was a subject of desire.

I felt angry at the people, books, and articles that told me this experience would be painful, asymmetrical, and violating. Yet they were not wrong. They were accurately describing the language they were speaking and the dynamics it created. Penetration, by its dictionary definition, was a form of force. To get fucked was to be ruined and damaged. I had a sheath, and a sword was entering it. That Lacan quote came back to me: "There is no woman who is not excluded by the nature of things, which is the nature of words."[6] The nature of the words used to describe sex had shaped the nature of the act. It had shaped the limited ways people felt they could go about it – and the uncomfortable, intrusive experiences many women had.

I grew determined to change the nature of words so we could change the nature of things. To change the way we spoke about ourselves so we could have different bodies, different bonds, different lives. To change the way we imagined women so that instead of being sheaths for others' swords, we could finally live life for ourselves.

On Octopussies

Another year later, I was working as an editorial assistant for a feminist theory journal when I proofread an essay: "On

Octopussies, or the Anatomy of Female Power" by Gerard Cohen-Vrignaud. It described the octopus as a symbol of the engulfing vagina, from Victor Hugo's *Toilers of the Sea* – a book about sailors scared of being swallowed by a giant octopus – to *The Little Mermaid's* Ursula and *James Bond's* Octopussy.[7] The octopus in *Toilers of the Sea* had "a raging sexual appetite in search of libidinal satisfaction," Cohen-Vrignaud wrote. It was so stereotypically masculine, yet in such a feminine way. It collapsed this very binary. The paper went on to describe a trend in nineteenth-century France where women wore their hair like tentacles – a style known as the "follow-me, young man" – symbolizing the desire to lure in those who caught their eye. Like the egg with the sperm.

The insight I'd had in class several years prior solidified: The vagina's status as an active force, rather than a passive hole, was not feminist wishful thinking. It was an image that had lived in the collective unconscious for centuries, even as it was repressed. No, women were not born to be objects. Our language and culture had made us so. Yet even in the midst of that, there was a language of sorts – the language of symbols and stories – that simply could not deny our subjectivity.

Another six years later, I interviewed Sue Jeiven, a tattoo artist in Brooklyn, for an article. I had never wanted a tattoo. Yet as she described a client who got a seascape on his arm just before quitting his day job to sail around the world, I felt inspired. Not just because I was about to give up my New York apartment to travel, but also because I remembered the octopussy and all it stood for: that sense of adventurousness, independence, and freedom in exploring the wild ocean, in reaching out to the object(s) of your desire. Before I knew it, I was asking Jeiven, "Would you tattoo an octopus on my arm?"

We met up for a brainstorming session and decided on an image of an octopus swallowing a ship. It would go on my left shoulder, reminding me that I'm an active subject who engulfs, not a passive object that gets penetrated. As Jeiven turned my skin into art, I told a story to distract myself from the needle, a tale that shaped her illustration. It was the story of how I met my partner at the time, how I engulfed him into my life. "It looks like you," he told me when I showed him the tattoo. "Grabbing on to what you want."

Being It All

Today, I sometimes wonder if I still want the tattoo. I question whether it matches the way I see myself now. I do not wish to perform the dominating role that men have been cast in. I do not wish to turn the tables on men, to attack them and swallow them whole. I do not wish to lure my prey in a forceful or manipulative manner. I wish to evade the predator/prey paradigm entirely. I wish to create harmony, not flip around an adversarial dynamic.

And sometimes, I wish to be fucked. If subjectification means always being in charge and never letting go, that ruins the fun of it. The term "subject" ironically stems from the Latin word *subiectus*, which means "lying under" or "below."[8] You can hear this connotation in modern use as well: A queen and king's subjects are below them. It is almost as if being a subject means being an object. This paradox is perfect. A subject is someone who feels comfortable as an object. Who feels safe surrendering. Who can be seen and fucked and inhabit her body and heart at the same time. Who knows she'll never lose her subjecthood. A subject feels powerful enough that she need not assert power over others.

Is my octopus asserting power over the poor shipwrecked sailors? Perhaps not. When I take another look, I notice an ambiguity: Though she holds the ship, she lies below it, like a true *subiectus*. And it's unclear what she'll do next. Will she swallow it whole into her (w)hole? Or will she simply sit with it elevated in her arms, enjoying the mariners' company as she protects them from the waves? The image's true meaning lies in the ambiguity. It represents all that a woman can be: a caring protector, a vicious destroyer, a creature simply looking to amuse herself. She is so strong, she need not overpower. One might say, in BDSM lingo, that she is topping from the bottom, dominant and submissive at the same time.

That is real life. Even in just one moment, we cannot always fit into one category: subject or object, above or below. A submissive is called a "sub," a word not unlike "subject." My hope is that subjectification, rather than denouncing objecthood, paves a way out of the dualistic thinking that compels people to choose one or the other. I, for one, do not want to choose. I want to try everything, to be everything. To marry my work. To be a devoted housewife. To cover myself in jewels and lace. To buy a partner satiny underwear. To have dinner on the table when my spouse comes home, and a plate laid out in front of me when I do.

I want it all – not just to have it all, but to be it all. If women can only exist in one term of a binary, one side of a verb, how can we ever be subjects in the full sense of the word? How can anyone?

Dancing With Words

Anarchist writer and activist Emma Goldman is sometimes quoted as saying, "If I can't dance, I don't want to be part of your revolution." Philosopher Jacques Derrida interpreted this to mean that we cannot confine a woman to one place, writing: "That which will not be pinned down by truth ... is, in truth, feminine."[9]

I myself don't want to be part of the revolution if I cannot dance with language, if it will pin me down. I need room to pirouette between punctuation marks, to leap over letters, and to limbo under lines dividing false dichotomies. I am not looking to rigidly reverse our sentences to contain a female subject and male object. I am looking to open possibilities for actions that defy the "male subject, female object" structure, including those that look beyond "male" and "female." There is no truth about what is feminine – or masculine – except that it cannot be pinned down by truth. We are all everything.

One step in this revolution in how we speak and act, however, is affording women the subject role in more statements, whether the verb is "look," "desire," or something unrelated to sex. I have focused on sex because how we view sex shapes how we view bodies and, consequently, people. But this must be done in all areas. We can work toward equality in the bedroom and the boardroom and every room by changing how we frame the narrative: to talk more about what women desire and less about what men desire from them. To talk less about what women look like and more about what they look at. To refrain from defining women and let them define themselves. To stop trying to fix women and work together to fix the world.

We are still allowed to write ourselves into the object role. But even then, we are subjects writing the sentence: "I write." With each verb in this book, with each active-voice chapter, I am writing myself into being. If the nature of things is the nature of words, we can change how things work through the words we write and speak. We can even change nature, not just as we conceive of it, but as we conceive it. If we write women into the active voice, if we conceive our children and brainchildren from "hell yes," what comes out of us will have a wholly different constitution.

Does woman exist? That's up to us. That depends on the stories we write. That is why I write: to speak myself into existence. To inhabit the active voice. Women are speaking themselves into existence each moment. It's up to us if we listen or if we think, "she doesn't know" or "she is out of her mind." I cannot tell any woman how to define herself. But what I can say is this: Woman can only exist as everything. We cannot exist as "the feminine." We cannot exist as the moon or sun. Woman cannot exist as the engulfer or the penetrated, as the commodity or the consumer. Because that is not existence. That is non-existence. That is erasure, confinement, self-denial. As long as we attempt to define a woman, she will not be afforded the right to exist.

A woman is simply this: She is the one writing herself into being. She is someone who begins a sentence with "she," fills in the rest with all she feels and thinks, then writes a new one. We must leave the question of what a woman is open-ended. We must let women themselves fill in the blanks. We must let each woman be a subject and an object as she wants, but always the author of the sentence.

Does woman exist? She always has and never will. Bodies have always existed. The minds and hearts that live in these bodies, with their endless and inimitable stories, have existed. Yet the moment we try to fit a woman into the dictionary, she will create a new language. Any subject will. "I" is not meant to be defined. Even the dictionary leaves much room for self-definition.

I (pron): the one who is speaking or writing.[10]

Anyone, anything can be that one. And nobody can ever be The One. Nor would we want to. There is freedom in being undefinable. In escaping illumination. In dancing. English cannot do a person justice. It will never capture us all, with its so-called dualities that are really singularities paired with negations, its slicing of sentences into superior subject and inferior object. Still, we can become creative and use the language we know in new ways.

Today, society is structured around the metaphor of "man penetrates woman." It's the framework for gender in all areas:

Male subject, verb, female object. Man desires woman. Man dominates woman. Man owns woman.

Once we flip that fundamental sentence, what seemed like objective reality becomes just one interpretation. The female body goes from a passive source of pain to a powerful source of pleasure. We begin to question gender and all binaries. Queer sexualities no longer appear unnatural. Nor do people who buck gender roles. More sentences can be flipped.

Flipped, twisted, and reordered. And rewritten over again.

We need not invert every sentence, as long as we have space to hop around to different spots in it. And outside it.

Still, it's sometimes fun to rebel and switch up the usual ordering of words. When I get married, I'd like the officiant to say, "You may now kiss the groom."

I hope one day, there will be weddings, non-monogamous commitment ceremonies, and everything in between where subject and object positions are shared.

As in, "You may now kiss each other."

Notes

Preface
1. Google Dictionary (2023). "Objectification."

1 I Walk: My Path Out of Objecthood
1. Jacques Lacan (1990). *Television: A Challenge to the Psychoanalytic Establishment*. Norton.
2. Jacques Lacan (1975). *Le Séminaire, Livre XX. Encore, 1972–73*. Seuil.
3. Ibid.
4. Perry M. Rogers (2003). *Aspects of Western Civilization: Problems and Sources in History*. Pearson.

2 I Feel: My Body's Size Doesn't Matter Because I Have a Big Heart
1. Alison Goldman (2012). "What Men Think about Women's Bodies." *Glamour*, https://www.glamour.com/gallery/what-men-think-about-womens-bodies
2. Redbook (2017). "11 Surprising Things Men Do – and Don't – Notice about Your Body." *Redbook*, https://www.redbookmag.com/love-sex/relationships/a12889/what-guys-notice
3. Cosmo team (2006). "Feel Great Naked." *Cosmopolitan*, https://

www.cosmopolitan.com/uk/love-sex/a532/feel-great-naked
-67203

4. Sara Halprin (1995). *Look at My Ugly Face: Myths and Musings on Beauty*. Viking.

5. Carol Emery Normandi and Lauralee Roark (2001). *Over It: A Teen's Guide to Getting Beyond Obsessions with Food and Weight*. New World Library.

6. Rebecca Traister (2005). "'Real Beauty' – Or Really Smart Marketing?" *Salon*, https://www.salon.com/2005/07/22/dove_2

7. Dove US (2013). "Dove Real Beauty Sketches | You're More Beautiful than You Think (3mins)." YouTube, https://www.youtube.com/watch?v=XpaOjMXyJGk&ab_channel=DoveUS

8. Dove Indonesia (2015). "Choose Beautiful." YouTube, https://www.youtube.com/watch?v=W07P3i5Yaak&ab_channel=DoveIndonesia

9. Lane Bryant (2015). "We're Taking Back the Definition of Sexy. Who's With Us? #ImNoAngel." Facebook, https://www.facebook.com/watch/?v=10153404856407018

10. Alanna Vagianos (2015). "14 Women Pose Naked to Redefine 'American Beauty' on Their Own Terms." *The Huffington Post*, https://www.huffpost.com/entry/women-pose-naked-to-redefine-american-beauty-on-their-own-terms_n_55ae8994e4b0a9b94852ad67

11. "How to Enter" (2022). Big Beautiful Women Pageant International, https://bbwpageantinternational.com/about-us; "Areas of Competition" (2022). Miss Voluptuous Pageants, https://www.missvoluptuouspageants.com/competition

12. Zach Johnson (2015). "Jon Stewart Mocks Media's Focus on Caitlyn Jenner's Appearance: 'Your Looks Are the Only Thing We Care About.'" *E! News*, https://www.eonline.com/news/662664/jon-stewart-mocks-media-s-focus-on-caitlyn-jenner-s-appearance-your-looks-are-the-only-thing-we-care-about

13. Carter Brown and Diamond Stylz (2020). "Interview with Carter Brown and Diamond Stylz." University of Minnesota Libraries, Jean-Nickolaus Tretter Collection in Gay, Lesbian, Bisexual

and Transgender Studies, https://umedia.lib.umn.edu/item
/p16022coll97:204

14. EFF YOUR BEAUTY STANDARDS (@effyourbeautystandards)
(2021). "@a.m.hanna." Instagram, https://www.instagram.com
/p/CX4tsPEg-Zs

15. EFF YOUR BEAUTY STANDARDS (@effyourbeautystandards)
(2018). "Indeed." Instagram, https://www.instagram.com/p/Be
-4Bx-lj18

16. Melissa A. Fabello (2015). "What If Body Positivity Doesn't
Work? How about Body Neutrality?" *Ravishly*, https://www
.ravishly.com/2015/08/21/what-if-body-acceptance-doesnt
-work-how-about-body-neutrality

3 I Reveal: Freeing the Person Behind the Nipple

1. Leah Rose Chernikoff (2014). "Talking Nipple Selfies with Cara
Delevingne and Jourdan Dunn." *Elle*, https://www.elle.com
/fashion/news/a19343/nipple-selfies-cara-delevingne-jourdan
-dunn

2. WILLOW (@OfficialWillow) (2015). "When did the women's
body start being something to hide?" Twitter, https://twitter
.com/OfficialWillow/status/558635492007505920

3. Barry R. Komisaruk, Nan Wise, Eleni Frangos, Wen-Ching Liu,
Kachina Allen, and Stuart Brody (2011). "Women's Clitoris,
Vagina, and Cervix Mapped on the Sensory Cortex: fMRI
Evidence." *The Journal of Sexual Medicine*, https://www.ncbi
.nlm.nih.gov/pmc/articles/PMC3186818

4. Cleveland Clinic (2022). "Benefits of Breastfeeding," https://
my.clevelandclinic.org/health/articles/15274-benefits-of
-breastfeeding

5. Laura Mulvey (1975). "Visual Pleasure and Narrative Cinema."
Screen, https://academic.oup.com/screen/article-abstract/16
/3/6/1603296

6. Sara M. Lindberg, Janet Shibley Hyde, and Nita Mary McKinley
(2006). "A Measure of Objectified Body Consciousness for
Preadolescent and Adolescent Youth." *Psychology of Women*

Quarterly,   https://journals.sagepub.com/doi/10.1111/j.1471
-6402.2006.00263.x

7. Valentina Boursier, Francesca Gioia, and Mark D. Griffiths
(2020). "Objectified Body Consciousness, Body Image Control
in Photos, and Problematic Social Networking: The Role of
Appearance Control Beliefs." *Frontiers in Psychology*, https://
www.frontiersin.org/articles/10.3389/fpsyg.2020.00147/full

8. Jenny Kutner (2014). "'Maybe America Just Needs a Big Blast
of Boobies': Lina Esco Tells Salon about Her Topless Crusade
to Free the Nipple." *Salon*, https://www.salon.com/2014/12/16
/maybe_america_just_needs_a_big_blast_of_boobies_lina_esco
_tells_salon_about_her_topless_crusade_to_free_the_nipple

9. Lina Esco (2013). "Why I Made a Film Called *Free the Nipple*
and Why I'm Being Censored in America." *The Huffington Post*,
https://www.huffpost.com/entry/free-the-nipple_b_4415859

10. Gotopless.org (2022). "Topless Laws," https://gotopless.org
/topless-laws

11. Jenn Selby (2014). "Scout Willis Topless Instagram Protest:
Bruce Willis and Demi Moore's Daughter Opposes Female
Nudity Policy." *The Independent*, https://www.independent.co.uk
/news/people/scout-willis-topless-instagram-protest-daughter
-of-bruce-willis-and-demi-moore-demonstrates-against-social
-media-policy-on-female-nudity-9452552.html

12. Rihanna (@rihanna) (2014). "'@TheFashionLaw: . @Scout_
Willis is protesting Rihanna's Instagram ban and looks hot
while doing it." Twitter, https://twitter.com/rihanna/status
/471788131973222400; Caitlin White (2014). "Miley Joins
#FreeTheNipple with a Completely Topless Instagram Photo."
MTV, https://www.mtv.com/news/y6sqs9/miley-cyrus-topless
-photo-instagram

13. Gothamist (2017). "NSFW Photos: Women 'Free The Nip' for
10th Annual Go Topless Parade In NYC," https://gothamist
.com/arts-entertainment/photos/nsfw-photos-women-free-the
-nip-for-10th-annual-go-topless-parade-in-nyc; Christopher
Mathias (2014). "NYC Book Club Goes Topless 'To Make

Reading Sexy,' Succeeds (NSFW PHOTOS)." *The Huffington Post*, https://www.huffpost.com/entry/topless-book-club-new -york-photos-nsfw_n_5267320

14. Tish Weinstock (2015). "Free the Nipple Icelandic Style." *Vice ID*, https://i-d.vice.com/en/article/a3g7mk/free-the-nipple -icelandic-style

15. Anne Branigin (2022). "An Adidas Ad Showed Bare Breasts. Is That Liberating or Exploitative?" *The Washington Post*, https:// www.washingtonpost.com/lifestyle/2022/02/10/adidas-bare -breast-ad

16. Freethenipple (2016). "Use promo code: 'thanks' for 20% off today! @ Freethenipple.com." Instagram, https://www.instagram .com/p/BM4nYRkhwDv

17. Alice Newell-Hanson (2015). "Topless Feminism Is Not the Only Feminism." *Vice ID*, https://i-d.vice.com/en/article/8xnvz3 /toplessness-vs-feminism

18. *Playboy* (2020). "Riley Ticotin: Playmate," https://www.playboy .com/app/riley_ticotin; Esquire Editors (2015). "10 Popular Instagram Models Bare it All for Treats! Magazine (NSFW)." *Esquire*, https://www.esquire.com/style/mens-fashion/news /a40443/instagram-models-naked-treats-nsfw

19. Annie Martin (2016). "Kim Kardashian Defends Nude Selfie: 'I Am Empowered by My Body.'" *UPI*, https://www.upi.com /Entertainment_News/2016/03/09/Kim-Kardashian-defends -nude-selfie-I-am-empowered-by-my-body/7531457556434

20. SI Swimsuit (2018). "In Her Own Words: SI Swimsuit Models Celebrate More than Just Their Bodies in Candid Project." *Sports Illustrated*, https://swimsuit.si.com/swimnews/in-her -own-words-sports-illustrated-swimsuit

21. Erin Vanderhoof (2018). "Meet the First Sports Illustrated Swimsuit Issue of the #MeToo Era." *Vanity Fair*, https://www .vanityfair.com/style/2018/02/sports-illustrated-swimsuit -metoo-era

22. Eyewitness News (2021). "Family Says Daughter's 2nd-Grade Teacher Ripped Hijab Off Her Head in NJ School." *ABC*, https://

abc7.com/teacher-pulls-off-hijab-muslim-maplewood-seth
-boyden-elementary-school/11103242

23. Frantz Fanon (2004). "Algeria Unveiled." In *Decolonization: Perspectives from Now and Then (Rewriting Histories)*. Ed. Prasenjit Duara. Routledge.

24. The Daily Show with Trevor Noah (2016). "Dalia Mogahed: Understanding American Muslims and the Media's Coverage of Terrorism." Comedy Central, https://www.cc.com/video/ju44t3 /the-daily-show-with-trevor-noah-dalia-mogahed -understanding-american-muslims-and-the-media-s-coverage -of-terrorism

25. Jacques Lacan (1990). *Television: A Challenge to the Psychoanalytic Establishment*. Norton.

26. Perry M. Rogers (2003). *Aspects of Western Civilization: Problems and Sources in History*. Pearson.

27. Film.com Staff (2010). "Interview: Hugh Hefner: Playboy, Activist and Rebel." *MTV News*, https://www.mtv.com /news/muotbx/interview-hugh-hefner-playboy-activist-and -rebel

28. Gail Dines and Eric Silverman (2022). "Hugh Hefner's Playboy Empire Was Built on the Abuse of Women." *Ms*, https:// msmagazine.com/2022/01/28/hugh-hefner-playboy-feminist -women-rape-abuse-sexual-assault

29. Michelle Smith (2017). "Playboy, Brooke Shields and the Fetishisation of Young Girls." *The Conversation*, https:// theconversation.com/playboy-brooke-shields-and-the -fetishisation-of-young-girls-85255

30. Maria Del Russo (2017). "How Hugh Hefner Helped Me Embrace My Sexuality." *Refinery29*, https://www.refinery29.com/en-gb /hugh-hefner-feminist-playboy-sexual-revolution

31. Planet Prudence | Self Love (@planetprudence) (2020). Instagram, https://www.instagram.com/p/B--MOZIAIih

32. Jaime M. Cloud and Carin Perilloux (2014). "Bodily Attractiveness as a Window to Women's Fertility and Reproductive Value." *Evolutionary Perspectives on Human Sexual Psychology and*

Behavior, https://wou.edu/wp/cloudj/files/2019/09/Bodily
-Attractiveness-Chapter.pdf

33. *The Christian Standard Bible* (2017). Holman Bible Publishers;
The Holy Bible: Contemporary English Version (2006). American
Bible Society; *The Holy Bible: English Standard Version* (2016).
Crossway Bibles.
34. Google Dictionary (2023). "Bosom."
35. Neotantra is a modern set of tantra-inspired beliefs and
practices originating from British colonialism in India. There
are many issues with the neotantra movement, which I describe
in Chapter 9. However, I am sharing this piece of neotantric
philosophy because it was helpful to me. See Diana Richardson
(2004). *Tantric Orgasm for Women.* Destiny Books.

4 I Look: Reclaiming the Dick Pic

1. Full Frontal with Samantha Bee (2017). "A Penis PSA." YouTube,
https://www.youtube.com/watch?v=BeWpX-ypSls&ab_channel
=FullFrontalwithSamanthaBee
2. Kristen Sollee (2015). "What Guys Think Happens When They
Send A Dick Pic." *Bustle,* https://www.bustle.com/articles/79177
-what-guys-really-think-happens-when-they-send-a-dick-pic
-according-to-buzzfeed
3. Ellie Krupnick (2015). "This Is What Women Really Think of
Dick Pics." *Mic,* https://www.mic.com/articles/110498/this-is
-why-guys-shouldn-t-send-women-dick-pics
4. FoxyBabeee_2021 (2021). "What the Fuck Is That?" *iFunny,*
https://ifunny.co/picture/what-the-fuck-is-that-like-what-you
-don-t-wMHSauFJ8
5. Rachel Zarrell (2014). "This Girl Had the Perfect Response to
an Unsolicited Dick Pic." *Buzzfeed,* https://www.buzzfeed.com
/rachelzarrell/hot-cheeto-with-the-powder-licked-off
6. Wickydkewl (2015). "Women React to Dick Pics." YouTube,
https://www.youtube.com/watch?v=F2ZnCrUvvKA
7. Nina Bahadur (2015). "This Is How Women React to Dick Pics."
The Huffington Post, https://www.huffpost.com/entry/women

-react-to-dick-pics-with-horror_n_6661402; Emma Cueto (2015). "This Is What Happens When Women React to Dick Pics." *Bustle*, https://www.bustle.com/articles/64009-women -react-to-dick-pics-video-is-hilarious-and-should-cure-guys-of -the-idea-their

8. Yael Bame (2017). "53% of Millennial Women Have Received a Naked Photo from a Man." *YouGov*, https://today.yougov .com/topics/society/articles-reports/2017/10/09/53-millennial -women-have-received-dick-pic

9. Jessica Ringrose, Kaitlyn Regehr, and Sophie Whitehead (2021). "Teen Girls' Experiences Negotiating the Ubiquitous Dick Pic: Sexual Double Standards and the Normalization of Image Based Sexual Harassment." *Sex Roles*, https://link.springer.com/article /10.1007/s11199-021-01236-3

10. Susanna Paasonen and Jenny Sundén (2021). "Shameless Dicks: On Male Privilege, Dick Pic Scandals, and Public Exposure." *First Monday*, https://firstmonday.org/ojs/index.php/fm/article /download/11654/10109

11. Seamus Duff (2017). "Harvey Weinstein 'almost died after gastric band failed at Naomi Campbell's party – and was nicknamed The Pig', Ex Driver Reveals." *The Mirror*, https://www.mirror .co.uk/3am/celebrity-news/harvey-weinsteins-ex-driver-recalls -11387121; Nick Pisa (2017). "'I DROVE MR SEX PIG' Harvey Weinstein's Former-Chauffeur Reveals More of the Film Chief's Sick Secrets.'" *The Sun*, https://www.thesun.co.uk/news/4738211 /harvey-weinsteins-driver-sex-claims

12. Jimmy Kimmel Live (2017). "Howard Stern on Harvey Weinstein." YouTube, https://www.youtube.com/watch?v=p3OuM8dY6Fw &ab_channel=JimmyKimmelLive

13. Late Night with Seth Meyers (2018). "Trump Backs Roy Moore; Charlie Rose Fired for Sexual Harassment: A Closer Look." YouTube, https://www.youtube.com/watch?v=mewW_pRSgEc &ab_channel=LateNightwithSethMeyers

14. This chapter does focus on men and, largely, women's relationships with them because the dick pic is such a gendered phenomenon.

There are additional places in this book where I speak of genitals in a gendered manner because I'm discussing them in relation to gendered tropes. I hope readers can forgive me and understand that my aim is not to further cement cultural associations between genitals and gendered traits but to acknowledge and unpack them. When I don't have the language or space to follow the letter of the law of inclusion, I still strive to stay loyal to the spirit of it.

15. Google Dictionary (2023). "Beauty."
16. Celebitchy (2009). "Jason Mraz: Men 'Don't Understand Your Addiction to Celebrity Gossip,'" https://www.celebitchy.com /54108/jason_mraz_men_dont_understand_your_addition_to _celebrity_gossip
17. *Seinfeld*, "The Apology" (2009). Season 9.
18. Molly Mulshine (2014). "Less Is More: The Hard Data on Men & Women's Sexting Preferences." *The Observer*, https://observer .com/2014/02/less-is-more-the-hard-data-on-men-womens -sexting-preferences
19. Robert Heinsohn (2015). "Why Are Male Birds More Colorful than Female Birds?" *Scientific American*, https://www .scientificamerican.com/article/why-are-male-birds-more-c
20. College of Biological Sciences (2015). "Frequently Asked Questions." University of Minnesota, https://cbs.umn.edu /research/labs/packer/faq#
21. Nature (2021). "Peacock Fact Sheet." *PBS*, https:// www.pbs.org/wnet/nature/blog/peacock-fact-sheet; Nicole Cosgrove (2022). "Male vs Female Peacocks: What's The Difference (With Pictures)." *Petkeen*, https://petkeen.com/male-vs-female -peacocks
22. Evolution Library (2001). "Tale of the Peacock." *PBS*, https:// www.pbs.org/wgbh/evolution/library/01/6/l_016_09.html
23. Pascal Gagneux (2023). "Penis Size and Morphology." Center for Academic Research and Training in Anthropogeny, https://carta .anthropogeny.org/moca/topics/penis-size-and-morphology
24. Josh Clark and Chuck Bryant (2020). *Stuff You Should Know*. Flatiron Books.

25. Sehoya Cotner and Deena Wassenberg (2020). *The Evolution and Biology of Sex*. University of Minnesota Library, https://open.lib.umn.edu/evolutionbiology

26. Daniel Bergner (2014). *What Do Women Want?: Adventures in the Science of Female Desire*. Ecco.

27. Abigail Anderson, Sophia Chilczuk, Kaylie Nelson, Roxanne Ruther, and Cara Wall-Scheffler (2023). "The Myth of Man the Hunter: Women's Contribution to the Hunt across Ethnographic Eontexts." *PLOS ONE*, https://journals.plos.org/plosone/article?id=10.1371/journal.pone.0287101

28. Christopher Ryan and Cacilda Jetha (2012). *Sex At Dawn: The Prehistoric Origins of Modern Sexuality*. Harper Perennial.

29. Film.com Staff (2010). "Interview: Hugh Hefner: Playboy, Activist and Rebel." *MTV News*, https://www.mtv.com/news/muotbx/interview-hugh-hefner-playboy-activist-and-rebel

30. Guerrilla Girls (1989). "Do Women Have to Be Naked to Get into the Met. Museum?" National Gallery of Art, https://www.nga.gov/collection/art-object-page.139856.html

31. Alexxa Gotthardt (2018). "Why Ancient Greek Sculptures Have Small Penises." *Artsy*, https://www.artsy.net/article/artsy-editorial-ancient-greek-sculptures-small-penises

32. Ruth Allen (2015). "The Difficulty of 'Defining Beauty.'" *Apollo Magazine*, https://www.apollo-magazine.com/the-difficulty-of-defining-beauty-british-museum

33. Elias N. Azar (2016). "Adonis." *World History Encyclopedia*, https://www.worldhistory.org/Adonis; V. Pirenne-Delforge and André Motte (2016). "Adonis." *Oxford Classical Dictionary*, https://oxfordre.com/classics/display/10.1093/acrefore/9780199381135.001.0001/acrefore-9780199381135-e-66

34. Amanda B. (2012). "When Did This Become Hotter than This." *Know Your Meme*, https://knowyourmeme.com/memes/when-did-this-become-hotter-than-this

35. Jonathan McAloon (2018). "Did We Miss the Point of One of the World's Most Famous Sculptures?" *Artsy*, https://www.artsy.net/article/artsy-editorial-point-one-worlds-famous-sculptures

36. Box Office Mojo (2022). "Magic Mike," https://www
.boxofficemojo.com/release/rl2657125889
37. Pornhub Insights (2017). "Girls Who Like Boys Who Like Boys,"
https://www.pornhub.com/insights/girls-like-boys-who-like
-boys; Justin Lehmiller (2017). "How Many Straight Men Watch
Gay Porn? And How Many Gay Guys Watch Straight Porn?" *Sex
and Psychology*, https://www.sexandpsychology.com/blog/2017
/4/5/how-many-straight-men-watch-gay-porn-and-how-many
-gay-guys-watch-straight-porn
38. Museum of Sex (2020). "NSFW: FEMALE GAZE," https://www
.museumofsex.com/portfolio_page/nsfw-female-gaze
39. Bellesa (2023). https://www.bellesa.co/videos
40. Lisa Wade (2014). "A Little Theory of Homophobia." *Sociological
Images*, https://thesocietypages.org/socimages/2014/12/28
/a-little-theory-of-homophobia
41. National Center for Health Statistics (2018). "Sexual Orientation
Among U.S. Adults Aged 18 and Over, By Sex and Age Group:
United States, 2018," https://www.cdc.gov/nchs/data/nhis
/sexual_orientation/ASI_2018_STWebsite_Tables-508.pdf
42. Flora Oswald, Alex Lopes, Kaylee Skoda, Cassandra L. Hesse,
and Cory L. Pedersen (2019). "I'll Show You Mine So You'll
Show Me Yours: Motivations and Personality Variables in
Photographic Exhibitionism." *The Journal of Sex Research*,
https://www.tandfonline.com/doi/full/10.1080/00224499.2019
.1639036
43. Truly, I'm not. Just as the male gaze doesn't actually represent
men, there's no "female gaze" to represent women. I am not
encouraging women to look at male bodies, which are just one
potential object of the gaze, but to discover and enjoy whatever
they like looking at.

5 I Ask: From Consent to Desire

1. Oxford English Dictionary (1989). "Consent," https://web
.archive.org/web/20211106040735/https://www.oed.com/oed2
/00047775

2. Consent Is Respect (2017). "Affirmative Consent Laws (Yes Means Yes) State by State," https://web.archive.org/web/20220507233701/https://affirmativeconsent.com/affirmative-consent-laws-state-by-state; Andrew Jeong (2022). "Under Spain's New Sexual Consent Law, Only Yes Is Yes." *The Washington Post*, https://www.washingtonpost.com/world/2022/08/26/spain-only-yes-law-sexual-consent

3. Samantha Rogers (2015). "How This School's Old Anti-Rape Poster Sparked New Controversy." *The Daily Dot*, https://www.dailydot.com/irl/anti-rape-poster-reddit-conversations

4. Inga Schowengerdt, Sharon Lamb, and Charlotte Brown (2021). "Problematizing Consent Campaigns in the #METOO Era." *Gender and Women's Studies*, https://riverapublications.com/article/problematizing-consent-campaigns-in-the-metoo-era

5. The United States Department of Justice Archives (2012). "An Updated Definition of Rape." https://www.justice.gov/archives/opa/blog/updated-definition-rape

6. Naomi Wolf (2002). *The Beauty Myth: How Images of Beauty Are Used Against Women*. Harper Perennial.

7. Susan Brownmiller (1975). *Against Our Will: Men, Women, and Rape*. Ballantine Books.

8. Centers for Disease Control and Prevention (2020). "Intimate Partner Violence, Sexual Violence, and Stalking among Men," https://www.cdc.gov/violenceprevention/intimatepartnerviolence/men-ipvsvandstalking.html

9. Michele C. Black, Kathleen C. Basile, Matthew J. Breiding, Sharon G. Smith, Mikel L. Walters, Melissa T. Merrick, Jieru Chen, and Mark R. Stevens (2011). "The National Intimate Partner and Sexual Violence Survey: 2010 Summary Report." Centers for Disease Control and Prevention, https://www.cdc.gov/violenceprevention/pdf/nisvs_report2010-a.pdf

10. Caroline Catlin (2016). "When You're a Woman Raped by a Woman." *Vice*, https://www.vice.com/en/article/7855zx/when-youre-a-woman-raped-by-a-woman

11. Justin Lehmiller (2020). *Tell Me What You Want: The Science of*

Sexual Desire and How It Can Help You Improve Your Sex Life.
Hachette Go. (The statistics I cite are also from a private email
exchange with Lehmiller.)

12. Leif Edward Ottesen Kennair, Joy P. Wyckoff, Kelly Asao, David
M. Buss, and Mons Bendixen (2018). "Why Do Women Regret
Casual Sex More than Men Do?" *Personality and Individual
Differences*, https://www.sciencedirect.com/science/article/pii
/S0191886918300539?via%3Dihub

13. Michael Safi (2016). "Sex and Consent: Poll Finds Victim-Blaming
Rife among Young Australians." *The Guardian*, https://www
.theguardian.com/lifeandstyle/2016/feb/22/sex-and-consent
-poll-finds-victim-blaming-rife-among-young-australians

14. Bari Weiss (2018). "Aziz Ansari Is Guilty. Of Not Being a Mind
Reader." *The New York Times*, https://www.nytimes.com/2018
/01/15/opinion/aziz-ansari-babe-sexual-harassment.html

15. Katie Way (2018). "I Went on a Date with Aziz Ansari. It Turned
into the Worst Night of My Life." *Babe*, https://babe.net/2018/01
/13/aziz-ansari-28355

16. Google Dictionary (2023). "Put Out."

17. Robin Hanson (2018). "Two Types of Envy." *Overcoming Bias*,
https://www.overcomingbias.com/2018/04/two-types-of-envy
.html

18. Ross Douthat (2018). "The Redistribution of Sex." *The New York
Times*, https://www.nytimes.com/2018/05/02/opinion/incels
-sex-robots-redistribution.html

19. Nicholas C. Borgogna, Emma C. Lathan, and Ryon C. McDermott
(2021). "She Asked for It: Hardcore Porn, Sexism, and Rape Myth
Acceptance." *Violence Against Women*, https://journals.sagepub
.com/doi/abs/10.1177/10778012211037378 (The statistics cited
are from a private email communication with Borgogna.)

20. AP (1989). "Defendant Acquitted of Rape; 'She Asked for It,'
Juror Says." *The New York Times*, https://www.nytimes.com
/1989/10/07/us/defendant-acquitted-of-rape-she-asked-for-it
-juror-says.html

21. Valeriya Safronova (2018). "Lawyer in Rape Trial Links Thong

with Consent, and Ireland Erupts." *The New York Times*, https://www.nytimes.com/2018/11/15/world/europe/ireland-underwear-rape-case-protest.html

22. Google Dictionary (2023). "Desire."

23. Perry M. Rogers (2003). *Aspects of Western Civilization: Problems and Sources in History*. Pearson.

24. OKCupid (2015). "A Woman's Advantage." OKCupid Dating Blog, https://theblog.okcupid.com/a-womans-advantage-82d5074dde2d

25. Jon Birger (2021). *Make Your Move: The New Science of Dating and Why Women Are in Charge*. BenBella Books.

6 I Create: My Body, My Voice

1. Yale Medicine (2022). "Endometriosis," https://www.yalemedicine.org/conditions/endometriosis

2. Abby Norman (2018). *Ask Me About My Uterus: A Quest to Make Doctors Believe in Women's Pain*. Bold Type Books.

3. Lorraine Johnson, Mira Shapiro, Sylvia Janicki, Jennifer Mankoff, and Raphael B. Stricker (2023). "Does Biological Sex Matter in Lyme Disease? The Need for Sex-Disaggregated Data in Persistent Illness." *International Journal of General Medicine*, https://www.tandfonline.com/doi/full/10.2147/ijgm.s406466

4. Maya Dusenbery (2018). *Doing Harm: The Truth about How Bad Medicine and Lazy Science Leave Women Dismissed, Misdiagnosed, and Sick*. HarperOne.

5. Joyce T. DiFranco and Marilyn Curl (2014). "Healthy Birth Practice #5: Avoid Giving Birth on Your Back and Follow Your Body's Urge to Push." *The Journal of Perinatal Education*, https://www.ncbi.nlm.nih.gov/pmc/articles/PMC4235063

6. Milli Hill (2021). *Give Birth Like a Feminist: Your Body. Your Baby. Your Choices*. HQ.

7. Google Translate (2023).

8. I am using the terms "birthing people" and "parents" to acknowledge that not all people giving birth are women. I also say "parents," plural, to emphasize the major role that partners

play in birth. In some places, I say "mothers" to discuss how the objectification of women specifically enters medical clinics.

9. Sally Placksin (2000). *Mothering the New Mother: Women's Feelings & Needs After Childbirth. A Support and Resource Guide.* William Morrow Paperbacks.
10. Melissa A. Thomasson and Jaret Treber (2008). "From Home to Hospital: The Evolution of Childbirth in the United States, 1928–1940." *Explorations in Economic History*, https://www.sciencedirect.com/science/article/abs/pii/S0014498307000241
11. Tracie White (2018). "Epidurals Increase in Popularity, Stanford Study Finds." *Scope*, https://scopeblog.stanford.edu/2018/06/26/epidurals-increase-in-popularity-stanford-study-finds
12. Our Health Service (2023). "Staying Active and Upright Positions during Labour," https://www2.hse.ie/pregnancy-birth/labour/preparing/staying-active-upright-positions
13. Tanya Djanogly, Jacqueline Nicholls, Melissa Whitten, and Anne Lanceley (2022). "Choice in Episiotomy – Fact or Fantasy: A Qualitative Study of Women's Experiences of the Consent Process." *BMC Pregnancy and Childbirth*, https://bmcpregnancychildbirth.biomedcentral.com/articles/10.1186/s12884-022-04475-8; Suzannah Weiss (2017). "These New Moms Say They Were Forced to Have C-Sections Without Their Consent." *Glamour*, https://www.glamour.com/story/new-moms-c-sections-without-consent
14. Ina May Gaskin (2003). *Ina May's Guide to Childbirth*. Bantam Books.
15. Ruth Zielinski, Kelly Ackerson, and Lisa Kane Low (2015). "Planned Home Birth: Benefits, Risks, and Opportunities." *International Journal of Women's Health*, https://www.ncbi.nlm.nih.gov/pmc/articles/PMC4399594
16. Molly Cora Enking (2018). "Women Are Being Cut during Childbirth without Need or Consent." City University of New York, https://academicworks.cuny.edu/cgi/viewcontent.cgi?article=1351&context=gj_etds#
17. Johns Hopkins Medicine (2022). "Episiotomy," https://www

.hopkinsmedicine.org/health/treatment-tests-and-therapies
/episiotomy

18. Hanna Ejegård, Elsa Lena Ryding, and Berit Sjogren (2008).
"Sexuality after Delivery with Episiotomy: A Long-Term Follow-
Up." *Gynecologic and Obstetric Investigation*, https://pubmed
.ncbi.nlm.nih.gov/18204265; Shiow-Ru Chang, Kuang-Ho
Chen, Ho-Hsiung Lin, Yu-Mei Y. Chao, and Yeur-Hur Lai (2011).
"Comparison of the Effects of Episiotomy and No Episiotomy
on Pain, Urinary Incontinence, and Sexual Function 3 Months
Postpartum: A Prospective Follow-Up Study." *International
Journal of Nursing Studies*, https://www.sciencedirect.com
/science/article/abs/pii/S0020748910002452; Lisa B. Signorello,
Bernard L. Harlow, Amy K. Chekos, and John T. Repke (2000).
"Midline Episiotomy and Anal Incontinence: Retrospective
Cohort Study." *British Medical Journal*, https://www.ncbi.nlm
.nih.gov/pmc/articles/PMC27253

19. Thomas W. Volscho (2010). "Sterilization Racism and Pan-Ethnic
Disparities of the Past Decade: The Continued Encroachment on
Reproductive Rights." *Wíčazo Ša Review*, https://www.jstor.org
/stable/40891307; Our Bodies Ourselves (2022); "A Brief History
of Birth Control in the U.S.," https://www.ourbodiesourselves
.org/health-info/a-brief-history-of-birth-control

20. Karina M. Shreffler, Julia McQuillan, Arthur L. Greil, and David
R. Johnson (2015). "Surgical Sterilization, Regret, and Race:
Contemporary Patterns." *Social Science Research*, https://www
.ncbi.nlm.nih.gov/pmc/articles/PMC4297312

21. Trevor Kirczenow MacDonald, Michelle Walks, MaryLynne
Biener, and Alanna Kibbe (2021). "Disrupting the Norms:
Reproduction, Gender Identity, Gender Dysphoria, and
Intersectionality." *The International Journal of Transgender
Health*, https://pubmed.ncbi.nlm.nih.gov/34918009

22. Julie Compton (2019). "Trans Dads Tell Doctors: 'You Can Be
a Man and Have a Baby.'" *NBC News*, https://www.nbcnews
.com/feature/nbc-out/trans-dads-tell-doctors-you-can-be-man
-have-baby-n1006906

23. Trevor MacDonald, Joy Noel-Weiss, Diana West, Michelle Walks, MaryLynne Biener, Alanna Kibbe, and Elizabeth Myler (2016). "Transmasculine Individuals' Experiences with Lactation, Chestfeeding, and Gender Identity: A Qualitative Study." *BMC Pregnancy and Childbirth*, https://bmcpregnancychildbirth.biomedcentral.com/articles/10.1186/s12884-016-0907-y

24. Pandora Pound, Rebecca Langford, and Rona Campbell (2016). "What Do Young People Think about Their School-Based Sex and Relationship Education? A Qualitative Synthesis of Young People's Views and Experiences." *BMJ Open*, https://bmjopen.bmj.com/content/6/9/e011329

25. Daniel Bergner (2014). *What Do Women Want?: Adventures in the Science of Female Desire*. Ecco.

26. Paul Joannides (2022). *The Guide to Getting It On*. Goofy Foot Press.

27. Gabrielle Blair (2022). *Ejaculate Responsibly: A Whole New Way to Think about Abortion*. Workman Publishing Company.

28. Jenny A. Higgins, Jessica N. Sanders, Mari Palta, and David K. Turok (2016). "Women's Sexual Function, Satisfaction, and Perceptions after Starting Long-Acting Reversible Contraceptives." *Obstetrics and Gynecology*, https://pubmed.ncbi.nlm.nih.gov/27741195

29. Crystal Raypole (2021). "Does Birth Control Affect Your Sex Drive? Here's What You Should Know." *Healthline*, https://www.healthline.com/health/birth-control/does-birth-control-affect-sex-drive

30. Andrew Goldstein, Caroline Pukall, Irwin Goldstein, and Jill Krapf (2023). *When Sex Hurts: Understanding and Healing Pelvic Pain*. Hachette Go.

31. Allison Behringer (2018). "Episode 1: Sex Hurts." *Bodies*, https://www.bodiespodcast.com/resource-pages/2018/8/28/episode-1-sex-hurts

32. Erin Blakemore (2019). "The First Birth Control Pill Used Puerto Rican Women as Guinea Pigs." *History*, https://www.history.com/news/birth-control-pill-history-puerto-rico-enovid; The

Pill (2022). "Eugenics and Birth Control." *PBS*, https://www
.pbs.org/wgbh/americanexperience/features/pill-eugenics-and
-birth-control

33. Leigh Senderowicz (2020). "Contraceptive Autonomy:
Conceptions and Measurement of a Novel Family Planning
Indicator." *Studies in Family Planning*, https://onlinelibrary
.wiley.com/doi/10.1111/sifp.12114

34. Oxford Learner's Dictionaries (2022). "Control," https://www
.oxfordlearnersdictionaries.com/us/definition/english/control

35. Loretta Ross (2006). "Understanding Reproductive Justice:
Transforming the Pro-Choice Movement." *Off Our Backs*,
https://www.proquest.com/docview/197138754

7 I Want: Why Buy the Cow When You Can Both Be Free?

1. Hip Online (2004). "Ciara – Goodies," https://www.hiponline
.com/645/ciara-goodies.html

2. *Liberated: The New Sexual Revolution* (2018).

3. Caitlin Flanagan (2006). "Are You There God? It's Me, Monica."
The Atlantic, https://www.theatlantic.com/magazine/archive
/2006/01/are-you-there-god-its-me-monica/304511

4. King James Bible (2017). Green World Classics.

5. Christopher Ryan and Cacilda Jetha (2012). *Sex at Dawn: The
Prehistoric Origins of Modern Sexuality*. Harper Perennial.

8 I Touch: Feeling Myself, the Other

1. The Editors and Rachel Varina (2022). "28 Masturbation Tips
That'll Maximize Your Pleasure." *Cosmopolitan*, https://www
.cosmopolitan.com/sex-love/advice/a1602/solo-sex

2. Jenny Block (2014). "The Most Important Thing Teen
Girls Should Do But Don't: Masturbate." *Jezebel*, https://
jezebel.com/the-most-important-thing-teen-girls-should-do-
but-dont-1563444100

3. Logan Levkoff (2012). "5 Reasons Every Woman Should Consider
Sex for One." *The Huffington Post*, https://www.huffpost

.com/entry/female-masturbation-sex-for-one_b_2213593; Faye M. Smith (2023). "Female Masturbation Techniques for Mind-Blowing Orgasms – and Why Getting Off Empowers Women." *Woman and Home*, https://www.womanandhome .com/health-wellbeing/sex/female-masturbation

4. Laci Green (2013). "Laci's Guide to ORGASM." YouTube, https:// www.youtube.com/watch?v=AepqPbvpsvo&ab_channel=lacigreen

5. Dorian Solot and Marshall Miller (2007). *I Love Female Orgasm: An Extraordinary Orgasm Guide*. Da Capo Press.

6. Alexander K.C. Leung and Lane M. Robson (1993). "Childhood Masturbation." *Clinical Pediatrics*, https://journals.sagepub .com/doi/abs/10.1177/000992289303200410

7. Emily Nagoski (2015). *Come as You Are: The Surprising New Science that Will Transform Your Sex Life*. Simon & Schuster.

8. Luce Irigaray (1985). "This Sex Which Is Not One." In *This Sex Which Is Not One*. Cornell University Press.

9. Carlin Ross (2013). "'Getting to Know Me' in Ms. Magazine." *Dodson and Ross*, https://www.dodsonandross.com/articles /getting-know-me-ms-magazine

10. Carlin Ross (2012). "The Power of Sisterhood." *Dodson and Ross*, https://www.dodsonandross.com/articles/power-sisterhood

11. Laura Bogush (2018). "Just Show Up for Yourself." *Dodson and Ross*, https://dodsonandross.com/articles/just-show-yourself

12. Betty Dodson (2015). "How Can I Stop Female Ejaculation?" *Dodson and Ross*, https://dodsonandross.com/articles/how-can -i-stop-female-ejaculation

13. Betty Dodson (2018). "Do You Believe the Female Sex Drive Exceeds the Male Sex Drive?" *Dodson and Ross*, https://www .dodsonandross.com/articles/category/creating-sexual-desire

14. Betty Dodson (2014). "Will a Vibrator Desensitize My Clitoris?" *Dodson and Ross*, https://www.dodsonandross.com/articles/will -vibrator-desensitize-my-clitoris

15. Carlin Ross (2013). "Orgasm: Men vs. Women." YouTube, https://www.youtube.com/watch?v=t1Vy3nUsd78&ab_channel =CarlinRoss

16. Betty Dodson (2014). "Will a Vibrator Desensitize My Clitoris?" *Dodson and Ross*, https://www.dodsonandross.com/articles/will-vibrator-desensitize-my-clitoris

17. Ruth La Ferla (2020). "You Are Your Safest Sex Partner. Betty Dodson Wants to Help." *The New York Times*, https://www.nytimes.com/2020/03/26/style/self-care/betty-dodson-masturbation.html

18. Arielle Pardes (2015). "7 Secrets of Female Masturbation." *Men's Health*, https://www.menshealth.com/sex-women/a19547144/7-secrets-female-masturbation

19. Shere Hite (1976). *The Hite Report: A National Study of Female Sexuality*. Seven Stories Press.

20. Alfred Kinsey (1998). *Sexual Behavior in the Human Female*. Indiana University Press.

21. International Society for Sexual Medicine (2023). "What Are Multiple Orgasms? How Common Are They?" https://www.issm.info/sexual-health-qa/what-are-multiple-orgasms-how-common-are-they; Morgan Mandriota (2023). "Yes, Men Can Have Multiple Orgasms: A Step-By-Step Guide." *MindBodyGreen*, https://www.mindbodygreen.com/articles/multiple-orgasms-for-men-guide

22. Google Dictionary (2023). "Naturalize."

23. Natasha (2015). "The Transformation of the Women Is Beautiful." *Dodson and Ross*, https://www.dodsonandross.com/articles/transformation-women-beautiful

24. Carlin Ross (2012). "The Power of Sisterhood." *Dodson and Ross*, https://www.dodsonandross.com/articles/power-sisterhood

25. Laura Bogush (2019). "A Gathering of Goddesses." *Dodson and Ross*, https://www.dodsonandross.com/articles/gathering-goddesses

9 I Define: Embody Your Divine Self

1. Laura Barcella (2014). "The Strange Truth about Orgasmic Meditation." *Refinery29*, https://www.refinery29.com/en-us/2014/03/63548/meditation-cult

2. Gary Schubach (2011). "TEDxSF – Nicole Daedone – Orgasm The Cure for Hunger." YouTube, https://www.youtube.com /watch?v=BZjRH1FmxfM&ab_channel=GarySchubach

3. Kendall Fisher (2015). "Dalai Lama Says If There Is a Female Dalai Lama in the Future, She Must Be 'Attractive' or She Is 'Not Much Use.'" *E! News*, https://www.eonline.com/news/699153 /dalai-lama-says-if-there-is-a-female-dalai-lama-in-the-future -she-must-be-attractive-or-she-is-not-much-use

4. Ibid.

5. Ellen Huet (2018). "The Dark Side of the Orgasmic Meditation Company." *Bloomberg*, https://www.bloomberg.com/news /features/2018-06-18/the-dark-side-of-onetaste-the-orgasmic -meditation-company

6. Ibid.

7. Nastaran Tavakoli-Far (2020). "Things Get Dark." *The Orgasm Cult*, https://www.bbc.co.uk/programmes/p091jn0h

8. Netflix (2022). *Orgasm Inc.*

9. Molli Mitchell (2022). "What Happened to OneTaste? Inside Female Orgasm Company." *Newsweek*, https://www.newsweek .com/what-happened-onetaste-nicole-daedone-orgasm-inc -netflix-1757854; Ellen Huet (2018). "FBI Is Probing OneTaste, a Sexuality Wellness Company," *Bloomberg*, https://www .bloomberg.com/news/articles/2018-11-13/fbi-is-probing -onetaste-a-sexuality-wellness-company; Guardian Staff and Agencies (2023). "US Founder of 'Orgasmic Meditation' Startup Indicted on Forced Labor Charges." *The Guardian*, https:// www.theguardian.com/us-news/2023/jun/06/onetaste-nicole -daedone-sex-abuse-cult-charged

10. David Deida (1997). *The Way of the Superior Man*. Sounds True.

11. GriffinMind (2022). "Andrew Tate High Value Men vs Women TateSpeech." YouTube, https://www.youtube.com/watch?v= hsLyQfCLeRw&ab_channel=GriffinMind

12. Bill Chappell (2023). "Andrew Tate Is Indicted on Human Trafficking and Rape Charges in Romania." *NPR*, https://www

.npr.org/2023/06/20/1183176707/andrew-tate-indicted-human
-trafficking-rape-romania

13. Anna Rova (@annarova) (2022). "I was always the cool girl."
    Instagram, https://www.instagram.com/p/CmDTyfvSmEa
14. Keith Ablow (2015). "J. Crew Plants the Seeds for Gender
    Identity." *Fox News*, https://www.foxnews.com/health/j-crew
    -plants-the-seeds-for-gender-identity
15. Mama Gena (2022), https://web.archive.org/web
    /20221208234751/https://mamagenas.com
16. Thomas P. Lowry and Thea Snyder Lowry (1976). *The Clitoris*.
    Warren H. Green, Inc.; Carly Cassella (2022). "We May Finally
    Know How Many Nerve Endings Are in The Human Clitoris."
    Science Alert, https://www.sciencealert.com/we-may-finally
    -know-how-many-nerve-endings-are-in-the-human-clitoris
17. Mama Gena (2018). "Violence Flourishes Without the Feminine,"
    https://mamagenas.com/violence
18. Regena Thomashauer (2016). *Pussy: A Reclamation*. Hay House,
    Inc.
19. I'm aware that one of the theorists this book draws from, Luce
    Irigaray, also suggests in her writing that women operate the
    way vulvas operate. I personally disagree with some of her work,
    too, and read it more symbolically than literally.

10 I Bleed: A Girl Becomes an Object Becomes a Subject

1. Thomas Laqueur (1992). *Making Sex: Body and Gender from the
   Greeks to Freud*. Harvard University Press.
2. Sigmund Freud (2017). *Three Essays on the Theory of Sexuality:
   The 1905 Edition*. Verso Books.
3. Girls Not Brides (2017). "Periods and Child Marriage: What
   Is the Link?" https://www.girlsnotbrides.org/articles/periods
   -child-marriage-link
4. Dartmouth Medical School (2008). "Etymology of Abdominal
   Visceral Terms," https://humananatomy.host.dartmouth.edu
   /BHA/public_html/resources/etymology/Pelvis.htm

5. WordReference.com (2023). "Mater" and "Matter," https://www
.wordreference.com

6. WordReference.com (2023). "Man," https://www.wordreference
.com

7. Catherine Malabou (2022). *Pleasure Erased: The Clitoris Unthought*. Polity.

8. Ntozake Shange (2022). "we need a god who bleeds now." *Voetica*, https://voetica.com/voetica.php?collection=2&poet= 829&poem=7163

9. Louis Althusser (1984). "Ideology and Ideological State Apparatuses." In *Essays on Ideology*. Verso.

10. I acknowledge that many women deal with real pain and support them in utilizing whatever helps them, including Band-Aid solutions. My issue is not with these products' existence or use but with their PR. See Suzannah Weiss (2020). "We Need to Stop Normalizing Period Pain." *Folks*, https://folks.pillpack.com /we-need-to-stop-normalizing-period-pain

11. rupi kaur (@rupikaur_) (2015). "Thank you @instagram for providing me with the exact response my work was created to critique." Instagram, https://www.instagram.com /p/0ovWwJHA6f

12. Sarah Ogden Trotta (2013). "5 Reasons Why Menstruation Is Awesome (Despite What We're Told)." *Everyday Feminism*, https:// everydayfeminism.com/2013/02/menstruation-is-awesome

13. Lara Cardoso (2020). "Everything You Need to Know about the Moon Cycle and Your Period." *Diva*, https://divacup.com/moon -cycle-and-your-period; Funk It Wellness (2020). "Seed Cycling with the MOON," https://funkitwellness.com/blogs/seedcycling /seed-cycling-with-the-moon

14. Tariro Mantsebo (2019). "Learning to Honour Our Sacred Menstruation." *Girls Globe*, https://www.girlsglobe.org/2019/05 /27/learning-honour-sacred-menstruation

15. UNICEF (2018). "FAST FACTS: Nine Things You Didn't Know about Menstruation," https://www.unicef.org/press-releases /fast-facts-nine-things-you-didnt-know-about-menstruation

16. Kathryn Watson (2019). "Period Syncing: Real Phenomenon or Popular Myth?" *Healthline*, https://www.healthline.com/health/womens-health/period-syncing; Suzannah Weiss (2017). "Surprise: Your Period Probably Doesn't Sync Up to Women You Hang Out With." *Glamour*, https://www.glamour.com/story/surprise-your-period-probably-doesnt-sync-up-to-women-you-hang-out-with

17. Meg Walters (2021). "Is There Really a Connection Between Your Menstrual Cycle and the Moon?" *Healthline*, https://www.healthline.com/health/womens-health/menstrual-cycle-and-the-moon; Maria Cohut (2021). "Menstrual Cycles and Lunar Cycles: Is There a Link?" *Medical News Today*, https://www.medicalnewstoday.com/articles/menstrual-cycles-and-lunar-cycles-is-there-a-link

18. Leandro Casiraghi, Ignacio Spiousas, Gideon P. Dunster, Kaitlyn McGlothlen, Eduardo Fernández-Duque, Claudia Valeggia, and Horacio O. de la Iglesia (2021). "Moonstruck Sleep: Synchronization of Human Sleep with the Moon Cycle under Field Conditions." *Science*, https://www.science.org/doi/10.1126/sciadv.abe0465; Rachel Nall (2019). "What Are the Benefits of Sunlight?" *Healthline*, https://www.healthline.com/health/depression/benefits-sunlight

11 I Grow: The Politics of Pubes

1. Tami S. Rowen, Thomas W. Gaither, Mohannad A. Awad, E. Charles Osterberg, Alan W. Shindel, and Benjamin N. Breyer (2016). "Pubic Hair Grooming Prevalence and Motivation among Women in the United States." *JAMA Dermatology*, https://jamanetwork.com/journals/jamadermatology/fullarticle/2529574

2. Otto J. Placik and John P. Arkins (2014). "Plastic Surgery Trends Parallel *Playboy* Magazine: The Pudenda Preoccupation." *Aesthetic Surgery Journal*, https://academic.oup.com/asj/article/34/7/1083/256333

3. Marina Hyde (2013). "How Sex and the City Made Pubic Lice an

Endangered Species." *The Guardian*, https://www.theguardian
.com/lifeandstyle/lostinshowbiz/2013/jul/04/sex-and-city
-pubic-lice-endangered

4. The Vulva Gallery (2022). "Vulva Portraits & Personal Stories,"
https://www.thevulvagallery.com/stories

5. Dodson and Ross (2022). "Vulva Gallery," https://dodsonandross
.com/vulva

6. Betty Dodson (2018). "First Time Orgasm." *Dodson and Ross*,
https://www.dodsonandross.com/sexfeature/first-time-orgasm

7. Roger Friedland (2011). "Looking through the Bushes: The
Disappearance of Female Pubic Hair." Spirituality, Political
Engagement, and Public Life Social Science Research Council,
https://www.academia.edu/3552167/Looking_Through_the
_Bushes_The_Disappearance_of_Female_Pubic_Hair

8. Ellie Krupnick (2012). "Jennifer Love Hewitt 'Maxim' Interview
Reminds Us She's Still Vajazzling (PHOTOS)." *The Huffington
Post*, https://www.huffpost.com/entry/jennifer-love-hewitt
-maxim-vajazzling_n_1326401

9. Team Coco (2012). "Jennifer Love Hewitt Teaches Conan about
'Vajazzling.'" YouTube, https://www.youtube.com/watch?v=
DLgfEilskfc&ab_channel=TeamCoco

10. Thomas W. Gaither, Mohannad A. Awad, E. Charles Osterberg,
Tami S. Rowen, Alan W. Shindel, and Benjamin N. Breyer (2017).
"Prevalence and Motivation: Pubic Hair Grooming among Men
in the United States." *American Journal of Men's Health*, https://
www.ncbi.nlm.nih.gov/pmc/articles/PMC5675231

11. Nadine Ajaka (2017). "The Casualties of Women's War on Body
Hair." *The Atlantic*, https://www.theatlantic.com/health/archive
/2017/02/the-casualties-of-womens-war-on-body-hair/514983

12. Marianna Cerini (2020). "Why Women Feel Pressured to
Shave." *CNN*, https://www.cnn.com/style/article/why-women
-feel-pressured-to-shave/index.html; Smithsonian (2023). "Hair
Removal." https://www.si.edu/spotlight/health-hygiene-and
-beauty/hair-removal

13. Roger Friedland (2011). "Looking Through the Bushes: The

Disappearance of Female Pubic Hair." Spirituality, Political Engagement, and Public Life Social Science Research Council, https://www.academia.edu/3552167/Looking_Through_the _Bushes_The_Disappearance_of_Female_Pubic_Hair

14. Debra Herbenick, Vanessa Schick, Michael Reece, Stephanie Sanders, and J. Dennis Fortenberry (2015). "Pubic Hair Removal among Women in the United States: Prevalence, Methods, and Characteristics." *The Journal of Sexual Medicine*, https://www .sciencedirect.com/science/article/abs/pii/S1743609515327326

15. Alanna Martine Kilkeary (2022). "How to Shave Pubic Hair If You Have a Vagina." *Teen Vogue*, https://www.teenvogue.com /story/how-to-shave-your-pubic-area-safely

16. E. Charles Osterberg, Thomas W. Gaither, Mohannad A. Awad, Matthew D. Truesdale, Isabel Allen, Siobhan Sutcliffe, and Benjamin N. Breyer (2016). "Correlation between Pubic Hair Grooming and STIs: Results from a Nationally Representative Probability Sample." *Sexually Transmitted Infections*, https:// pubmed.ncbi.nlm.nih.gov/27920223; Alexandra M. Klann, Jessica Rosenberg, Tanran Wang, Samantha E. Parker, and Bernard L. Harlow (2019). "Exploring Hygienic Behaviors and Vulvodynia." *Journal of Lower Genital Tract Disease*, https:// www.ncbi.nlm.nih.gov/pmc/articles/PMC6591092

17. Billie (2022). "Billie Introduces the Pink Tax Rebate," https://web .archive.org/web/20221207041522/https://mybillie.com/pages /pink-tax

18. Nood (2022). "Permanent Hair Removal in 8 Weeks," https:// www.trynood.com/pages/shaving-lander

19. Nood (@trynood) (2022). "In as little as 8 weeks, you can kiss shaving goodbye for good!" Instagram, https://www.instagram .com/p/CkeelAqLmqs

20. Suzannah Weiss (@suzannahweiss) (2022). "Hand is raised!" Twitter, https://twitter.com/suzannahweiss/status /1595466235357319169

21. Nood (@trynood) (2022). "It's time to dust off the cobwebs in your cauldron and flash the bats off your broomstick!"

Instagram, https://www.instagram.com/p/Cj_r587NdkQ; Nood (@trynood) (2022). "Don't let the clingy bush haunt you!" Instagram, https://www.instagram.com/p/CkwZYYOpalf

22. Suzannah Weiss (@suzannahweiss) (2022). "Because even when no one is looking, the male gaze is still lurking behind every corner..." Twitter, https://twitter.com/suzannahweiss/status/1599427217489944576

23. Billie (2023). "The Rules of Body Hair," https://mybillie.com/pages/the-rules-of-body-hair

24. Global Cosmetics News (2021). "Gillette Venus Launches New Pubic Hair and Skin Collection alongside #SayPupic Campaign." YouTube, https://www.youtube.com/watch?v=o3YQ5hmTfos&ab_channel=GlobalCosmeticsNews

25. Gillette Venus (2021). "New Gillette Venus for Pubic Skin and Hair," https://web.archive.org/web/20221205214312/https://www.gillettevenus.com/en-us/pubic-care

26. Patricia Obst, Katherine White, and Ebony Matthews (2019). "A Full Brazilian or All Natural: Understanding the Influences on Young Women's Decision to Remove Their Pubic Hair." *BMC Womens Health*, https://www.ncbi.nlm.nih.gov/pmc/articles/PMC6921585

27. Paul Enzlin, Kaat Bollen, Sofia Prekatsounaki, Liesbeth Hidalgo, Leen Aerts, and Jan Deprest (2019). "'To Shave or Not to Shave': Pubic Hair Removal and Its Association with Relational and Sexual Satisfaction in Women and Men." *The Journal of Sexual Medicine*, https://www.sciencedirect.com/science/article/abs/pii/S1743609519311166

28. Catriona Harvey-Jenner (2015). "The Orgasm Gap is REAL – Women Are Losing Out." *Cosmopolitan*, https://www.cosmopolitan.com/uk/love-sex/sex/news/a34410/female-orgasm-survey

29. Go Ask Alice (2015). "What to Do With Pubic Hair?" Columbia University, https://goaskalice.columbia.edu/answered-questions/what-do-pubic-hair

30. This is especially true for trans women, who may be misgendered

or harassed for having body hair. See Bel Olid (2022). *Hairless: Breaking the Vicious Circle of Hair Removal, Submission and Self-hatred*. Polity.
31. Stefan G. Lechner and Gary R. Lewin (2013). "Hairy Sensation." *Physiology*, https://journals.physiology.org/doi/full/10.1152/physiol.00059.2012
32. Audre Lorde (2017). "Poetry Is Not a Luxury." In *Sister Outsider: Essays and Speeches*. Crossing Press.

12 I Care: Sexual Empowerment Sells
1. Ali Finney (2019). "Fillers Are Injecting Themselves into the Wellness Convo and Honestly, It's Awesome." *Well + Good*, https://www.wellandgood.com/dermal-fillers-stigma
2. Ibid.
3. The brand has since downplayed its ability to disguise the vulva's taste and scent and now focuses on other uses like STI prevention, thanks to feedback from myself and others.
4. DeoDoc (2023). "About Us," https://deodoc.com/pages/about-us
5. Gillette Venus (2023). "New Gillette Venus for Pubic Hair & Skin," https://web.archive.org/web/20221205214312/https://www.gillettevenus.com/en-us/pubic-care
6. Lenora E. Houseworth (2021). "The Radical History of Self-Care." *Teen Vogue*, https://www.teenvogue.com/story/the-radical-history-of-self-care
7. Allie Jones (2016). "Lo Bosworth Wants to Solve Your Vagina Problems." *The Cut*, https://www.thecut.com/2016/10/lo-bosworth-wants-to-solve-your-vagina-problems.html
8. Love Wellness (2023). "Vaginal Health Kit," https://lovewellness.com/collections/vaginal-health/products/the-vaginal-health-kit
9. David Frederick, H. Kate St. John, Justin R. Garcia, Elisabeth A. Lloyd (2017). "Differences in Orgasm Frequency Between Gay, Lesbian, Bisexual, and Heterosexual Men and Women in a U.S. National Sample." *Archives of Sexual Behavior*, https://digitalcommons.chapman.edu/psychology_articles/74
10. Michael Barnett (2017). "How RB is 'Closing the Orgasm Gap'

with Durex." *Marketing Week*, https://www.marketingweek.com /rb-looking-close-orgasm-gap-durex

11. RB (2016). "K-Y® Intense® Is Giving Women a Reason to Fake It No More." *PR Newswire*, https://www.prnewswire.com/news -releases/k-y-intense-is-giving-women-a-reason-to-fake-it-no -more-300308691.html

12. K-Y's press release cites a textbook, but after communicating with that textbook's authors, I discovered there is no known research behind the statistic. See Suzannah Weiss (2018). "What a Fake 'Female Orgasm' Statistic Says about Gender Bias." *The Establishment*, https://medium.com/the-establishment /what-a-fake-female-orgasm-statistic-says-about-gender-bias -591985f8d68c; International Society for Sexual Medicine (2023). "What Are Multiple Orgasms? How Common Are They?" https://www.issm.info/sexual-health-qa/what-are -multiple-orgasms-how-common-are-they

13. O Shot (2017). "Let's Talk Vaginas with Cindy Barshop, Dr. Carolyn Delucia, MD, FACOG, & Olivia," https://oshot.info/lets -talk-vaginas-with-cindy-barshop

14. Sigmund Freud (2017). *Three Essays on the Theory of Sexuality: The 1905 Edition*. Verso Books. My remarks on the penis vs. phallus also stem from a conversation with historian Thomas Laqueur.

15. Luce Irigaray (1985). "This Sex Which Is Not One." In *This Sex Which Is Not One*. Cornell University Press.

16. Natalie Gil (2017). "Women Are Putting Glitter in Their Vaginas & Doctors Are Concerned." *Refinery29*, https://www.refinery29 .com/en-us/2017/06/161871/vagina-glitter-bomb-doctor-health -warning

17. Jen Gunter (2017). "Don't Put Ground Up Wasp Nest in Your Vagina." *Dr. Jen Gunter*, https://drjengunter.com/2017/05/16 /dont-put-ground-up-wasp-nest-in-your-vagina

18. Elizabeth Gulino (2022). "I Got a Vajacial So You Don't Have To." *Refinery29*, https://www.refinery29.com/en-us/vajacial -treatment-steps-benefits-cost

19. Amy Schlinger (2016). "Khloé Kardashian Says to Put Vitamin

E on Your Vagina. So Should You?" *Glamour*, https://www
.glamour.com/story/khloe-kardashian-says-to-put-vitamin
-e-on-your-vagina-so-should-you; Kelsey Castanon (2017).
"Khloé Kardashian Has an 8-Step Skin Routine – For Her
Vagina." *Refinery29*, https://www.refinery29.com/en-us/2017
/03/144703/khloe-kardashian-vagina-facial-beauty-routine

20. Joan Riviere (1999). "Womanliness as a Masquerade." In *Female
Sexuality*. Ed Russell Grigg. Routledge.

21. Mary Ann Doane (1992). "Film and the Masquerade: Theorizing
the Female Spectator." *The Sexual Subject: A Screen Reader in
Sexuality*. Ed. Mandy Merck. Routledge.

22. Maude (2023), https://getmaude.com

23. Bellesa (@bellesaco) (2022). "The thrust effect." Instagram,
https://www.instagram.com/p/CmcRspCv1Cq

24. Bellesa (@bellesaco) (2022). "Help." Instagram, https://www
.instagram.com/p/ClXTVMYuoR4

25. Bellesa (@bellesaco) (2023). Instagram, https://www.instagram
.com/p/CrrDms3Oo40; Bellesa (@bellesaco) (2023). "Reminder
xx." Instagram, https://www.instagram.com/p/CxYUmPIREUr

26. Bellesa (@bellesaco) (2022). "Just some food for thot babe."
Instagram, https://www.instagram.com/p/ClkIvqpOYIC

13 I Receive: Sex Work as Play

1. Marie Solis (2021). "Sex Workers Made OnlyFans Valuable –
Then It Sold Them Out." *The Verge*, https://www.theverge.com
/2021/8/23/22638310/onlyfans-ban-explicit-content-payment
-processing-visa

2. Google Dictionary. (2023). "Work."

3. Global Network of Sex Worker Projects (2017). "Sex Work
as Work," https://www.nswp.org/sites/default/files/policy_brief
_sex_work_as_work_nswp_-_2017.pdf

4. Angela Jones (2016). "I Get Paid to Have Orgasms: Adult
Webcam Models' Negotiation of Pleasure and Danger." *Signs:
Journal of Women in Culture and Society*, https://www.journals
.uchicago.edu/doi/10.1086/686758

5. Angela Jones (2019). "Sex Is Not a Problem: The Erasure of Pleasure in Sexual Science Research." *Sexualities*, https://journals.sagepub.com/doi/abs/10.1177/1363460718760210
6. Norval Morris and Gordon J. Hawkins (1969). *The Honest Politician's Guide to Crime Control*. University of Chicago Press.
7. There is some data suggesting that one benefit of legalizing sex work is reduction of sexual violence. Still, we wouldn't need sex workers to curb sexual violence if it weren't so prevalent. We can do better than perpetuate a culture that prizes male violence, then send violent men to sex workers. See Huasheng Gao and Vanya Petrova (2022). "Do Prostitution Laws Affect Rape Rates? Evidence from Europe." *The Journal of Law and Economics*, https://www.journals.uchicago.edu/doi/abs/10.1086/720583
8. Alain Corbin (1987). "Commercial Sexuality in Nineteenth-Century France: A System of Images and Regulations." In *The Making of the Modern Body: Sexuality and Society in the Nineteenth Century*. Eds. Catherine Gallagher and Thomas Laqueur. University of California Press.
9. Paul Nathanson (2014). "Letter: Prostitution Is, at Worst, a 'Necessary Evil.'" *The Montreal Gazette*, https://montrealgazette.com/opinion/letter-prostitution-is-at-worst-a-necessary-evil
10. Global Network of Sex Worker Projects (2017). "Sex Work as Work," https://www.nswp.org/sites/default/files/policy_brief_sex_work_as_work_nswp_-_2017.pdf
11. Authentic consent applies not just to sex workers but to others who may have sex without enthusiasm, such as couples trying to conceive. See Nadine Thornhill (2020). "Why I'm Not Always Enthusiastic about Enthusiastic Consent." YouTube, https://www.youtube.com/watch?v=VAvWRaXm3iE&ab_channel=NadineThornhill
12. Victoria Bateman (2023). *Naked Feminism: Breaking the Cult of Female Modesty*. Polity.
13. Such stigma hurts sex trafficking survivors as well; many refrain from reporting their traffickers out of fear that they themselves could be punished. See Suzannah Weiss (2016). "When Sex

Trafficking Victims Go to Prison." *Ravishly*, https://www.ravishly
.com/2016/12/28/when-sex-trafficking-victims-go-prison

14. The View (2015). "'Women Get Paid to Have Sex All the Time' through Material Things, Raven-Symoné says. Do You Agree?" Facebook, https://www.facebook.com/watch/?v= 10153032197431524

15. Shubham Kamble (2022). "Mind-Blowing OnlyFans Statistics (2022)." *Other Way Round*, https://otherwayround.net/onlyfans -statistics/#OnlyFans-User-Statistics; Lorena Castillo (2023). "OnlyFans Gender Statistics and Trends in 2023." *Gitnux*, https://blog.gitnux.com/onlyfans-gender-statistics

14 I Like: You're Just Not That Into Them

1. Bethany Heitman (2010). "How to Feel Sexy All the Time." *Cosmopolitan*, https://www.cosmopolitan.com/lifestyle/advice /a3095/feel-so-freakin-sexy-0709/

2. Ellen Scott (2017). "I Wore Sexy Underwear for a Week to See If It Made Me More Confident." *Cosmopolitan*, https://www .cosmopolitan.com/uk/fashion/style/a9575074/i-wore-sexy -underwear-for-a-week-to-see-if-it-made-me-more-confident; Isabella Silvers (2019). "5 Women and Non-Binary People on When They Feel Their Sexiest." *Cosmopolitan*, https://www .cosmopolitan.com/uk/love-sex/a26564570/women-on-when -they-feel-sexiest/

3. Naomi Wolf (2002). *The Beauty Myth: How Images of Beauty Are Used against Women*. Harper Perennial.

4. Regena Thomashauer (2016). *Pussy: A Reclamation*. Hay House, Inc.

5. Clint Carter (2014). "8 Reasons Guys Love It When You Orgasm." *Women's Health*, https://www.womenshealthmag.com/sex-and -love/a19942250/guys-love-when-you-orgasm

6. Cosmo Frank (2015). "8 Reasons He Really Wants to Make You Orgasm." *Cosmopolitan*, https://www.cosmopolitan.com /sex-love/news/a47459/reasons-he-really-wants-to-make-you -orgasm

7. Catriona Harvey-Jenner (2015). "The Orgasm Gap is REAL – Women Are Losing Out." *Cosmopolitan*, https://www.cosmopolitan.com/uk/love-sex/sex/news/a34410/female-orgasm-survey
8. Greg Behrendt and Liz Tuccillo (2009). *He's Just Not That Into You: The No-Excuses Truth to Understanding Guys*. Gallery Books.
9. Layla Martin (@thelaylamartin). "Have you made this dating mistake?" Instagram, https://www.instagram.com/p/ClFIegkPvb9
10. Greg Behrendt and Liz Tuccillo (2009). *He's Just Not That Into You: The No-Excuses Truth to Understanding Guys*. Gallery Books.

15 I Write: Inhabiting the Active Voice

1. I'm taking poetic liberty here, as the essay does not explicitly explore the intersubjectivity of the two labia; it evokes them to illustrate how a woman is neither one nor two. It does discuss the non-hierarchical relationship between the clitoris and vagina. See Luce Irigaray (1985). "This Sex Which Is Not One." In *This Sex Which Is Not One*. Cornell University Press.
2. She may have also been referencing a quote by Catharine MacKinnon that I learned soon after writing this book – "Man fucks woman; subject verb object" – which appears in: Catharine MacKinnon (1982). "Feminism, Marxism, Method, and the State: An Agenda for Theory." *Signs*, https://www.jstor.org/stable/3173853
3. Google Dictionary (2023). "Fuck."
4. Google Dictionary (2023). "Penetrate."
5. Emily Martin (1991). "The Egg and the Sperm: How Science Has Constructed a Romance Based on Stereotypical Male–Female Roles." *Signs*, https://web.stanford.edu/~eckert/PDF/Martin1991.pdf
6. Jacques Lacan (1975). *Le Séminaire, Livre XX. Encore, 1972–73*. Seuil.

7. Gerard Cohen-Vrignaud (2012). "On Octopussies, or the Anatomy of Female Power." *Differences*, https://read.dukeupress.edu/differences/article-abstract/23/1/32/60646/On-Octopussies-or-the-Anatomy-of-Female-Power

8. Online Etymology Dictionary (2019). "Subject (n)," https://www.etymonline.com/word/subject

9. Christie V. McDonald (1982). "Jacques Derrida and Christie V. McDonald: Choreographies." *Diacritics*, https://www.proquest.com/openview/cfa7a804b335f25eadff10a5f898a99e/1

10. Merriam-Webster (2023). "I," https://www.merriam-webster.com/dictionary/i